Advance Praise

"(*Strong Glass*) renders childhood perspective so convincingly. The sensory details—the fragrant lilac bushes, the savor of penny candy in the neighborhood movie theater, rainbows of stained-glass in her father's shop—create a nostalgic softness that makes the darker revelations all the more unsettling... The metaphor of glass—clear yet fragile, reflective yet capable of distortion—serves as a fitting symbol for memory itself: what we see, what we think we see, and what may lie just beneath the surface.

—Suzie Housley, *Midwest Book Review*

In *Strong Glass*, a memoir of her struggle to break free from her troubled home in mid-twentieth century Appalachia, Roblyer paints a probing, reflective portrait of family and the fierce, fragile bonds that link us to one another... Her narrative explores the landscapes of generational poverty, mental illness, and social ostracism, all with a gritty determination both to exorcise the dark grievances of the past and to understand how they can shape–but not necessarily determine–our present experience."

— Gregory O'Dea, Professor of English Literature Emeritus, The University of Tennessee at Chattanooga

"M. D. Roblyer writes such tangled pain with such hard truth and a clarity that will illuminate—even heal—the terrible secret sorrow that resides in many."

—Summer Dawn Hammond, *The Impossible Why*

"...the author's compelling prose is deeply empathetic, and her quest to connect with herself and others is one from which we all can learn."

—Tracy Yokas, *Bloodlines: A Memoir of Harm and Healing*

"*Strong Glass*... reads like a riveting novel."

— Sherry Poff, President, Chattanooga Writers' Guild

Strong Glass

Strong Glass

A Memoir of Escaping the Dark Mirror of Family History

M. D. Roblyer

First Edition

Casebound ISBN: 978-1-62720-662-4
Paperback ISBN: 978-1-62720-663-1
Ebook ISBN: 978-1-62720-664-8

Library of Congress Catolog Number (applied)

Design by Eleanor Salvatore
Editorial Development by Abby Szypula and Caroline Drennen
Promotional Development by Eleanor Salvatore

Published by Apprentice House Press

Loyola University Maryland
4501 N. Charles Street, Baltimore, MD 21210
410.617.5265
www.ApprenticeHouse.com
info@ApprenticeHouse.com

For my family, Bill and Paige,
who make the music so I can write the words,
and my parents Servatius (Spates) Lewis Roblyer and
Phrona Catherine (Francis) Roblyer,
who willed me some of their gifts
and all their ghosts.

Disclaimer

Except for the histories of my dead relatives, what I report here are what action researchers call "lived experiences." That is, I describe what happened based on my own perceptions and colorings of memories. I tell the events truly, as I remember them and as much as they can be verified with established facts. In search of accuracy, I have plundered the memories of others and clocked hundreds of hours on Ancestry and Newspapers.com. If this book contains any errors of truth or fact, they were inadvertent and unintentional. NOTE: To protect their privacy, my siblings' names and those of most still-living persons are pseudonyms.

Published Excerpts

Stories from *Strong Glass* have appeared in modified form in the following publications:

1. "Bread of Life" appeared in Issue 1067 of *Bewildering Stories:* https://www.bewilderingstories.com
2. "Hall of Mirrors" appears online at TrashLight Press: https://trashlightpress.com/
3. "Battle Over the Bulge" appeared online in the July 3, 2025, edition of *Bright Flash Literary Review:* https://brightflash1000.com
4. "Cat Fight" won second place in the Chattanooga Writers Guild Three-Way Contest for Nonfiction and appears in the Fall 2025 Chattanooga Writers Guild *RidgeCut* Anthology. (Available on Amazon)
5. "Apex Moments" won first place in the June 2025 Chattanooga Writers Guild Nonfiction Contest and appears online: https://chattanoogawritersguild.org/

Contents

Prologue

Slumped over my Toyota's steering wheel in the garage of the snug North Florida bungalow my husband Bill and I shared, I wasn't lamenting how the brokenness in my life reflected my fractured childhood; the idea had never occurred to me. This was merely the end of another twelve-hour workday at the university, and as usual, I lingered in my car, focusing on how the next few hours might cast a sliver of light onto my dark mood.

I pictured Bill, home hours earlier from work at the same university, joyously making dinner in our bright, herb-fragrant kitchen. He would be energized and whole-body vocalizing to one of his vinyl LPs—Beethoven and AC/DC were favorites—accompanied by the familiar clatter and rattle of pots, pans, and dishes. When I slogged in the door, I'd unburden myself once again about the worst aspects of my job and all the reasons I'd quit if only the money weren't so good. *Let me tell you the crap that went down today at that place.*

Wine glass in hand, he'd be ready with long, understanding hugs and improbable puns in a bid to buoy my mood. While I organized the work I'd do later that evening, he'd quickly get dinner on the table. He hadn't mentioned that morning what we'd eat; I envisioned maybe roast pork and apples or his chicken chili with the homemade corn bread that always won praise from our friends. Maybe he'd surprise me with a new dish. Talking little, we'd wolf it down so I could work until midnight and get a few restless hours of sleep before it all began again.

Those sensory images of brief respite were enough to pry me out of my car. As I pushed open the front door of the house with my armload of books and papers, I took an eye-blinking moment to register the dark silence that met me. Then my gaze fell on an unexpected object in the foyer.

I was about to snap, "Bill, what the hell's this suitcase doing here?" when he appeared, car keys in hand. I hadn't seen him so somber since his mom died, but he had that same elegiac look. In the calm, matter-of-fact teacher voice he used to tell students their behavior was unacceptable, he began to explain why he was leaving me.

"Peggy, you can't think it could go on like this. You come home and speak to Cecil sweeter than you do to me." At the mention of his name, our round white cat raised his head from his favorite spot on our sofa, and I could swear he smiled.

"Every day you seem to find some reason to explode at me—and, my God, Peggy, it's so unpredictable!" He shook his head, his face sunken with sorrow, but his tall frame erect and determined. "You come home mad, and you talk to me like whatever happened at work was my fault, and everything I suggest just makes it worse. I've tried to understand you, to make you happy. At first, I was sure I could, but these last few years have shown me I was wrong.

"I love you; God knows I always have, but—I. Can't. Take. Any. More." He punctuated these last words with his fist on the back of the sofa. "If this is the way the rest of our life will be, I'm out of here." His car keys jangled as he gestured toward the packed bag.

I listened open-mouthed, staring first at Bill, then the suitcase. Suddenly I was an actor who had forgotten the next line. I knew he was right, and I had no words. He was an expert at fixing things, but he couldn't fix the misery I had brought with me into our marriage no matter how hard he tried. Now, seven years in, he was ready to stop trying. The scene he was describing was familiar, dialog from an old play I had seen so often and pushed away from memory. Instead of an evening of singing, dinner, and consolation, I was propelled back to a time I hated and a place I had tried so hard to leave.

I was thirty-five and had been hitting personal achievement targets since I was a teenager, beginning with fleeing my tormented parents and the quaint and claustrophobic Appalachian village where I grew up. Our corner of Western Maryland saw its finest hours when big industry like the Celanese plant in Cresaptown, where we lived, was called on to help win the World Wars. My parents had been there since the 1920s and never left when the jobs faded away, not that staying or going would have made any real difference in their narrative. They were captives in a larger story and, I was to learn, so was I.

My father feared poverty more than he worried about dying, and had he lived to see it, I knew he would have been proud—and a little astonished—at just how fast I had come from having nearly nothing to more than I needed. But he would have shaken his head mournfully at how I was spending my earnings. Bill and I feasted once a month from the early-bird menu at a casual-dining restaurant and paid a maid every two weeks to tidy our three-bedroom house. We had just celebrated our first luxury purchases: a brand-new Sony video cassette player and our first cassette, our only one for the next year. We watched it with popcorn nearly every weekend.

Dad would have been alarmed at these small indulgences. I

could just hear him moaning, "Those kids spend money like it grows on trees." But oh, how he would have loved Bill, my mirror opposite, a man so playful and exuberant that he drew others to him like party lights on a warm summer night. He had drawn me, too, so obsessed with marrying me that he talked me into it, but even he could never make a dent in my angst. I even chafed at his perpetual good mood. *How could that man be equally content working with university architecture students as he had been teaching middle-school industrial arts when we first met?*

I married for love, but first I earned for myself the financial independence my mother had drilled into me I would need if love left. I had overcome every obstacle, accomplished every goal I set, and the path before me glowed with possibility. So why was I always so angry? And why was I holding Bill hostage to my wrath?

At first, the suitcase made no sense to me. *He's gonna leave me just like that, after he always swore we were perfect for each other? And didn't everyone else agree, even my sister Cindy, always so vigilant for my happiness?* I had known it, too, from the first weekend Bill had begged me to spend with him in his Miami hometown, bicycling through the sudden fragrance of low-hanging orchids in Fairchild Gardens, slow dancing after dinner in the Coconut Grove. At first, I resisted how well-matched we were—I wanted no more romantic entanglements to slow me down—but I finally succumbed to the lure of our indefinable mutual magnetism.

We had traveled far in our few years together. After I finished my doctorate and he a master's degree at Florida State University, we bought a small house north of Tallahassee, which Bill skillfully remodeled before we traded up to a larger one. We agreed on everything, even a choice to remain childless and focused on careers. We sorrowed tragedies like his mother's death, celebrated successes together, and each won better-paying jobs and promotions. We worked as a team and prospered as a couple. In my view, our union was as good as it could possibly be. *Marriages mature. You can't be gaga-happy constantly.* But there was no circumventing that sinister suitcase. I, who was usually so quick to answer criticism with verbal acid, had no words. *How could something so perfect have turned out so wrong?* Irony crowded my brain.

As I tried to make sense of what was happening in the present, the past jerked into my mind. My mother rails accusations at my father, "Why, Spates? Why do we have to live this way?" My father stands sullen, glowering; then a screen door bangs like a gun, and his rage explodes, echoing out across the valley.

I believed I had outrun my family history of restless discontent and unpredictable fury, but Bill and his suitcase forced me to admit that the traumas of my youth had legs that could stride through time. I saw at once that I was re-enacting with Bill a role I had seen so often in my childhood. That shock of illumination landed quickly, but there were many more to come. As I continued examining the past I had fled, the deeper I fell into my family background, further and further down into the generations-long, dark mirror of its history.

Was it possible for "things to be different," as Bill demanded? How could I confirm what I didn't know? I grasped at once that the past I assumed I had left far behind was buried inside me and had to be exhumed. Yet I feared what I might unearth.

For those with fraught childhoods, the past is a fractured mirror, reflecting a repeating pattern of warped images far into the future. By facing that mirror once again, could I rebuild my image strong and whole, or would I be destined to replay the same mistakes that had brought me toes over the edge of losing Bill and all we had achieved?

Yes, I was afraid of going back, but I was more afraid not to, and so I was led down that shadowy trail, Scrooge-like, by my own ghosts. From that long journey there would be no respite, only the rare grace of insight along the way and the path behind me illuminated by revelation.

First Part

Preflight

Chapter One

Small World

When I first opened an interrogation of my past, I believed life began for me when I was born on a dramatic Easter Sunday. I was the little girl Mom told me she had prayed for after my two brothers came along. But neither of their births had meant days of labor as mine did, and she impatiently paced the halls in the Memorial Hospital in Cumberland, Maryland, trying to persuade me to emerge and be pampered. Even at the beginning, I was fighting her wishes, auguring a clash of wills that continued throughout our lives.

The story of my birth as my mother dramatized it for me became a lively full-color movie I enjoyed playing out in my mind. Dr. Brings was peeling a hardboiled, dyed Easter egg as he strolled down the obstetrics ward before heading off to church. When Mom began to scream in pain from her hospital bed, he snapped, "Oh, shut up, Catherine," not believing this was finally it after all her false alarms. Anyone who knew her was aware of how she liked to exaggerate everything. Dr. Brings didn't have time to change his clothes before I arrived, so he delivered me in his Sunday best.

Mom hadn't wept during that long labor, but she described the nurse's surprise after they showed me to her. "Look, now she's crying!" the nurse laughed as tears rolled down my mother's face. I've always thought her relief that the ordeal was over was mingled with joy at the birth of a girl-child, though it didn't turn out the way she expected.

She named me Margaret Dale, but I never learned from where she plucked my first name. It was a common enough one for little girls at that time, and perhaps she liked that Margaret means "pearl." Or maybe her mother's West Virginia family, the Roys, had mentioned that Saint Margaret was the female patron saint of Scotland, where her family hailed from.

I always knew where I got my middle name. "You're Dale after Dale Evans," she had announced proudly when I was very young, and I was delighted because my friends and I always watched the Roy Rogers and Dale Evans Show on TV and begged to see all their movies. They were a famous Hollywood couple, but Dale was already a successful actress and businesswoman before meeting Roy. Mom admired Dale because she was a strong, independent, career woman, which seemed to be Mom's vision for me.

Peggy is a diminutive for Margaret by way of Meggy, and to my father I was always Peggy Dale. Margaret sounded formal and boring to me, while Peggy was a fun and carefree girl that everyone liked and wanted to be around. I always introduced myself as Peggy if Mom wasn't there, but Mom always called me Margaret. My siblings fell in line with her wishes and still call me Margaret to this day. Jamaica Kincaid has written, "To name is to possess," and that was my mother's first claim on me, her creation. My dueling names may have been an early signal of a growing discord between my parents.

My father's draft card disclosed that he was only five feet, four inches and 130 pounds, but he always seemed big to me, not only because I was small, but also because of his giant's bellow when his anger woke. My indelible memory of him was a bespectacled, balding old man with a weathered face and a perpetually worried expression, but I ran across yellowed photos of him in his twenties with fair complexion, winning smile, and a tousle of light-brown hair. "Oh, yes, he was good-looking back then," Mom sighed when I remarked on the contrast between those photos and the Dad I knew. My brother Bobby also assured me, apparently on good authority, "Dad was bull-strong, you know." He held up clenched hands. "Fists of steel."

I don't recall Bobby hanging around our house much in my childhood. He was nine years older than me, and my own recollections of him from that time are few. When we were adults though, he loved regaling me and anyone else who would listen with stories of his childhood in our village of Cresaptown. It lay about seven miles down winding, two-lane McMullen Highway (a.k.a. Route 220) from Cumberland, Maryland, which was nicknamed the Queen City when it was the state's second-largest urban center after king-sized Baltimore.

"Every minute I wasn't in school, I roamed all over Cresaptown, exploring everything, finding out what was going on, talking to everyone I met," Bobby mused, eyes glowing. "I sure knew more about what was happening in Cresaptown than Mom or Dad, I can tell you that." Even with the weight of eighty years on him, the memories of his adventures animated his face, and he became again that young adventurer.

"When I was eleven, I wanted to be the first in our family to fly. One Saturday I hitched rides to Mexico Farms Airport south of Cumberland and talked a local pilot into taking me on a joyride around Allegany County."

"Didn't any of your friends go with you?" I mentally calculated the dangers.

"No, not that time, but we did spend a lot of time at the railroad tracks behind our house smoking cigarettes." He chuckled, shaking his head. When I accompanied him on his first visit to the oncology doctor when he was in his late seventies, Bobby admitted he had started smoking when he was twelve and had a pack-a-day habit until he was thirty when he said God told him he had to quit.

Our brother Fred, three years younger than Bobby and six years older than me, was more studious and dutiful and around the house more, so Mom often made him into my unpaid babysitter. She also entrusted Fred with tracking down the adventurous Bobby, not to retrieve him but to serve as her informant. One summer afternoon when Bobby was smoking with friends at the railroad tracks, he began a treatise on what a little rat-snitch his younger brother was.

"Why I'll bet if I looked down in that gulley right now," Bobby huffed, "he'd be there listening to us." They all leaned over and looked down, and there was Fred staring up at them. Bobby must have brought up that event to me dozens of times over the years, and even as an old man, he was still steaming at Fred for being Mom's stoolie. I don't think Fred ever picked up on that anger; he always shared the same story for laughs. Not that I blame Fred for doing what Mom directed. We'd all have been afraid not to, though I often wonder why he didn't just say, "I couldn't find him."

When I was about six, I learned that Mom didn't completely trust Fred either. He described with some irritation how Mom reacted when he showed her some change he had found.

"You stole it, didn't you?"

"No, Mom, really," he protested. "I found it on the ground near the Skelley's on my way home from school."

I always trusted my mother's opinion, so I had to ask. "Well, did you steal it?"

"Of course not!" Fred snapped, throwing me a sharp look. "And If I find any money again, I'll never tell her."

I got to be the baby of the family for four years, until my mother placed a blanketed bundle on the sofa and called, "Margaret, come here." As I approached, Mom made introductions. "Come meet your sister Lucinda." I looked down at the bundle and observed, "Her eyes are so big," and Mom laughed. When I was a teenager, Fred made it clear that Mom wasn't laughing when she first realized she would have a "surprise child."

"Mom told me she considered shooting herself with one of Dad's guns."

That news stunned me. "Oh, no, Fred! Why would she do that?"

Fred shrugged. "Hard to say. You know Mom. Maybe she didn't want to be tied down to the house any more than she already was."

I've wondered why she would confess such musings to her son. More of her drama? Or was she impressing on him how unhappy she was, trying to justify how she treated Dad?

A typical day in my childhood began with morning sounds I dreaded.

"You're trying to make me your slave, Spates!" Mom wails from their bedroom. I'm out of my deep sleep.

My father rumbles reply. "Woman, leave me in peace! I'm the one who's a slave, going out there to that freezing shop every day to put food on your table!" I'm fully conscious now, ready for another day of sullen anger and abrupt outbursts when they were in the same room. Even absent a morning fight, my body woke up rigid as I lay in bed anticipating them.

The finale was Dad slamming the screen door, retreating across the driveway to labor over stained glass windows in our family business, the Art Glass Company. Or he would retrieve one of his guns from the small apartment above his shop and withdraw to the grassy bank behind it, releasing explosions out across the railroad tracks, across the Potomac River and into the valley beyond. Despite all the verbal combat, I never saw my father strike my mother. The yelling was merely a libretto for the bellicose opera that was their marriage.

When I was very young, it didn't seem to matter if my morning began with household turmoil. I skipped outside to a day of delights in my small world. Released to wander our yard with instructions not to leave it, I encountered the redolence of spring-blooming honeysuckle hanging from trellises skirting the back porch steps and found wonder in the tall, white-and-purple lilac bushes at the far edge of our small backyard. Great, full-bosomed divas, the bushes waved their leafy arms about at the touch of a breeze. Lilacs blooming in spring and summer wafted a light fragrance over me as I played. Even now, the scent of lilacs always sends me back to Cresaptown, looking up at the lilac ladies in small-child wonderment, awed by their size and beauty and the drama of their motion. Heavy blooms of pink and white peonies nodded regally in summer breezes all along one side of the house. I remember my childhood world as perfumed and pastel-painted.

Valley View Drive was lined with small dwellings like the one where I grew up, many built by the hands of those who lived in them. Dad and his dad, my Grandfather Robert, built ours in the mid-1920s when Cresap Park was established adjacent to the Cellulose and Chemical Manufacturing Company property. The plant opened in 1918, but its operations, along with hiring, picked up speed in 1922 when it developed the first cellulose acetate yarn, which it dubbed Celanese, a portmanteau of "cellulose" and "ease." The company officially changed its name to the Celanese Corporation of America in 1927, but to everyone in the area, it was simply "the Celanese."

Cresaptown's gradual spread from Cresap Park was no coincidence; families of a growing workforce preferred to live close by so they could walk to work swinging their domed, metal lunchboxes. Cresap Park, then all of Cresaptown, filled up with families of Celanese workers.

❧

One rainy day, I wandered into my parents' bedroom and noticed a colorful two-foot square stained-glass window of a Bible surrounded by lilies. Mom found me gazing up at its colors, and when I pointed to it, she picked me up to touch the glass and trace my fingers along the leading. "Daddy made this," I murmured softly.

"No," Mom corrected, "His father, your Granddaddy."

Though I always identified the Art Glass Company with my father, who worked it with one other man, my grandfather had founded the company twenty years before I came along. Most other Cresaptown men were shift laborers at the Celanese.

Our flat, grassy backyard ended in a bank that began as a gentle slope but ended quite suddenly in a steep, sheer drop-off of perhaps fifteen feet, with railroad tracks cutting through below the cliff it formed. On tiptoe, I could just catch sight of smoke rising from each passing steam engine, though the tracks were too far below to see the train itself. Our street's Valley View Drive name reflected the beauty of its location, offering glimpses of the Potomac River past the railroad tracks and a vista of green hills. It did not, however, capture how the noise of every Baltimore & Ohio or Western Maryland train rumbling through that stretch of track reverberated off the cliff, their train whistles resounding and echoing throughout the valley, creating a wailing din. Though it seems strange to think of it now, the trains' close-by thunder and whistle screams were familiar and comforting as I lay in bed at night, my own Cresaptown lullaby, and I drifted into sleep content.

Our neighborhood was unlocked screen doors and five-year-olds allowed to wander and explore, but I didn't have adventuring in my blood like Bobby. For me, excitement was being allowed the hundred-yard ramble from our house to where my best friend, Gail, lived on Meadow Avenue. Gail's father, Lester, had been a prisoner of war in a German stalag and was then a successful banker, living the middle-class dream. He literally worked bankers' hours and sat on boards of directors for our church and Cresaptown government, while my father was creating and installing church windows and cutting mirrors or glass panes for local homes and never had time for such things.

Only propinquity can explain why Gail and I gravitated toward each other as best friends because we contrasted in almost every possible way. I was a thin, towhead-blond, blue-eyed tomboy; my favorite play involved running games and playing in dirt or mud on a bank opposite the platform where my dad's glass shipments were offloaded. Gail was brown-eyed and darkhaired, a "girly girl," shy, timid, and plump, no doubt the result of her mother's tasty fare.

Gail's home was as small as ours but far different from the simmering chaos of my own, with its parental clashes and four children laughing, teasing, yelling, and barging in and out noisily.

"For Godsakes, Bobby, don't slam the screen door!"

With Lester at the bank, Ruth had only Gail and her older brother Dick to manage, and she liked them quiet and close to home.

I preferred spending time at Gail's home, staying there until Ruth, her homemaker mother, began to inquire, "Peggy, won't your mom be missing you?" Ruth kept an attractive, orderly household and made well-balanced, nutritious meals. I hung around hoping she'd ask me to stay for lunch or a sleepover. On my first overnight at Gail's, I puzzled over how the bed was made. "Why two sheets?"

From Gail's mother, I learned that many people had a top and bottom sheet for more comfortable sleeping; we used only the bottom one. Saving time and money, not comfort, was the rule in our house.

Every part of Gail's house was a marvel to me. Her living room was cooled in summer by one of the first window air conditioning units in our neighborhood. In their methodically arranged attic space hung plastic bags with the family's off-season clothes, and Gail's mom had set aside a play space there for her and her toys. I was impressed that her father had painted the basement floor high-gloss gray, the better to keep it clean. The close-clipped lawn in the back of their house leading down to their weeping willow tree seemed a cover tableau from *Better Homes and Gardens*, whose issues were arranged just so on her shiny living room coffee table.

Once I chirped, "Mama, can Gail come over to play?" But she shook her head.

"You go over there, honey. I don't want that kid carrying tales to Ruth."

Our household turmoil couldn't have been secret from Ruth or anyone else in the neighborhood, but I have little doubt now that Gail's mom was happier to have her daughter well away from it. I'll never know if Mom was aware of the differences between our house and Gail's, let alone whether it fed into her growing discontent with her situation. I just know she gave me whatever she could, and that was enough for me, at least for a while.

Chapter Two

Margaret, the Pearl

My mother made me feel as if I was the pearl inside my own crusty little oyster-world. I thought myself her favorite child, a common enough opinion among young children, but maybe more likely true in my case because I was the little girl she had yearned for, her only daughter until Lucinda, the unexpected child, arrived four years later. It strikes me now that she was bringing to life a portrait of the perfect childhood, though now I recognize it was more a coveted self-portrait. I think she wanted to teach me as she had not been taught, dress me as she had never been dressed, and shower on me the love she had not known. I was to have the childhood she never had. Her brown eyes that could stab always softened when she looked at me.

At bedtime, Mom hugged me in her lap and sang and read to me to grow my imagination and love of language. She once bragged that she taught me to read before I began school and seemed to have her mind set on my reflecting her own self-perceived childhood precocity.

I memorized all the stanzas of "Froggie Went a Courtin'" and quickly began riffing other verses for "The Alphabet Song," a letter-learning ditty that began, "B-I bye, B-Oh bow, B-I biddy bye B-Oh bow biddy bye bow, B-U boo biddy bye bow boo, boo." As she sang "The Ballad of Molly Malone," I could envision a young woman wheeling her wooden fish cart through Dublin, but I made my mother laugh by asking why Molly's ghost might have wanted to do that long after she left the job.

Over and over, I begged her to sing her favorite old country songs about love and loss. As Mom's voice rose, I pictured the weeping Native American maiden waiting in vain for her brave warrior to return from war in "Little Red Wing," and the train engineer killed in the "Wreck of the Old Number 9" the night before he could marry his sweetheart so dear.

"Margaret, you're crying." She was incredulous, then concerned. "I'd better stop."

"No, Mama, sing it again!" I couldn't get enough of hearing about couples who loved each other so much. I wasn't seeing a lot of that in my own home.

Characters from the poems and stories she read to me from the *Children's Book of Illustrated Literature* fed a mind hungry for the imagery of exotic people in faraway lands. "Aladdin" and the *Velveteen Rabbit* occupied a parallel universe to my own, and just as real. I believed that *Small Rain*, a book of illustrated Bible verses by Jessie Orton Jones had been written about me, my siblings, and my friends, so similar were its children's faces to ours. One image was a very young little girl in the flower-trellis-framed doorway of her home gazing out wistfully, one forefinger in mouth, her small white cat beside her. I was convinced that I was that little girl.

Mom sewed seersucker sunsuits and gingham dresses for me (which later became hand-me-downs for Lucinda) and plied me with whatever gifts she could to make me feel equal to any other child in my circle, though some of her gifts didn't work out as she intended.

In the 1940s and 1950s, movie theatres held promotions to draw in families with children, giving out live fuzzy yellow baby ducklings or baby chicks dyed with pastel colors to take home in small cardboard boxes with holes. My mother had to know the mess they would make, but she couldn't refuse my pleas. Perhaps she even thought a pet would be educational. I brought home two ducklings whom we dubbed Cheep and Peep.

Ducks don't make great pets or playmates, so after a month or so, I forgot my fuzzy ducklings completely. They roamed over our yard until my father pointed out that Peep and Cheep had become full-grown white ducks, walking around quacking amiably and leaving layers of duck doo-doo in their wake.

"Catherine, these birds have to go," Dad protested. "I can't have customers stepping in this crap."

One morning, I realized the mess had disappeared and so had Peep and Cheep. When I asked my mother where they were, she pointed toward up the hill to our neighbor on Valley View Drive.

"They were making too much of a mess around the yard," she explained gently, "So they went to live with Mrs. Riffey. But you can visit them whenever you want." When I declared I wanted to visit right now, she waved her permission.

Mrs. Riffey was a tall woman about my mother's age who always seemed to appear in an old, faded kitchen apron with large front pockets. She smiled genially when I showed up at her door inquiring about my feathered companions. "Of course, Peggy Dale, come on in."

She opened her screen door and led me back to her kitchen, as I tried to puzzle out why she would keep ducks inside her house. We arrived at her pantry and opening its doors she announced, "Here they are."

I looked around on the floor, but she pointed to a high shelf where two pale, featherless-and-headless duck bodies floating in jars sent me bawling out the front door and gave me nightmares. When Mom figured out what had happened, she marched quick-step out the door and up the hill. The wrath that came down on Mrs. Riffey that day must have been akin to what God was said to have visited on the iniquitous. Mom seemed to feel that Mrs. Riffey had intentionally chosen a particularly brutal way of sharing the news of my pets' demise. Mom tried to make Cresaptown a sheltered place for me to grow up, but distress grew like a weed in my own home, and other kinds of hazards found me outside of it.

Mom was generous and protective of me, but she always described Dad as a miser, and that's how I came to view him. Even our wounds had to be what he considered serious to take us to a doctor; otherwise, he deemed it a frivolous use of funds.

Riding with bare feet on the front of Fred's bicycle as he steered it out our driveway, I managed to get my foot tangled in the spokes. I suppose I was lucky I escaped with only some deep cuts. Quite an argument ensued when Dad refused to let Mom take me in for treatment for my mangled foot as I sat there whimpering with my foot in a pan of water.

"It will get infected!" she railed. "She needs a tetanus shot!"

He hesitated only a moment before dismissing that argument. "Naw, she'll be okay," he concluded, looking down at my bloody foot turning the pan of water a deep pink. "Just put some iodine on it."

Mom painted minor injuries with orange mercurochrome; major ones got brown iodine. Hearing that I had a major wound made me wail louder, but Dad remained unmoved. I got the iodine, and I did not get an infection, though over seventy years later, you can still see the scar.

How hard Dad worked to get the money for our doctor visits or the food on our kitchen table was always lost on me; I took it all for granted, as most kids do. But most of all, I was blind to the erroneous perceptions about my parents I was absorbing, ideas that would later damage my chances for a happy marriage.

My mother allowed movies to nurture my childhood imagination, and it was cause for celebration for Fred and me when she decided I was old enough to accompany him to Cresaptown's "The Park," a small movie theatre about three-quarters of a mile away. Even if it meant babysitting a little sister to do it, Fred could get out of the house and see his friends and whatever was playing on the big screen. Less than a dollar covered both our movie tickets and penny candy, a small price to allow my mother a break from two of her brood.

I came to dote on the predictable regimen of this outing, which always included a stop at Lucas' American Gas Station on the McMullen Highway for a nickel's worth of penny candy. Short and squarely built, Mr. Lucas always wore oil-stained overalls and an open, friendly expression, but he looked especially happy when he was doling out our candy.

Mr. Lucas' store boasted a dazzling array of confections. They beckoned behind a convex-glass-fronted display case adorned with small fingerprints from children pointing to their favorites. I always wrestled with the problem of which teeth-rotting treats to select. Fred and I had to share them between us, which further complicated the selection process. Mr. Lucas' display tempted us with chewy Bit-o-Honey and Mary Jane, black licorice sticks, sugar-coated licorice-jelly "babies," and squares of white divinity shot through with colorful jellybean-like pieces. There were also multi-colored sticks of sweetened coconut, chewy Tootsie Rolls, and for last-until-the-main-feature sucking, root-beer barrels or jawbreakers. The choice was a byzantine problem that always threatened to make us late to the movie. Combined with the orange marshmallow circus peanuts and sugar-coated orange jelly slices my dad shared from his stash of favorites, the shape of my teeth by the time I was ten should have surprised no one. Dad's shiny silver filling on a front tooth may also have reflected his own love of confections.

At The Park, I sat where Fred always put me, around the center of the theatre, while he sat in the front row with his friends. Once I sauntered down to visit him but found that watching the movie from there was like following a tennis match, whipping my head right and left to follow the action. Sitting further back by myself worked out well for everyone.

Just as I began to worry that it would never begin, the theatre faded to dark, and the long, red-velvet curtains on either side of the stage swept back from the center. A cartoon or *Three Stooges* short came first, sometimes followed by an episode of a serial like *King of the Rocket Men*.

The main feature might be a slapstick comedy with Abbot and Costello or Francis the Talking Mule, or a science fiction feature film like *Creature from the Black Lagoon*. Once the show was *Invaders from Mars*, a dark tale about a child's nightmare-come-true that introduced new terrors into my psyche and sent me crying down the aisle to Fred.

"Geez, Margaret, it isn't real. Look at the zippers in the creatures' backsides."

"Y-yes, I guess so. Can I sit with you now?"

Mom assumed Fred understood the "keep-her-with-you-at-all-times" mandate she had long ago given meant that he and I would always sit together in the theatre. She did not reckon on the lure of sidelong glances from teenage girls or the unparalleled fun of sitting with one's male friends, probably arguing raucously over which actress had the biggest boobs. I was usually left alone with talking mules or Martian creatures.

One trip offered more drama than anything on the movie screen. My eyes were glued to it when a miracle occurred. My portion of the penny candy had long since been consumed, but suddenly the sky opened and rained down a candy bar into my lap. A full-sized Clark Bar in all its chocolate-covered, peanut-butter crunchiness, just for me! As I looked around, I saw that the treat could have come only from a man seated by himself in the row in front of me. I was a well-brought up child, so I leaned forward, tapped him on his shoulder, and whispered, "Thank you." He turned slightly and nodded. I think I saw him smile.

Shortly after that, the movie ended, and Fred returned to collect me. When he saw my chocolate-covered mouth and the Clark Bar, his eyes widened. "Where'd you get that?"

The man must have vamoosed when he saw my brother coming, but I described him, and Fred immediately knew who it was. He tried to take the partially eaten bar from me, but I threw a fit and people turned to stare, so he grabbed my chocolate-smeared hand and headed for home. When we got to the house, I skipped up the steps ahead of my brother and excitedly boasted to Mom the story of my candy miracle.

When Fred opened the screen door, she turned on him, teeth clenched, her face bright red. "Who was it?" she snarled.

"Oh, Mom, it must have been Mr. Smith; he's harmless," he

began, but he got no more out before the torrent began. She retreated a step from Fred and clenched her hands across her breast, as though she were afraid of what she might do if she were close enough to grab him.

"Mr. Smith!" she shrieked. "That filthy man? My God, boy, don't you have any sense at all? Think what could have happened! And where were you during all this?"

After railing at my brother, she turned to me. I was crying even before she took away the remainder of my miracle candy bar and threw it in the garbage can with the eggshells and coffee grinds.

Rather than yelling at me, she sat in a kitchen chair and pulled me gently onto her lap, her voice dropping to the register I was used to when she spoke to me. With her small cloth handkerchief, she dabbed at the tears on my hot cheeks and quieted me before exacting a promise that I would never again talk to or accept candy or anything from a "total stranger."

After that, I seldom went to movies and only with her. No candy.

I don't know how old I was when I was hospitalized, and no one remembers why, but my memory of the experience is vivid. I could not understand why my mother had to leave me there at night, and I screamed and tried to climb out of the crib when I saw that she was gone. To calm me, one nurse picked me up in her arms and walked around to show me other children in the ward, all quiet and asleep in their beds, but I was having none of it. Mom returned in the morning to find me red-eyed and worn out from sobbing, sitting in my crib covered over with a netting that the nurses had used as a last resort to keep me immobilized.

"What the hell are you doing to her?" she yelled as the amazed nurses started backing away from her. The tiger mom's cub had been caged. She took me home that day.

Everything in my early childhood convinced me that my mother was my protector-savior goddess. She ruled my world, and I feared nothing. Who could have predicted the one danger from which she couldn't shield me?

Chapter Three

The Pillow and the Pie

The space above my father's glass shop was a hall of mirrors. Framed and unframed pieces of every size were propped along the walls facing each other, repeating images rendering the narrow room gigantic. When I stood before them, I saw a dizzying number of reflections of me, one behind the other, fading into the distance, the so-called infinity effect. Most captivating to me were the gold-framed antique ones waiting to be refinished, called re-silvering, because reapplying silver nitrate on the back of the glass is what endows it with reflective quality. In these old mirrors, I saw blotchy, imperfect echoes of myself, and in dim light it appeared as though shadows of other figures stood behind me. My shadow ghosts did not look benevolent.

In these old mirrors, age determined the amount of damage. When I stood before those so old that they'd lost most of their reflective silver, I could see little clear detail even in my own face. Like the darkened mirrors, age has done damage to my memory of some details of events that were to shatter my worldview, but the essence of what happened is etched clearly in my mind.

Even if no friends were around to play kick the can or

hide-and-seek, or if the weather was bad and I tired of wandering the house or coloring on the back porch, I had a catalog of other fun activities. One arrived in the form of a large cardboard box that my mother emptied of its dozens of toilet paper rolls and left on the porch to throw away. I hauled it back into the living room, turned it upside down, propped it open on one side with books or a shoebox, and played games underneath it. Then I turned it open-side-up, crawled into it, and lurched merrily around on the floor like a cardboard car, which kept me so busy she let it stay there for months afterwards as my plaything.

But this was a fine, sunny morning, and I was impatient to begin a round of outside fun. I liked to explore the bank behind the lilac trees and tool shed where my father tossed glass remnants from his work creating stained-glass church windows in his shop. I looked for pretty pieces of ruby or aureate gold I could hold up to the sun and look through, or the rare find of stained glass "jewels," the small, round, faceted pieces that usually appeared in my father's window designs at the intersection of four square or rectangular pieces. I once showed Dad one I had found, and he offered me a penny for each one I returned to him, as they could be reused and would have been thrown out in error. I had in mind finding enough jewels to buy myself a tasty treat from the neighborhood store near Gail's house.

I must have been just shy of six when my mother chose a day when the house was empty except for me and my year-old sister, Lucinda—whom we called Cindy—was playing happily in the bedroom we shared. After breakfast, I was preparing to skip out the door when Mom called me into her bedroom, picked me up in her arms, and set me down gently on her bed. The pink-and-blue flowers on her white chenille bedspread always intrigued me; my own chenille bedspread had plain white flowers. With my index finger, I began to trace the outlines of the pastel flowers as she sat beside me.

"Margaret Dale," she began, taking me by my arms and turning me to face her, "I want to talk to you. Sweetheart, is someone touching you where they shouldn't? You can tell me."

Her worried face observed me closely for signs of recognition or relief, but on my countenance, she found neither. I shook my head, "No, Mama." I had no idea what she was talking about, but thinking the matter closed, I made to slide off the side of the bed and run outside. Mom took hold of my arms to keep me there on the bed facing her.

This was long before the development of methods to interview children who may have been sexually abused, and she had no experience doing such an interrogation anyway. She had only her own personal experience, and it's unlikely anyone had asked her such a question when she was my age and wished they had. Would she have known how to answer? Thinking back as a grown woman, maybe she thought she would, and so believing, she asked me.

The perplexed look on my face must have shown her she was not getting through to me that she was trying to help me. She continued to probe, framing the same question in different ways, trying to communicate to me that I had been violated and that she was my advocate.

"I won't be upset with you, Margaret," she asserted, her rising voice belying her words. "I know someone has been touching you somewhere they shouldn't. Just tell me who it is."

I already said no. Why was my answer not right? What should I say? I sat squirming, uncomfortable with the shapeless dimensions of the situation, its dark edges revealing no sure path into a resolution for the problem. Mom seemed impatient, and I longed to tell her what she wanted to hear, if only I knew what it was. I wriggled out of her grasp and lay back on the bed, turning over the puzzle in my mind. Finding no answer in the space my child's short attention span allotted to it, I drifted into a daydream, her voice fading into the background.

Then quite suddenly, a pillow was on my face, pressing down, covering my nose, my mouth, my eyes. I could not breathe. My small legs flailed helplessly as I tried to throw off the soft but relentless obstruction. Her irritation must have sparked into a blaze of exasperation. Was she trying to shock me into seeing the seriousness of the situation? Or did she suddenly conclude that a little girl's life was being ruined and, powerless to stop it, felt it was better to end that life now before it turned out warped and ugly? Or did her actions begin as one motive and become another? In those airless, sightless seconds as she held down the pillow and listened to my muffled cries, she had time to make, unmake, remake a decision.

Who can say why she did it? We never spoke of the episode, though I never forgot it. By the time I was old enough to collect words and thoughts to form a question, it had become fused together with the hundreds of her other strange and inexplicable acts into the image I had of her as an unpredictable, irrational person whose ire you must take care not to arouse.

Just as suddenly as it came, the pillow was gone, and I struggled to sit up. The panicked look on my face and rising tears told her she had to take a new approach.

"Tell me who touched you," she cajoled, "and I'll give you a nickel to buy a pie."

Now this was a carnality I was familiar with. A pre-packaged, handheld pie from the neighborhood store was one of my favorite treats.

"Can I have the whole thing for myself?" I sobbed, a little joy coming back into my shattered life. "Can I have apple?"

I could almost taste the sweet, mushy fruit and cardboard crust of that manufactured pastry.

"Yes, yes, just tell me! Was it your father?"

I pictured Dad's shocked face and the quick rage that would surely follow. I shook my head.

"Your brother Fred, then? Was it him?"

Sobbing and terrified, I agreed it was the innocent and unsuspecting Fred. I could deal with his anger; my mother had some control over what he might do to me. I nodded through my tears. The look on her face signaled that I had, at last, supplied the required answer.

"And where did he touch you?" She seemed relieved that the truth had come to light.

Yet another question I could not answer! As I cast about anxiously for what might satisfy her, she pointed to my female private area. "Was it on your teenie?"

Again, I agreed, thankful that I had not only landed on a response that would end this captivity and torment by this new and frightening version of my mother but would also allow me to have a wonderful, promised treat. I got the nickel and skipped off to buy the pie and finally begin my day. I lingered on the road home as long as possible.

Fred came back from school to a screaming torrent of accusation and rebuke usually reserved for my father. His vehement denials that he had not and would never think of doing such a thing to me or anyone may have convinced her only that she had accused the wrong male family member. Later when she had left the house to help a customer in my father's shop next door, my brother confronted me.

Fred towered over me. His whole body, usually so slack and relaxed, was taut with anger. "Why did you tell her such a lie?" he hissed. "What were you thinking?"

I was caught between two volatile forces. He would never hit me or even scream at me because Mom would hear, but I didn't relish living with his anger either. I burst into tears and explained as best I could in my child's language that I had been forced into this knowingly false charge. He seemed to understand and stalked off. I never mentioned the pie.

Vivid nightmares began to visit my sleep, one repeating often. I perch at the edge of the maroon overstuffed sofa in our living room, my small legs dangling, and I look down idly at a marble ashtray on a metal stand beside me. As I watch with an inarticulate terror that only a small child's mind can conjure, the ashtray's marble patterns begin to move around, stirring into misty plumes that rise out of the tray. I see that the plumes threaten to become shadowy creatures like those behind me in the mirror hall, and terrified out of my mind, I fall from the sofa and try to rise and flee. But my feet do not obey my command, and I stumble and fall. With the shadowy ghosts about to overtake me, I wake shrieking and crying for my mother, my comforter, the cause of my terrors. Other nights, I sailed over the green hills past the Potomac River, only to plummet suddenly and wake as if I had fallen from the firmament.

Sometimes lying half-awake at night, everything in my room appeared far away. I would call out to my mother to come in and reassure me that I would not fade away into the background and be unable to reach out and touch anything solid again. The possibility that she could have caused any of my night alarms would never have occurred to her. My view of her as my protector-savior goddess had been destroyed, and that eroded faith changed me. If I could not trust her, who could I trust?

When I began first grade at Cresaptown School later the same year, I found a place that restored coherence in my chaotic mind. I loved everything about school, and school seemed to love me back. Everything ran along predictably, and each day, each month, offered the same agreeable sequence. My teachers' comments glowed with praise, and Mom seemed pleased, so I was relieved. Who wanted to rouse the dark wrath I had seen in her?

Later that year, I ambled home after the last bell through yellow-and-rust-colored trees in a gathering dusk to find both my parents and sister gone and Fred my babysitter. His voice was shaking, his face drawn. "Cindy somehow climbed inside that empty cardboard-box of yours." I tried to envision her wobbling around the living room floor in it as she had seen me do so often.

"The box fell over, and her head caught the sharp corner of the piano."

My face went cold. "H-how bad is it? Will she be okay?"

"I don't know. Mom and Dad took her to Memorial Hospital in Cumberland. We'll have to wait until they get back."

I wandered about the house unable to think of much else besides my sister. Sometimes I stood sentinel at the back door at the driveway to catch sight of Dad's truck, waiting for word on whether she was alive or dead. She was too young to be much of a playmate, but she was a cheerful presence in our home and, unlike me, always seemed to be happy and smiling.

They were still not back by the time Fred made me go to bed. When I woke in the morning, Mom assured me Cindy would be fine. "She'll need rest and quiet for a couple days. She's sleeping now."

Before making me get dressed for school, Mom allowed me to look in at Cindy as she slept in our parents' room, and I glimpsed a white-bandaged head.

Now a new nightmare, more frightening than walking shadows or falling from the sky, haunted my sleep and drifted into my waking hours. I dreamed my mother had killed my sister and cut her up. Somehow, she put her back together, but I could see the red lines in her skull where Mom had reassembled her like a jigsaw puzzle. I woke up wailing but dared not tell anyone the exact shape of my anxiety, saying only that I dreamed Cindy was hurt again.

My nightmare gave narrative to my unconscious fears. I recalled the pillow incident, but Fred and I examined the position of the piano and its sharp corners and deemed it plausible that an accident had occurred just as Mom described. But my terror was born of not knowing, of being certain of nothing—a fear that became a shadow I would never outrun.

That year, my view of Mom as my protector-savior goddess faded away and fear took its place. Only later would I learn of events in her own past that haunted her and drove her to take the actions that destroyed my childhood innocence.

Chapter Four

I'll Fly Away

So much of my mother's early life is unknown and unknowable. If some of her actions were charged crimes in which motive and intent had to be proven, the case would have to be dismissed for lack of evidence. After the appearance of The Suitcase that changed my life, I searched for details of her early life but found no letters and few documents, no witnesses alive who could give first-hand, unbiased testimony that is more than mere guesses about what happened to her or to her mother, Floda Mae Pryor. Nothing remained to lend the clarity I craved. *The Mystery of the Missing Mothers*. Though I don't know their whole background, I have uncovered clues as to why Mom was unable to outrun the darkness cast over her life, a shadow that was later willed to me.

When I was a teenager, Dad gave me a ride to Cumberland in the Art Glass Company truck, and as usual, we didn't talk much. As we passed the Rose Hill Cemetery where Mom's father was buried, my father suddenly jerked a thumb towards it. "Blackjack's in there. Did you know that?"

My maternal grandfather Lewis had acquired a nickname not due to his poker proficiency but his weapon of choice. As a young man, he carried a blackjack to deliver blunt-force trauma to anyone accusing him of cheating.

"Yeah," I exhaled. Talking with my father about my mother made me uncomfortable.

"He fooled with her, you know." He glanced over at me quickly to see if I understood. So many decades before the "Me Too" movement, the word abuse was not even used by anyone we knew to describe what Mom had endured as a child.

"Yeah, I know," I mumbled, looking away from him, though, of course, I didn't really understand. I assumed it wasn't anything good, but I had my own problems and didn't want to shoulder hers.

Not long after, I asked Bobby about what Dad had divulged, and he turned away, embarrassed. "Of course not, Margaret. Granddad was a great, bighearted kind of guy."

"Blackjack was?" His nickname alone seemed to belie Bobby's view.

"Yeah, he was. I visited him once when I was a kid, and he took me on a tour all around South Cumberland. Cafes, bars, pool halls—I saw it all."

"But don't you think what Mom told Dad could be true? Dad thought it was."

"Nah, Mom is just crazy. She makes up stuff like that."

He was saying that her claim of abuse was just some of Mom's usual drama, dredged up to cultivate pity, and I gathered that Fred agreed with him. With her children in denial and her husband an enemy, all that was left to Mom was to try her best to forget it all, burying all that shame and guilt and anger deep down, a volcano at her heart.

As far as I know, no one in our family ever asked my mother directly for her story for fear of opening a Pandora's box of demons, unsettling her volatile mood. If I had asked her, I suspect she would have made it as vivid as she had my birth story. Though now she is long dead, I see her short, plump frame stepping forth out of the dark mirror to describe her childhood. We sit across from each other at the kitchen dinette in the small, sparsely furnished house where I grew up. She would be wearing her usual faded cotton housedress, a dish towel in her lap, and her never-still hands constantly touching the metal table or repositioning the green milk-glass salt-and-pepper shakers or Autumn Leaf sugar bowl. As she speaks in her precisely grammatical English, her bright brown eyes dart about the room, taking in everything, making certain she misses no tasks or children that need attention.

Mom clears her throat and begins. "Mama took me to visit her people the Roys, who lived in those dusty hills around Hambleton, West Virginia. I was so young—maybe five or six—that I don't know how many times we went. Whenever Mama could get away from that devil Blackjack, I guess. Mama would ask one of the Roy cousins to come get us because Daddy had no car. Daddy always said driving made him too nervous." Her brown eyes close, and she falls silent for a few moments.

Shaking herself out of her reverie, Mom continues. "I don't know where the Roys were before they got to West Virginia. I heard the family came over from Scotland but were a mix of Scottish, Welsh, and English. The clan patriarch was Isaac Paul Roy, who worked on the railroad but later became a shift worker in the local 'rubberworks' or tire factory. My family and your father's people usually had a manageable handful of children, as your father and I did, but Isaac had eleven kids with his first wife, Martha Wilfong, wore her out, and married another, Mary Susan Pennington Ketterman, and had three more with her." She clucks her tongue in amazement. "He also adopted three of her

Ketterman children from Mary Susan's previous marriage. My mother, Floda, was the last of Martha's children."

Mom suddenly laughs, recalling the joy in the Roy home. "That was one boisterous place! The cousins and I ran around the house playing games and exploring the woods surrounding their place. And there was so much food—biscuits and bacon and fresh eggs from their chickens, homegrown tomatoes and vegetables—three meals every day and always plenty for everyone. Of course, I was oblivious to all the work that all those kids and all that cooking meant for Grandma Roy and the other womenfolk. Remember that story I wrote, 'The Hill Wife'? That was based on one of the Roy's neighbors."

My mother's voice is wistful. "I never wanted to go back to Blackjack's house. It made me sad when Mama cried most of the way back to Cumberland." She falls silent and her face recedes into shadow.

Did Mom view her time at the Roys in the same idyllic haze as I do my earliest years in Cresaptown, before the family's wretchedness began to shape my story? Though Mom was born in Cumberland, it seemed to me she saw her grandparents Isaac and Mary and the other Roys as her real family and her mother's birthplace as her native soil.

The protagonist in Mom's short story "The Hill Wife" is a West Virginia teenager surviving a hard life and harder husband in the pitiless poverty of rural Appalachia. A gentle, sensitive soul, she is worn out and weary, isolated in a ramshackle hovel with too many children to care for. Each morning, she wakes to prepare a breakfast of biscuits and potatoes and eggs fried in lard, one of three cheap, heavy meals she will make that day, each one filling you out without filling you up. Each day's work begins but never ends as she hauls up bucket after bucket of water from the creek for drinking, cooking, and washing in a home with no electricity or appliances. In between, she washes dishes, changes babies, and scrubs by hand all the family's clothing and cloth diapers, stopping only to squash the fat, green worms that prey on her small vegetable garden. Each night, full of pain mental and physical, she faces the sexual demands of her brutish husband.

For months, the man rejects and ridicules her one plea: that he build her a small porch in the back of the shack where she can sit for a few moments each day to gaze at the river and valley and green mountains beyond them and dream her own dreams. "You ain't got time for sitting around on your fat ass," he scoffs.

One night when she is physically spent and facing another of her husband's sexual assaults, she makes an excuse to leave the bedroom and returns with her husband's shotgun. She gives him both barrels.

Later the sheriff arrives. Knowing of her husband's violent, abusive nature and seeking to help her avoid jail, he gently questions her. "Did he threaten ya, Ellie? Was he beatin' ya again?" The young hill wife looks down at her rough, old woman's hands and smooths her thin cotton nightgown over her knee. "I done it," she replies softly, "because he wouldn't build me no back porch."

"Hillbilly hell" is how my mother's story impressed me, and it painted as grim a picture of life for rural, hill-country women as Robert Caro's biography of Lyndon Johnson's youth and early political life did for the Texas hill-country ones. Caro made the case that electrification of the area that LBJ represented in Congress was a key part of his rise to power. Caro's chapter "The

Sad Irons" described women "worn out before their time . . . old at forty, old at thirty-five, bent, and stooped, and tired" from their work as housewives and farm wives. The chapter title refers to how women had to haul wood, start a fire in a wood stove, and heat up blocks of iron with wooden handles for the ironing—irons that could slip and sear flesh. He wrote, "The women of the Hill Country called them 'the sad irons.'" With all the hauling water and wood, washing by hand, and childcare in a home without electricity, the whole life sounded sad to me.

Life in the West Virginia Mom wrote about in "The Hill Wife" must have been just like the Texas that Caro described. Even in 1935, fewer than ten percent of West Virginia farms were electrified; rural areas got it last. Floda and her relatives would have known only a life of housework—washing, ironing, cooking, canning, cleaning, childcare—without electrical power. Even when West Virginia did get electricity, few rural families could afford electrical appliances like stoves, washers, and irons. Even powered washers required that many women still had to haul water to fill them by hand. Many homes could not afford telephones, and those that could often took messages for neighbors.

I never looked at my electrical appliances the same way after reading "The Sad Irons," and I never viewed Grandmother Floda's life the same way after reading "The Hill Wife." I perceived it was Mom's tribute to Floda and all the other women in her family who emerged from the unforgiving struggle for survival of body and soul. Was Mom also writing about herself? To me her story meant that a life drained of hope or respite could cut open the sensitive vein in a woman and drain it out into care of children, house, and husband until there is nothing left inside but dry ache and a desire for escape, even the escape of death. The only way women like Martha Wilfong could get some rest was to die.

One of Mom's favorite old hymns was "I'll Fly Away," which she used to sing in our kitchen before I could understand the despair she must have been feeling. Its refrain echoes the desperate longing of women like herself and her mother. "When the shadows of this life have gone, I'll fly away. Like a bird from prison bars has flown, I'll fly; I'll fly away."

Floda Mae died over twenty years before I was born, but I met her in my mother's story. Did she once view Blackjack as her path out of that hard life? I conjure an image of her to stand before me, a sad-eyed wraith in a thin, ankle-length dress, cotton bonnet, and faded apron, all stitched by hand. She holds a small cloth handkerchief. If I could speak to that ghost, I would ask her to tell me her own story. We would sit on the rickety steps of the Roy's unpainted front porch, her young face eerily like my own mother's, but more flaccid. Her brown eyes are gentle and profoundly melancholy, her voice so quiet I must bend toward her to hear her words.

"I was borned in Dry Fork, West Virginia," Floda whispers. "I ain't sure how Lewis got up to Dry Fork from where he was raised up in Byrdstown, Tennessee. I think maybe the railroad sent him through Jellico to Lexington or even to Cincinnati, and then he worked the spur up through West Virginia.

"He seemed like such a kindly man when I met him. When I learned I was in the family way by him, he told me we'd marry his next trip up through Hambleton and said he'd even adopt Zelda, my two-year old baby. He finally got around to the marrying part after Phrona Catherine was borned. We stood up 'afore the Keyser, West Virginia, Justice of the Peace, who married us legal in 1919. Keyser was fifty mile north of Dry Fork, but I think my uncles was gettin' impatient with how long it was takin' Lewis to marry me, and they tole him they'd be totin' shotguns next time they saw him, so he wanted to stay clear of the Roy boys.

"Phrona Catherine was borned in 1918 at my cousin's house in Whitmer, West Virginia. I should have knowed it was a bad sign to have a chile in that bad pandemic year." Floda's eyes mist over with a faraway gaze. "It was so cold that winter that when Cousin Luther fell sick of the grippe, Mama fetched that baby inside the oven for a spell to keep him warm. 'Course the oven weren't hot or nothin', but in the evenin' it still give him warmth enough to save his life.

"Good as his word, Lewis made my Zelda a Pryor after we was married, and in 1922, we and the girls settled in Cumberland, Maryland. The house was big and had 'lectric lights and water flowin' right in the kitchen!" She shook her head, recalling the wonder of it. "We was so happy at first, but it didn't take long afore I found out what Lewis was doin' to my little Zelda, and I was beggin' my daddy to take her back to West Virginia. It 'bout broke my heart to let her go."

Floda's shoulders slump, and she dabs at her eyes with her handkerchief. I envision possible scenes of how Floda found out what her husband was doing. Did she walk in on him as he was molesting Zelda? Did a neighbor share a suspicion? I never learned. The facts died with her.

Floda's ghost continues, "I didn't know what else to do. I had to get her out of there, to give her a chance. But I couldn't save Phrona. She was Lewis's chile, and he wouldn't turn loose of her. But I guessed what he had in mind for her."

She weeps into her hands, the sound fading with her as her face retreats into darkness. But there's more to tell, so I conjure my mother to come forth and finish the story.

Mom's voice is low and bitter. "Unlike the hill wife, my

mother didn't slaughter Blackjack like the animal he was; I wish she had. The cousins would probably have helped her. Instead, my last memory of my mother was when she proposed what I know now was a strange kind of play. I still remember her words. 'Phrona, let's bang pots and pans against the wall.'

"Some in the Pryor family said that Blackjack's dissipated life left him with a venereal disease, which he passed on to my mother, and the disease took her mind. But I have always thought she was driven mad when she realized she was bringing children into the world she could not protect from the monster she had married. I suppose no one really knows. I just know I never saw her alive again." Mom buries her face in her dishtowel and begins to sob.

Might a frustrated and despairing Floda have used histrionics as catharsis for her anguish, as her own daughter Phrona later would? In the early 1920s, it was all too easy for someone to "put away" a troublesome family member, especially a female, and Blackjack might have tired of Floda's drama and had her committed. Mom was never told what became of Floda, but I sent away for documents that showed my grandmother died in a Baltimore mental institution. There were rumors she gave birth again before she died—some said it was twin boys—though no child survived long. Floda's tragedy was over at twenty-eight. Phrona was eight.

Floda lived and died in obscurity, and her gravesite heaps mystery on mystery. Blackjack is buried alongside his second wife Blanche in the Rose Hill Cemetery in Cumberland, but Floda lies in Wellersburg, West Virginia, about twelve miles outside that Maryland city. Even in death, Blackjack banned Floda from his presence. She lies alone, no other family members with her, save one.

One overcast day after a long search, I located her resting place and discovered two names on her gravestone: Floda Mae Pryor and Ambrose Pryor. (Ambrose was Blackjack's middle name.) The stone says that Ambrose lived about two years and died before Floda, but no one in our family had heard of him, and neither Maryland nor Pennsylvania records held any trace of his birth. Floda's disappearance was also a mystery to Phrona; no one explained why her mother vanished so suddenly. My mother knew only that Floda's nurturing presence was no longer there. She was alone with the monster.

I've often thought that if Floda hadn't become so ill, she might have been able to shield my mother from Blackjack or appeal to the Roys to force Blackjack to let her join them, as they had Zelda. Now I see that Floda's death set in motion events that caused a cascade of deepening shadows on our family's future.

One of Blackjack's grandchildren by his second wife, Blanche, filled in some of the details for me that Mom may not have known. "He abused any little girls he could get to," she declared. "I know he molested my aunt and cousins, as well as other little girls in the family or neighborhood. When I asked my mom about her dad being a pedophile, she denied it. 'Oh, no, he never did things like that to anyone. He just liked little girls.'" Her denial of what her own daughter knew seems more repression than reliable fact.

When I heard those details, it made sense to me that the Grandfather Pryor my brother Bobby knew was a "great guy." Blackjack "just liked little girls."

Mom's ghost wipes her eyes with the dish towel before finishing her story. "Three years after my mother died, my Daddy married the widow Blanche who brought two of her children to live with us, including her little girl, Elsie. I think Blanche wanted to be a good mother to me, but I was still grieving my own Mama, my angelic Floda. I wailed into my pillow every night; no one could console me, which I know annoyed Daddy." Mom smirks grimly. "When Blanche fell pregnant the next year, I begged Daddy to let me live with the Roys and my half-sister Zelda in Hambleton. He finally agreed. By then I had outgrown his preferences; he probably had Elsie to occupy him." As Mom's face fades from my sight, I want to run after her to comfort her, to tell her that now I understand, as I never did while she was with me. But she is already gone.

I believe Mom escaped to the Roys because she was desperate for a way out of Blackjack's presence, but I also think she was searching for acceptance, yearning to recover the limitless love of the mother who was taken away so young. A year living with the Roys must have taught her that her answers did not lie in the dusty hills of West Virginia. She wanted no part of the "hill wife" role to which it consigned the poor among its women. Returning to Blackjack and Blanche in Cumberland, she continued her search for a better life, a place of respite where she could find relief from the pain and dream her own dreams.

Chapter Five

The Fence

When I was around seven or eight, Mom got the idea she needed to enclose the backyard, perhaps to protect Cindy and me from straying too far or maybe to prevent customers from wandering over from the shop. Or ever conscious of appearances and what people thought, maybe she felt that a tall, white picket fence around the entire house would signal to our neighbors that we had truly achieved the Ozzie-and-Harriet dream. Of course, Harriet would never have talked to Ozzie the way Mom spoke to my dad.

Mom had a few frugal habits from the Depression years. She made bars of soap from leftover soap fragments before modern times made it a trendy product, and she always barked at us to turn off lights when we left a room. I never knew what shampoo was until I was in college; we always used those bars of soap on our hair. But she was also a steadily flowing fountain of ideas for spending money—a new living room suite, a picture window for the bedroom. For a short time, our kitchen boasted an Ironrite Mangle Iron for pressing clothes. The Ironrite was courtesy of one of Dad's customers, installed on a trial basis. Bobby explained that Dad did it to please one of his customers who sold the devices, but I remember Mom loved it and begged Dad to buy it.

"Look, Margaret, how easy it is to work," exclaimed my delighted mother.

Indeed, it did look like a child could operate it and so, intrigued by the novelty, I asked, "Can I try?" Mom showed me how to place a wrinkled pillowcase on the steaming bed, lay a damp dish towel over it, and close the lid down to press them both. I was impressed, but even I could have told her that Dad wasn't going to buy that Ironrite.

"We're the only ones in Cresaptown to have one," she crowed. "My ironing will be done in half the time." She'd have saved time all right. With that Ironrite she'd have been able to turn over most of the ironing to me.

Two weeks later, the Ironrite vanished. I feel sure Dad only tried it to please his customer; he never would have bought it, any more than he would have gotten her an electric washer. When she asked for such things, she may have seen them as a practical time-saver, as well as a boast to the neighbors, but knowing Dad as I did, he viewed them as extravagances.

Mom also tried mightily to persuade Dad to build her a fence around the yard, but as usual, my father was adamant: no fence. And as usual, that didn't stop my mother, who apparently decided on a "forgiveness-is-easier-than-permission" route.

One morning after breakfast, when Dad had left for a days-long window job, she gave fifteen-year-old Bobby her orders. "Bobby, I'd like you to build a fence for me." He knew it wasn't a request. "Sure, Mom, just show me what you want." Bobby always maintained he didn't know Dad had already nixed the idea, but I found that hard to believe.

Mom pointed out to Bobby some nice boards she had spotted

in the shop's storage area, and a few days later, we had a tall fence blocking off our yard from the driveway. She probably planned for Bobby to paint the fence, then build "Fence Part 2" around the rest of the yard. Bobby, telling me the story years later, admitted that he was quite proud of his handiwork and eager for Dad to come home and see the design and construction he had done all by himself. He envisioned him and Dad standing together admiring it, hoping Dad might say, "Nice job, Son!" and give him a proud look or rare clap on the back.

I don't remember being there when my father arrived, so I got this description later from Bobby. He and Mom were in the kitchen and heard the truck engine as it roared into the driveway, followed by the crashing sound as it hit the fence. When Dad pulled into the driveway and the fence came into view, he backed up the truck, put it into gear, and went for the fence at ramming speed. My mother and brother hared out to the back porch and, as they stood there staring, Dad backed halfway out of the driveway and came forward to crash into the fence again. Bobby gaped unbelieving at the wreckage of his proud creation as Mom cried, "Spates, my God, what have you done?" and Dad, his rage spent, lay over the steering wheel of his dented truck and cried bitterly, his hands pawing helplessly at his balding head. When I arrived on the scene later and saw the fence and my distraught father, I filed the episode under the heading of Parent Battles and crept inside.

When I asked Mom what had happened, she seemed genuinely worried and muttered something like, "Just stay out of his way when he's like this, Margaret. I never know what he'll do." By evening, the broken pieces of Bobby's proud creation had been carted away, collateral damage of my parents' conflict.

I have come to believe that when Dad saw the fence, it

triggered a PTSD episode from another period in his life, years before he had even met my mother. That time was 1930 when the first full year of the Great Depression began with the October 1929 stock market crash. Unemployment and poverty like no one alive had ever experienced were spreading like a contagion throughout the country. My brother Bobby narrated to me my father's experiences of that time so often and in such vivid detail that I can hear my father telling it.

Dad emerges from the dark mirror just as I remember him. Flannel work shirt, faded overalls, lined face gazing at me with those worried eyes. I sense he is glad I want to talk with him, that now I am interested in hearing his story as I never was when he was alive.

We are in the dim light of his shop on an overcast day, yet I see him clearly, as if we were really there together. He clears his throat and makes that quick "tss tss" sound with his teeth he always did before beginning a story. He hitches up a pant leg, places a work-booted foot on the stair up to his office, and leans an arm on his leg as he clasps his hands together—a casual male-stance I have seen him take dozens of times when he talked with customers—before starting to speak.

"The first time I knew what a Depression was all about was the winter after the Black Friday stock market crash. By December 1929, Pop's customers weren't comin' around as much, and he told me he didn't have any work for me. Said I should go out and find my own. I was pretty confident because I was strong and had never known a time when I couldn't find some way to make money. Work was just startin' to disappear all over the country, but I didn't know that; none of us did. I was an unskilled, nineteen-year-old kid with a sixth-grade education, but I just knew I could find something." He looks down at his work boot and shakes his head. After a moment, he picks up the story again.

"I spent a good while lookin' before I found a job 'on spec' in January 1930, workin' for a local developer named Opie Annan. Opie hired a bunch of us guys to dig underground ditches and drain fields for septic tanks in a new housing development. Told us we'd be paid when the money started comin' in on home sales. I wasn't happy about that arrangement, but it was all I could find, so I took it and felt lucky to get it. A bunch of men applied, but I was young and muscular, so I was one of the fellers picked. Opie assured us he'd be workin' hard sellin', and he'd be able to pay us by the spring.

"Those were some of the coldest days in my memory, but we worked twelve or more hours every day of that winter diggin' through ground that was snow covered and then iced over. Opie didn't have any back hoes or nothin' like that, so we used pickaxes and shovels to break up that hard dirt. It got so frozen that we could dig all day and only make it through a few feet.

"By spring of 1930, Opie hadn't been able to sell a single homesite. He couldn't meet his mortgage, let alone pay us, and he had to abandon the whole project. When he broke the news, he couldn't even look at us; he was so ashamed. All that work, and we never got a penny out of it." Again, my father looks down, regarding his hands, and pauses for a moment before continuing.

"A couple of the guys were pretty hot about it, said they'd take it out of Opie's hide, but that was just talk. Most of us just felt beaten down. To make matters worse, I couldn't find anything else, and I went all over that area for months askin' every place I could find. No one needed a hired man. One guy offered a nickel a cord for choppin' wood, but a feller could break his back doin' that and make hardly anything, so I turned that down. A lot of the Cumberland stores started closin', and the ones still open had NO WORK signs in their windows.

"None of the churches were buyin' or replacing' windows. Just nailed up boards if windows broke. Pop had almost no money comin' in and the three other kids to feed, so he told me he couldn't afford to have me there, that I'd have to move out. Mom and Pop's house was the only home I'd ever known, but I understood. He couldn't take care of everyone."

Dad's voice falls silent as I consider the reality of those times.

Driven by the dearth of jobs and failing businesses in the early 1930s, the increasing ranks of homeless men and women became an army of the desolate, traveling from place to place in search of jobs. My father joined them when he had just turned twenty years old.

Dad's stories of those fearful days and nights seemed like dark fairy tales of a foreign land, but it was our country between 1929 and 1939 during the Great Depression. Men, women, and children left places they had lived all their lives and went on the road, looking for either handouts or work. To move from town to town, many hobos, as they were called, adopted a dangerous, sometimes fatal mode of transportation. Dad would later describe to Bobby his days of "riding the rails," or jumping into boxcars as they rumbled slowly through towns or stopped to load and unload freight.

Railways hired guards called "bulls" to use whatever means they saw fit to dissuade hobos from boxcar-hopping, and when hobos did manage to reach a new town, local police often employed their own measures to keep them from staying long. Towns already had their own ranks of homeless, jobless families, many of whom had built make-shift encampments dubbed Hoovervilles (after the President they blamed for the Depression). These slums were springing up around the country, and transient hobos represented a further drain on an already-failed local economy.

Dad hopped one of the Western Maryland cars that stopped in Cumberland and joined other lines headed south. I conjure his ghost once again to continue his story.

"A couple dozen of us were in one boxcar, including a few kids travelin' alone and one guy with his wife and three kids. When we reached a Florida town one night and opened the car door, we found ourselves lookin' down the barrels of a dozen rifles as the local sheriff and his deputies and bulls surrounded us. Some of the kids traveling alone started cryin'; I hadn't heard them cry before that.

"'Y'all have just one chance to go back where you come from,' the sheriff barked, waggin' his rifle at us, 'or I'll set the dogs on you. If you live through that, I vow I'll throw you into my jail, and God help you then.'

"Peggy Dale, I don't think you could understand how that made me feel. I wanted to help those kids, those women, but I couldn't even help myself."

As Dad takes out his handkerchief to wipe his eyes, I imagined that sheriff going to church on Sunday, taking his Bible with him. Maybe his pastor preached from the Gospel of Matthew about the last judgement. "Depart from me, ye cursed, into everlasting fire, prepared for the devil and his angels: For I was hungry, and ye gave me no meat: I was thirsty, and ye gave me no drink: was a stranger, and ye took me not in." That sheriff must have known the words, but I guess he couldn't see how it applied to any of those people. Maybe he just didn't care.

Dad continues, "They made us walk out to the edge of town and turned us loose. Another young feller and I decided to take the sheriff's advice and head back North. By that time, I'd been travelin' over a year and never found one job. Ever'place was just as hard up as Cumberland, and the folks were all just as broke as I was. Whatever food we managed to get was from families that grew their own, and even they were near as bad off as us. I was also sick, so I was gettin' pretty weak." Dad's voice falls silent again.

Sick, heartsick, and hungry, Dad must have been as low as he had ever been. He never said how long they were walking, probably weeks or months. He must have known the despair in the cry of the old African American spiritual. *Sometimes I feel like a motherless child, a long way from home.*

Dad picks up his story. "The other feller and I hitched rides whenever we could but mostly, we walked. I can't blame folks for not pickin' us up. We must have looked pretty rough by then after sleepin' in woods along the way and no place to clean up. One morning we woke up under a tree. Frost was everywhere; we knew winter was comin'. Cold, hungry, and bug-bitten and nothin' to eat for days, we were so weak I said to the other feller, 'If we don't find somethin' to eat today, we're gonna die tonight.' We saw a path to a river and mostly slid down it, hopin' to get a drink of water and maybe find somebody who would give us a fish.

"We saw an old Black man fishin' by the stream, and he turned around, looked us over, and said, 'Y'all are 'bout the hongriest boys I ever done seen.' He didn't have any food for us, and fish weren't bitin', but we talked a while 'bout how bad things were for the country and how hard it was on poor folk. I told him I was from Cresaptown in Western Maryland, and I didn't think I'd ever see home again.

"After we talked with this man and had a drink of water from the river, we felt a bit rested, so I said goodbye and reached out to shake his hand. When I drew it back, the man had left a dime in my palm. He said it was a gift, and we should buy a loaf of bread. That would fill us up. We were okay after that. The other feller went his own way soon after we shared the bread, and I continued up towards Maryland."

I never heard my father speak about a spiritual life or any such abstractions, but I know he was a lifelong member of the Cresaptown Methodist Church. He must have known the words the Bible says Jesus spoke to his disciples by the sea: "I am the bread of life: he that cometh to me shall never hunger; and he that believeth on me shall never thirst." Dad never claimed that this old Black fisherman was an angel of God. Instead, he told his son Bobby how the gift of a dime was all that stood between him and starvation, and how a stranger gave two hobos the bread of life and the strength and will to go on.

By 1933, my father had made it as far as Baltimore where he found refuge in the city's Traveler's Aid Society, a national network of organizations designed to meet society's changing needs for poor travelers. During the 1930s, it aided thousands of individuals and families made homeless by the Depression and offered temporary housing and help ranging from healthcare to psychiatric services.

Through the TAS, Dad heard of a place that would give him work.

In 1933, the country's unemployment rate was 25 percent, and newly elected President Franklin Roosevelt established the Civilian Conservation Corps or CCC as part of his New Deal to create jobs, bolster the failed economy, and buoy a despondent populace. The program brought relief to young single men between seventeen and twenty-eight years of age by running work camps across the country, administering them much like military units. The program provided the men with free housing, food, and healthcare and paid them approximately $30 a month, most of which they had to send back home to their families.

Dad became one of thousands of homeless, unemployed young men the CCC enrolled, at the same time becoming part of what historian Jill Lepore called "a new American story." She wrote that "people from different parts of the country labored side by side, constructing roads and bridges and dams, everything from the Lincoln Tunnel to the Hoover Dam, joining together in a common endeavor . . ." Dad did his bit by helping build roads. At the end of two years, he had sent home about $720 (about $15,000 in today's money), saved $80 (about $1,700 today), and gained practical work skills. Bobby described to me Dad's lifelong reverence for FDR, whose New Deal policies saved his life. Healthy and strong once more, Dad headed back to meet his destiny in Cresaptown.

When Bobby recounted the story of Dad's Depression-era odyssey, it sunk in to me why Dad may have lost it when he saw the fence. Coming close to starvation shaped his psyche, as well as his spending habits. Everything he bought had a purpose, usually for his Art Glass Company work, and he socked away every dime he could so that his family could survive the hard times—and he knew hard times would return. I think that when he saw the fence, he saw what Mom did not: waste and frivolous use of expensive materials, and it enraged him.

Mom was only about ten when the Depression began, a kid who always had food on the table, so her experience was completely different from Dad's. I don't think she ever really "got" what those years did to him. Certainly, I was unaware of it until Bobby told me his stories, years after Dad's death. If I had known, might I have revered him for the resolute, resilient man he was? Or would I have been like her, still wanting my white picket fence?

Chapter Six

Art Glass Reflections

How old was I, I ponder now, when I became aware that everyone in my family were unpaid employees of the Art Glass Company? When the phone rang in the Art Glass shop, it also rang in our house, and from the way Dad stiffened and sprinted when he heard it, I learned early how vital it was that we answer it quickly at any hour of day or night. To my dad, a call meant a customer, and God help the person near the phone if they let it ring more than twice or stayed on longer than a minute for a personal call. Whether the call came as he was eating dinner or backing his truck out of the driveway, he scrambled to answer, and I saw my father's entire demeanor change from Dad to businessman.

I can't remember when my dad's identity and the business began to merge in my mind until they became the same—one could not exist without the other. Some customers also had trouble distinguishing between the two, a confusion for which Dad was at least partly to blame. He always answered the phone, "Art Glass," and some customers thought the company was named after him rather than his products. Sometimes a caller would ask, "Is this Art?" and Dad would reply good naturedly, "Yes, this is Art!" I think he humored their error because a firm mantra of the time was, "The customer is always right." Dad also knew that I wasn't the only one who didn't tolerate criticism well, so perhaps he did not want to correct anyone for fear of jeopardizing a good business relationship.

My sister and I found the confusion about the Art Glass name a source of high humor. Once when Dad was not at home, I answered the phone and a customer inquired, "Art there?"

I deadpanned, "You mean Mr. Glass?"

"That's the guy," replied the man. "He in?"

Cindy, overhearing all this, was one-part disbelief and the other parts laughing her butt off, but when my father heard of my joke, his face darkened. "Don't play around on the phone, Peggy," he warned in a tone I had never heard him use with me. This message was too important to dance around. He knew that the company was our life.

My brother Fred was never interested in learning Dad's work, but Bobby knew more about it than any of us due to what I feel was an unwise choice he made while a teenager. Like most states, Maryland had a law requiring kids to stay in school until they turned sixteen, though they could leave with parental approval. It was less enforced during the Depression, but in the economic boom that followed World War II, the government was back to beating the drum on high school completion. All the same, when Bobby was fifteen, our parents allowed him to quit school and go to work with Dad.

Bobby later proved as intelligent as any of us kids, so I've always felt his decision to quit school might have had something to do with an incident I heard about later. Bobby made what his teacher considered a smartass comment, and she exploded, "Bobby, you're not worth the powder to blow you up with!" I doubt that teacher knew that one of her verbal incendiaries may have altered the trajectory of an impressionable young man's life.

Though I regret the decision Bobby made about his education, it pleases me now to think that his life-long love of storytelling was sparked by the vivid tales that Dad regaled him with as they drove together on long trips to install church windows. Before Bobby joined our parents and ancestors behind the dark mirror, he repeated those stories often to me, his family, customers—to anyone willing to listen.

I lived with my father for nearly twenty years but knew little about him, his family, or his trade. For so many years after he died, Dad remained a shadowy figure in the background of my childhood world. For me, Bobby's stories brightened and clarified Dad's image like a refinished mirror.

"When Dad was born in 1910," Bobby once intoned, "his dad, our Grandfather Robert, was a brakeman. That was one of the lowest-paid—and most dangerous—of all railroad jobs. In an emergency, each railroad car had to be braked manually, so a brakeman ran atop moving cars and climbed down to release each of the brakes. You know that semicircle scar Grandad had on the left side of his head? He got that when he fell onto the tracks.

"Dad was born in 1910 in Turtle Creek, Pennsylvania, near Pittsburgh—close to where his parents lived at that time."

"Do you know where Dad got that weird first name?" I interrupted. Bobby shook his head, so I continued. "Dad's birthday was May 13, the Feast of Saint Servatius in the Catholic calendar. Grandma Adeline's family was French, and she was raised Catholic, so she named him Servatius after a French-Belgian saint. Isn't that funny?" Bobby seemed a little chagrined that I knew something he didn't know, so he merely shrugged and continued his own story.

"Dad hated his first name, and when he was a kid, his friends gave each other crazy nicknames. Not sure why they named one guy 'Nuts Clark.'" Here Bobby looked a little embarrassed, and I suspect he knew what the nickname referenced. "They called the other feller 'Snots Guzzlin' because he was always snifflin' and wipin' his nose. Dad got the name Spates, and it stuck."

As I puzzled over how they come to choose that name, Fred claimed it derived from "spuds," because Dad liked to build fires in the woods and bake potatoes or spuds. I feel that spuds to Spates is a bit of a phonic leap, but I have no other explanation. My father went by Spates for the rest of his life and even gave that name to his first son. Ironically, his son didn't like the name he was given any more than Dad had liked Servatius and ended up going by Bobby.

Dad was the eldest of Robert's four children, followed by his brother, Delos, whom we always knew as Uncle Doss. Then came sisters Beulah and Leona Agatha—Aunt Bee and Aunt Gay. Dad seemed to have absorbed his father's driving energy and may have acquired two of his other defining traits—self-reliance and persistence—from his early life with his demanding father. He carried another burden in addition to his odd first name. Dad's father made him leave school after sixth grade when he was only twelve years old to help support the family. As a young man, Dad took art lessons from a well-regarded Cumberland artist, and I heard he showed promise. But the demands of work made him cast art aside, and he was never able to develop that talent. Mom wasn't the only one to have regret for what might have been.

Young Spates revered his father and did whatever he asked. I later learned that Granddad did the same for his own father, my Great-grandfather Raymond, who had been wounded during the Spanish-American War and ended up living with his son. "Family helps family" could have been emblazoned on the Roblyer coat of arms, if we had been rich enough to have one.

Blackjack, Mom's father, also a railroad brakeman, was a slacker compared to our ambitious and entrepreneurial Granddad Robert. Always in pursuit of money-making schemes. Robert became a bootlegger, distilling moonshine in his basement during Prohibition. During one delivery a few miles from Cresaptown at the Fairgo (home to the Cumberland Fairgrounds), a customer produced a pistol during a dispute about prices. I envision a tense standoff playing out in headlights on a moonless night at the foot of Knobley Mountain. The close call must have made a distinct impression on young Spates. Supporting the family was one thing, but risking his life when it had only just begun was another entirely. When Dad refused to do any more such deliveries, my grandfather looked for other ways to pad the family income.

In 1925, Granddad Robert opened an auto garage outside Cumberland, Maryland. Learning auto-mechanic skills for the fledgling automobile field struck me as a smart move, and if the demand for auto repair had grown along with the size of his family, Robert eventually might have prospered in it. But there were not yet enough vehicles on the road to make a living at auto repair, so he kept hunting for more lucrative enterprises. When Dad gave Bobby the Art Glass Company origin tale, it became one of Bobby's favorite "Dad stories."

"Granddad found work with a man who had a contract to refurbish a local church's stained-glass windows. The contractor turned out to be either a con artist or an entrepreneur with a gambling problem—local opinions varied. He disappeared suddenly one night, leaving a box of what he had claimed were tools. Granddad opened the box to find it crammed with hymnals from the church attic.

"Granddad was good with tools but had no experience in glass work when the contractor offered him a job, but the church held him responsible for making good on the agreement. Granddad used what tools he had and learned on his own the skills needed to make the repairs. Dad and Uncle Doss were teenagers at that time, and Granddad put them to work, too."

Granddad must have had his eureka that glasswork was the fulltime money-maker he had been looking for. In 1926, he opened the Art Glass Company in Cresap Park, where our Great-granddad Raymond Roblyer owned land. Granddad Robert turned a serendipitous setback into a lucrative family business that my father later took over and ran until his death.

Dad was a glass man—not that he was fragile. Unless he was installing stained-glass windows in churches throughout Maryland and states around us, or cold-calling on churches with his notebook of work samples, he could be found daily from early morning until long past dark laboring in the bottom floor of the two-story Art Glass Company. Its concrete-block structure gloomed like a prison across the blacktop driveway from our house, and Dad had been serving time there since before I was born.

Forget any images that "glass shop" may conjure, any visions of brightly lit, spacious ateliers with plenty of windows to flaunt the shop's colorful products. Dad did most of his work in a suffocating space roughly the size of a small, two-car garage. It was crammed with sawhorse tables, rainbows of uncut stained glass, and equipment for cutting the fragile sheets and building church windows. With only a couple of dirty jalousie windowpanes, scant outside light penetrated. Illuminated by only a few bare lightbulbs dangling from the low ceiling, it was a dungeon of a place—cool in summers but menacing cold in winter. When I stood at the door and peered in, perhaps on orders to deliver a barked message from my mother—"Tell Spates lunch is ready"—the shop felt mysterious and unknowable to me, like him.

I watched Dad create church windows and cut mirrors for years without really seeing. I just wasn't that interested in any of it. I merely glanced at his worktable as I wandered around the place, casting about for something to fend off boredom if I had nothing to read and no one to play with. I'm not sure why I wasn't more curious. Perhaps because it was "men's work," a world I would never be a part of. Or maybe it was part of my mother's deliberate, determined effort to separate me from my father and keep me close to her.

Both Mom and Dad often warned me to stay out of the shop unless one of them was with me. If the Occupational Health and Safety Administration (OSHA) had existed back then, I have no doubt the Art Glass Company would have been fined, if not shut down. Glass pieces littered the floor and often cut workers' bare hands. Seeing my father with blood trickling from cuts on one or both of his dirty hands was commonplace. Unlike today's machines, none at that time had safety stops, and when my father cut wood pieces on a saw with an exposed blade, he warned me to stand back to avoid flying splinters.

In the early days, our neighbor Scottie Sarver, who had once been an unskilled machine wiper at the Celanese, was Dad's occasional employee. The Celanese had laid him off with the rest of the unskilled men at the end of the war, and he could find no other job. My father would pay him a pittance to do tasks like holding the bottom of a tall ladder as one of the other men climbed up to work on high church windows.

One evening, Dad banged open our screen door and rushed inside cursing and calling for his truck keys. Scottie stood at the door, his right hand gripping his shaking left one by the wrist, blood soaking through a dirty cloth around his finger and dripping on the porch. He had been using the table saw, and his hand had gotten in the way of the whirring blade, cutting off most of one finger. Shock was setting in, and his eyes were wide and unseeing as he held his bleeding, quivering hand. "It doesn't hurt; it doesn't hurt," he kept repeating until my father hustled him into the truck to get him to Memorial Hospital.

Traveling with my father on window installation trips could be just as hazardous as working in his shop because Dad always flew over the country roads. Speed may have been a holdover from his days as a bootlegger, but hours on the road also meant time taken away from work. The story goes that he drove so fast that Maryland state police could not catch him to issue tickets, instead mailing them to the house.

Looking back on the dangers involved in Dad's work, I am amazed he survived through my childhood. If his life had ended suddenly in those days, my life as I knew it would have been over, too. As bitterly as Mom complained about Dad, if he had died then, we all might have suffered the kind of poverty Dad knew as a young man.

Once—and only that once—when I was about fourteen, my father asked me to help him with his work. To finish the edges of a piece of glass or mirror, he used a continuous-belt sanding machine. The machine was electrical to keep it moving automatically, but the belt had to be wet manually by pouring a small, steady stream of water on it at the back during use. This prevented the edges from becoming too hot, which could break the glass or damage the silver coating on the back of a mirror. Ideally, it was a two-person operation: one person to keep the sanding belt moist and the other to do the sanding. Otherwise, he would have to make frequent pauses to wet down the belt.

"Peggy Dale, want to help me with this mirror?" Standing in front of the sanding machine in his work shirt and stained, sawdust-covered overalls, he gestured toward an oval mirror leaning against one of the worktables.

He had never asked me to help him, and I suppose I felt honored that he would trust me, a girl, to help with men's work. At the same time, I was leery of the loud, fast-moving machine. "What do I have to do?" He handed me a tall, stainless-steel can that had once held peas or corn but was now filled with water.

Dad instructed, "Just keep pouring this water on the back side of the belt. Don't pour too much and keep up a slow, steady stream, okay?" That seemed an easy enough task, but when he turned on that belt, the machine roared, and sparks flew out from the mirror as he expertly held its edges against the sanding belt. "Not too much, Peggy," he yelled over the machine's din. I pulled back as far as I could while still reaching the belt, and the noisy operation seemed to go on forever, though it lasted maybe half a minute.

I know I wasn't very good at it, but he seemed pleased to have a helper and maybe also some company. Now I think he might have been testing me to see if I could help with other such unskilled work in the shop, as his sisters had, and perhaps it was also an opportunity for us to get better acquainted. Later, I proudly announced to my mother that I had helped in the shop, and she shot me one of her black looks. "You stay out of there and keep away from that filthy old man." She set him straight, too, and he never asked me to help with anything again. That thwarted my last chance to know my father. Over the years, he and I practically became strangers.

A common sight at our house was brawny men emerging from panel trucks to unload eighty-pound cans of putty, flat boxes of leading for church windows, and jars of distilled water and chemicals for mirror re-silvering. Sometimes I would arrive home from school to find the entire driveway between our house and the shop filled with a wide tractor-trailer truck and straw scattered about the ground, as if an elephant had wandered in and parked there to have a snack. The semi was there to deliver a large, wood-slatted crate filled with window glass, mirror stock, and 4' by 8' sheets of variously colored stained glass separated by straw, later to be transformed into church windows—the "art" of the company's name. Dad helped delivery men place each glass crate atop pipes to roll out from the truck and onto a wooden platform at the end of the driveway.

Crates weighed 500-to-800 pounds, so transferring glass onto the platform required a strict protocol to keep the crate from crashing down and breaking the glass. Dad knew that one or two sheets would often be broken in shipment, but he got red-faced with frustration if he opened a case to find many shattered pieces. Too much breakage meant a delay in planned work and possibly lost revenue, though I never knew whether he had to eat the cost of that broken glass.

Most Art Glass Company revenue came from creating or repairing stained glass for churches—ecclesiastical windows—but the company did lots of other glass products. The most onerous of Dad's work had to be re-silvering mirrors, which was as complex as working with church windows, but a lot messier, and, because of the chemicals needed to strip off the old silver nitrate coating on the backs, even more dangerous.

When Dad went down in our cellar to resilver mirrors, he donned his heavy, rubber-coated apron, long rubber gloves, and helmet with a plastic visor. I found it a very impressive outfit. To me, it made him look like Captain Rocket in the pre-movie serials I saw at The Park theatre. When Dad removed the old silver nitrate with ammonia and stannous chloride—an intensely noxious and hazardous combination—the stench that rose from the cellar filled every room in the house.

"Stay out of the house today," Mom would warn. "Your father's trying to poison us again." She had little regard for what the chemicals might be doing to her husband. The smell that came up from the cellar into our kitchen was, indeed, overpowering, but she knew very well Dad was doing work that put food on our table. He eventually stopped re-silvering, maybe because of Mom's harping about the health risks, but more likely because the profit became too small.

The company thrived under my father, partly due to his image as an affable, good-natured, reliable business owner. That was the man outsiders saw. Whenever I told a friend's mother or father who my dad was, their face would light up. "Oh, yeah, I know Spates. What a great guy!" My friends agreed. "Your dad is so funny. I wish my dad were like him." They saw the guy who always had a smile ready for them and liked wordplay. He might wink at them and quip, "I think I'll spend a little time on my 'yatcht' (yacht) today." He thought mispronunciations hilarious.

My friends never saw the other side, the bear that could be abruptly roused to bellow with anger. Now I know his ongoing conflict with Mom had to have been the main reason for his sudden rages.

One summer evening when I was four or five and Cindy was tucked away in her crib, I was at the kitchen table dawdling over a nighttime glass of milk. Suddenly, there was a commotion from the bedroom, like furniture being jarred and pushed aside.

I heard something—maybe a chair—crashing to the floor just before my mother, clad in her cotton housedress, burst into the kitchen headed for the back screen door, chased close behind by my stark-naked father. She threw open the door and ran out, stopping on the back porch to glare at him.

"You stupid, filthy man. I can't bear any more of this! I can't! I'm not afraid of you! Go ahead and kill me, if you want!" Her face held a strange combination of fear and defiance. I wondered why she stood there, rather than running away.

"Woman, I'd love to! I've taken all I can from you!" Dad roared back from the kitchen, brandishing his fists.

Despite the violence of the situation, I was not so much afraid as amazed by the curious anomaly I saw on the lower half of my nude father. I stared at it open-mouthed, surprised and interested. Then my mother noticed me. "Spates," she cried, "The children!" He turned and met my astonished gaze, then stricken, retreated red-faced to the bedroom.

Over the years since I left that house, I have reflected on what could have brought two such disparate souls together. Dad was nine years older than Mom, and I never thought they had much in common except us kids. In my entire time with my parents, I don't recall either of them saying, "I love you," to each other or expressing any affection at all, but there must have been a time they believed they were as perfect for each other as my husband and I did when we married. My study of their lives yielded limited insight into the trajectory of their relationship. I did learn that the first thing they had in common was a Cresaptown bar called Cunningham's.

Chapter Seven

The Phrona Wars

A faded tattoo wrapped the muscle of my father's upper right arm. Among colorful inked ribbons and flourishes, you could just make out a name written in script: Gladys. When he was a young man, it must have made a proud declaration, a pledge that his feelings were deep enough to last forever. But by the time I was old enough to realize the anomaly it represented, its colors were washed out and most of the patterns receded into pale skin, fragments of a forgotten love song.

As a small child very much into coloring books, I was fascinated by the hues on my father's arm and puzzled over who could have painted that on him. When I first recognized it as a person's name, my innocent question was, "Daddy, who was Gladys?" but he blushed and tried to cover his arm, mumbling something about a friend from a long time ago. My mother, whose name was Phrona Catherine, had a more direct answer. "Some whore," she hissed. I had no idea what that was, but I knew better than to ask for clarification.

By the time I was six or seven, my father was also fading into the background of my life. I had accepted both my mother's scornful tone and the merit of her contempt for him. Only after learning from Bobby of Dad's colorful history was I able to add flesh to the pale image he had become—and learn more about Gladys.

❧

When Dad came back to Cresaptown after his rail-riding days, his parents, who had been getting CCC money from their son's paychecks, took him back. His luck continued to hold when he joined the 9,000-person workforce at the Celanese, now made prosperous by the parachute fabric it produced. Dad landed a job in the shipping department.

Mid-Depression, Dad was still wild enough to frequent a bar or two, but he had a steady job and perhaps was even ready to settle down. But like someone out of a 1980s ballad, he went looking for love in all the wrong places. In 1930s Cresaptown, the wrong place for Spates was Cunningham's Bar. Now we might call it a dive or juke.

Despite my mother's harsh opinions, I like to think of Gladys as a sweet-faced girl looking for whatever fun could be had in Depression-era Appalachia. When he met Gladys at Cunningham's, my father fell hard for her.

Bobby was delighted when Dad once offered, "Want to see photos of her?" But when he retrieved an album of those early days, he was heartbroken to find that Mom had torn out all the images of Gladys. *Still jealous after all those years.* Fred later showed me photos of young Spates and Gladys clinging to each other that had somehow survived Mom's green-eyed assaults on our albums.

I would love to have seen Gladys' face when Spates presented her his gaudily tattooed arm. Was she impressed with his ardor or appalled by his presumption? No other details about Gladys survived in our family lore. We know only that Dad's heart was broken, and he was left with a sad reminder of a lost love to carry on his skin for the rest of his life.

Phrona also came to Cunningham's, but I'll wager she wasn't just looking for fun, but a home of her own and a way out of her father's house. When Mom found Spates, maybe she thought he could be the provider and hard worker her father was not, and perhaps he saw in her a strong partner who could help him realize the future he envisioned—as his father Robert might have seen in the strong-willed Adeline; the women had temperament in common. In any case, Mom got Dad on the rebound from Gladys. Phrona was a young, immature eighteen, and Spates was an old man of twenty-seven.

One April day in 1937, with everything just starting to bloom, Spates and Phrona married in the United Brethren Church parsonage in South Cumberland. As they stood exchanging vows, each must have seen before them a partner who could help them achieve the life they wanted. The difference in their goals became apparent later, but on that day, when love was alive, all things must have seemed possible.

The way Bobby described it, our parents felt they had everything they needed to make a good start. Spates had a steady job at the Celanese, and they even had a place to live at his parents' house in Cresaptown, which must have appealed to Spates' thrifty bent. They began their married life in the home he and his brother had helped his father build in 1925, the one they threw him out of when the Depression began.

A Cresap Park-typical home of that time, it was about 1,000 square feet and had only the one bathroom, but one of its two bedrooms had elegant, white French doors that swung both ways, probably built according to Adeline's whimsical specifications. There was plenty of room by then. Doss had joined the Army

Transport Service and would go on to serve in the 101st Airborne in World War II. Aunts Bee and Gay were on their "starter marriages." But the house was unlucky for Spates from the start. Love would have no life for them there.

Bobby quite casually exploded the story on me. "I remember when Granddad came home to find Grandmom with a black eye."

"Wait, what? How did that happen?" Mom was always talking about how afraid we should be of Dad's anger, but here was yet another example of her own violence.

Bobby shook his head. "I have no idea. Some catfight, I guess. Anyway, two strong-willed, hot-tempered women in one house? That was a blow-up waiting to happen.

"Dad and Granddad huddled and decided that they would build another house for Mom and Dad on the lot next door, which Granddad also owned. They worked on it a little at a time on evenings and weekends when Dad wasn't at the Celanese. During the five years it took them to build, Mom and Dad rented a small house up the street that the neighborhood called 'the box.' I guess it was pretty small, even by Cresaptown standards."

By the time the house was built, my parents needed a bigger "box," as well as a larger salary, because my brothers had been born by then. The Great Depression was technically over by 1941, but the fear it instilled in my father never left him. He must have been grateful to have full-time employment, but his work loading and unloading trains that ran beside the plant was one of the company's lowest-paid unskilled positions—not enough to support a growing family and my mother's hunger for nice things.

Bobby loved telling the story of what happened next, and I loved hearing it. "Dad was always scanning the Celanese job listings, and he got excited when a position called 'Instrument Technician' appeared; it offered a salary three times what he was making at the loading dock. As you know, Dad was all about the money. When he read the list of qualifications, he knew instantly why it paid so much. The job called for instrumentation skills he had never even heard of. Dad had some machine skills from working with Granddad over the years, but the ones in this position required a lot more math and reading than he got with his sixth-grade education. That didn't stop him.

"The Celanese required in-person application, so Dad went to the manager in charge of the unit and handed him the form. Well, the guy glanced at Spates' background and laughed in his face. He tore up the application in front of him and yelled, 'Get out of here, you sad sack, and stop wasting my time!' Dad knew it had been a long shot, but he was determined."

"Did Mom help motivate him?"

"Dunno. Dad never mentioned that when he told me the story. He just said he was certain he could learn to do the job. When the position was still there on the next listing, Spates went back and applied again. He didn't get far into his spiel before the man again tore up the application and said something like, 'Goddamn it, Spates, are you as dumb as you look? No way you're ever gonna get this job, so get the hell out of my office and don't bother me again!'

"But Dad did come back. Word got around and workers began to gather to watch the fun. Of course, he got turned down again, but he came back again the next time the job was listed. By then, the size of the crowd had grown even bigger." Bobby laughed, "I can just hear the buzz, 'Hey, let's go! That poor bastard's gonna try it again!'"

I pictured a group of workers in flannel shirts and oil-stained denim overalls gathering to laugh and point and slap their knees. Celanese management got wind of the daytime drama, and since more-qualified applicants had not appeared, some higher-up decided that a man so determined to better himself would do it somewhere, if not at the Celanese.

Much celebrating must have ensued in both households the day Dad found out he had gotten his shot, but that was just the beginning. He knew how to do almost nothing of what the job required. Someone had placed another dime in his hand, but he had yet to figure out what to do with it to get the bread his family would need to survive hard times that were sure to return.

"How did he learn all that?"

"Dad told me he brought home manuals on the various tools and tasks of an Instrument Technician."

Dad's limited reading skills must have been supplemented by Mom's superior ones. I like to think of them sitting together, working as partners on the life they were building for themselves and their family. Maybe Dad practiced skills as she read the instructions aloud. Perhaps she smiled at him when he came home crowing that he had mastered a particularly complicated task. I can imagine her making pots of coffee for him in our old Drip-o-Lator as he worked into the night. I enjoy envisioning such things because what I saw later was so different. There must have been a time before the war between them began.

How many extra hours at work and how many evenings studying with Mom's help did Dad put in until he learned all he needed to know? He continued practicing until he became a highly skilled Instrument Technician. Bobby shook his head in disbelief, as well as admiration. "Dad mastered a job he shouldn't have been able to do at all." I figure that some of my strong will and perseverance must have come from him, though for both of us it was to become a double-edged sword.

When World War II began, the Celanese was one of the companies judged critical to the national defense, and Spates had a family to support. Both these facts must have figured into his decision to continue working there, rather than joining the regular military like so many of his friends and, of course, his younger brother. Doss, already serving in the Army, became part of the Normandy Invasion in France and the Siege of Bastogne in Belgium during the Battle of the Bulge. When I later asked my mother what Dad did during World War II, she sniffed, "He was in the National Guard." She made it sound like he was a coward.

Spates joined the Maryland National Guard in the 1930s as a bugler, and the Celanese was probably relieved that he continued in that role, but it must have been tough for Spates to have "war hero" Captain Roblyer for a brother. I've often thought my father might have wished he had also joined the Army instead of fighting in the Phrona Wars.

All the boys who made it home from Europe and Japan faced a different kind of conflict. The mid-1940s began the inevitable, painful transitions in the country's economy. In late 1947, the Celanese plant, the region's largest employer, was publicly denying rumors of massive impending layoffs while privately making plans to slash production.

Growing up and well into adulthood, I never knew much about the early days of my parents' marriage, even less about what happened before they met. Yet so much of what shaped me played out during those times. As a child, I witnessed perseverance that made my father drive himself relentlessly, past exhaustion, casting aside that demon, Self-doubt. Even if it were tasks he grew to hate, he couldn't stop. I was to absorb that ethic. Only later in my life would I realize that my mother was working hard to impress something else on me: that I should distrust my father.

I saw my parents behave like two countries with different histories and different worldviews, always suspicious of each other and always at odds. They screamed at each other in what might as well have been different languages across the chasm in their goals. Whether fed by her lack of control over family funds or marital struggles hidden from me, Mom's denunciations of Dad grew more frequent over the years, and her deep disgust and disdain for him became clear to me. When she talked to me about Dad behind his back, his official title was Filthy Old Man.

One late-summer afternoon, I wandered in the back door to find Mom cleaning some rhubarb at the kitchen sink as Dad sat at the table. She turned to me to deliver momentous news.

"Margaret, your father said you may have some money to buy sweaters for school this year."

I rarely got new school clothes, and I threw my arms around Dad's neck to hug him. "Thanks Dad!" I exclaimed. He beamed at me, but Mom shot me a warning look.

Later, she drew me aside to whisper, "Margaret, you don't need to hug that filthy old man like that. He might misinterpret it." I did not even think of challenging her.

After Mom was left distraught and agitated from arguing with Dad and he stomped off to the shop, it was always my job to console her. I once heard the screen door bang and peeked out of my bedroom to find her crying over the kitchen sink, dabbing at her eyes with a dishtowel. She wailed, "I told Spates it was just so hard, and he said, 'Aw, you wouldn't like it if it wasn't hard.' Why would he say something like that?" She hung her head and wept into her dish towel while I hugged her. I had no idea what he meant or why it distressed her so. Maybe she knew something about him I didn't. Incidents like these confirmed what she had worked so hard for years to impress on me: Dad really was a terrible person unworthy of being my father.

I came to feel if I did not take her side, she might reject me as she had him, and I think I feared that more than her anger. Sometime during my childhood, a rift opened between my dad and me and widened over the years until I forgot he was my father at all. To me, he became just the guy who yelled a lot and spent most of his time working.

Too late I learned that this long-running conflict had its roots in my mother's views of men, which began long before I was born. Dad likely knew what caused the split between him and me, but he died before I ever understood what was happening. I was considerably older before I grasped that I was not to blame. While he was alive, I always felt toward him as my mother had trained me to feel. He was the enemy, and I joined her battle against him.

Chapter Eight

Two Houses

When are the seeds of trauma planted and how are they nourished? In our family they seem to have taken root before any of us kids were born—maybe even before our parents were around—and I came to see they were fed by a volatile fusion of personal idiosyncrasies, historical circumstances, and pivotal decisions. The picture began to fill in for me the day I suddenly grasped that I had only a few vague memories of my grandparents.

I went to the oldest living source of family information. "Bobby, do you remember our grandparents?"

"Sure I do. I remember them all, except Mom's mother, who died when she was a kid. Fred and I knew Granddad and Grandmom Roblyer very well. You know we lived right next door to them for years, even after you were born. You probably don't remember them because of the big fight."

That sure sounded like our family, but I had never heard of this particular big fight until Bobby explained how it had happened.

Dad and Granddad built our house next to our grandparents, so close that they could stand in their yard and see Mom at her kitchen sink. The women had no use for each other, so living near her in-laws had to have ratcheted up my mother's natural intensity. Despite our physical proximity—or maybe because of it—an internecine war broke out suddenly and inexplicably sometime before I was born. No one alive knows what exactly started it or even how long it lasted. "Years," Bobby sighed. "I think it was some tiff between Mom and Grandma." I began calling it "The War of the Women."

I envision some stabbing personal comment like "You were never good enough for my Servatius" or "Keep your filthy husband away from my kids." Whatever the cause, the consequences of the split reverberated through our family like the sudden thunder that shook Cresaptown homes whenever the Allegany Ballistics Lab across the valley in Pinto, West Virginia, had a test or a rocket-fuel production accident.

Sometime around World War II, the families strung a low-voltage telephone wire between our two houses and installed an Army-surplus intercom, maybe a gift from Uncle Doss, who was in the Army. Family members used it to confer without leaving the comfort of their home. When the rift occurred, the line was cut and intercom boxes removed, a perfect metaphor for the severed communications between the families.

During the feud, Adeline and her childless daughter Beulah inexplicably started a neighborhood kids' club, a trendy activity of the era. My brothers, prohibited from visiting their grandparents, had to watch as local children streamed into the yard next door to enjoy games, cookies, and Kool-Aid. I was either not born yet or so young that I was unaware of it.

At some point during the split, Adeline sent Bobby a birthday card with a dollar bill in it. An attempt at détente? Bobby described how that went down.

"Me and my buddy Sonny stood there with our mouths

hanging open as Mom ripped up the card and threw the dollar bill on the ground. For a few seconds, Sonny looked from me to the dollar and back again. Then he snatched it up from the ground and skittered off before anyone could change his mind."

"I always recall Grandpa Robert's kindly blue eyes and that deep, semicircle scar on his bald head that he got from falling on the railroad tracks," Fred reflected. "He seemed to like nothing better than playing with his grandkids."

I have no such memories of Granddad, but I have a vague recollection of Grandma Adeline. My mental image is of a wrinkled old woman with sallow, drooping cheeks, pursing her lips as she crocheted doilies and smoked Tarleton cigarettes that sent up a perpetual halo around her head, though in my experience, she was no angel.

Shaking his head ruefully, Bobby recalled, "Grandma Adeline had a capricious and changeable nature, like a child. I remember one time she offered to take Fred and me to a drive-in movie. One-on-one time with grandparents would have been a treat, but a trip to a theatre where we might've had popcorn and candy? Were we excited! That evening, we dashed up to their house just before dusk with clean shirts and faces scrubbed. But Grandma had changed her mind."

"I'm just feeling so tired," she sighed, flicking a cigarette ash into the standing marbled ashtray beside her.

"We were both disappointed," Bobby chuckled, "but Fred was hoppin' mad. 'You son of a bitch!' He yelled at Grandma and whipped around to run away, but standing just behind him on the porch was Dad. That was a memorable ass-whipping. Our grandparents didn't propose any more drive-in trips after that."

Everyone in my family except Dad seemed to have a long memory when it came to affronts.

My only clear memory of Grandma Adeline comes from when I must have been four or five years old. I was standing before her wizened figure as she sat in an overstuffed chair in their living room smoking and crocheting, and my attention went to the fizzing drink in a short glass on the doily-topped table next to her. To me it resembled the fountain soda I had once tasted at the McCrory's soda-fountain counter in downtown Cumberland.

I pointed to it. "Grandma, what's that?"

Her small eyes narrowed. "Would you like a taste? You won't like it."

She helped me lift the fizzing drink to my mouth, the enticing effervescence tickling inside my nose before I sipped, but it was a good job I didn't get a big mouthful; I would have spit it out on her lap. Cackling, she took back the glass of Alka Selzer, set it down on the doily, and reached for her Tarleton.

Grandfather Robert had so little presence in my life that I remember almost nothing of him except the outline of his thin face and the half-moon scar on his head—and even that may be from what Fred described. As for my other living Grandparent, Blackjack, I recall only one brief encounter when he would have been about sixty-five and I about five.

Mom brought me to his house in South Cumberland, and he was sitting on an overstuffed chair in a dim-lit living room. "Margaret, this is your grandfather," she whispered, laying both her hands on my shoulders and holding me back just out of his reach. "Daddy, this is your granddaughter, Margaret Dale."

I gazed at his gray and sagging, unsmiling face and saw my mother's eyes, but there was no softness there. Perhaps I'm projecting onto my memory of that meeting what I later learned about Blackjack. Or was I really able to sense even then that the look he cast on me held something darker and more ominous than anything my childhood nightmares could have conjured? I remember only that I didn't like him.

No question or comment, just stared at me, unsmiling, with those evil-dark eyes. I don't know why Mom would have brought me there. Was it to taunt him? *Here is one little girl whose life you will not ruin.* I was glad we didn't stay long.

Recalling these memories filled in faces and narratives for some of those shadows behind me when I gaze into the mirror—all these strong, flawed, driven men and women that became part of me. I began to see in myself a reflection of those now-unseeing eyes, and a question became a refrain I would revisit often. How much of the image they willed me would I be able to change, and how much would I never able to outrun no matter how fast and how far I go?

The end of World War II changed everything for the country's economy, as well as for our family. By spring of 1949, the Celanese had announced a 1,500-worker layoff; more were to come. Other local industry layoffs landed a succession of body blows to the area economy and left the community reeling with uncertainty and anxiety not seen since the Great Depression. Hard times were returning.

But Spates, the man no one had even wanted to hire for the position, was now an expert technician and, with a wife and three children, one of the most ambitious and motivated of the Celanese employees. A year or so after the company began cutting back its Cresaptown production, they offered Dad his choice of moving to their Texas or New Jersey site because much of their

Maryland operations were being consolidated.

The Celanese's Cresaptown site would close thirty-five years later, though the enterprise that replaced it continues to be the single largest employer in the area. My father would appreciate the irony that the 250 acres where the Celanese had been became the North Branch Correctional Institution, a Maryland maximum security prison.

Fred recalled the moment of decision. "Mom and Dad sat at our kitchen table discussing what they should do. I'm not sure why they decided against moving."

I think I do. I believe my parents finally agreed on something. They saw that the Celanese layoffs that occurred in Cumberland could happen again in another place, perhaps even more extensively. Mom and Dad knew dozens of friends and neighbors who had been furloughed from the Celanese as well as other big employers like the Kelley-Springfield tire plant and B&O railroad. I think my parents decided it was better to turn toward a future they could control through their own hard work and enterprise—a Roblyer trademark—rather than leave their fate to the caprices of Celanese management.

The Art Glass Company, the business my grandfather had started, was thriving, but by then he was a worn-down sixty-three and hoping to retire soon. The men agreed that Dad would go to work for his father, who would eventually sell him the Art Glass Company. I was three years old when my parents threw in their lot with the fortunes of Western Maryland. The War of the Women was over.

After that, my father worked side by side with his father in tasks that formed the backdrop of my childhood. The labor was constant, often grueling, and considering the number of things that could go wrong with glass products, the profit margin had to be unpredictable. They still managed to make enough to support both families and gain a reputation well beyond Western Maryland.

Most Art Glass income came from stained-glass windows. When my grandfather mastered the practice, he became part of a line of artisans that began as far back as Roman times. Though stained glass is as fragile as any other glass, ecclesiastical windows can be quite strong. Depending on how they are made and barring injury from war or vandalism, they can last centuries. The oldest surviving sample, thought to have come from the Basilica of San Vitale in Ravenna, Italy, dates from the sixth century. Some, like the eleventh century Prophet Windows in Augsburg Cathedral in Germany, are still in place.

The stained glass my dad and his father created remains in churches throughout the region, as far away as Washington D.C., and Cape Charles, Virginia, and as close as our own Cresaptown Methodist Church. As I looked back in awe at the perseverance and resilience they summoned to create that legacy, I became grateful for whatever part of those qualities I inherited.

By the time I was five in 1952, the Art Glass Company's business was on fire with demand, continually expanding services and placing frequent ads in local newspapers. From 1951 through 1952, ads crowed, "We carry a full line of colored glass," "Glass tabletops cut to any size," and "Picture frames made while you wait." They offered to "futurize your old home" with then-trendy louvre or jalousie windows. Jalousies were parallel glass pieces or louvres joined on a common track that allowed them to be tilted open and closed like blinds to improve ventilation. Salesman that he was, my grandfather would not have informed customers that louvre windows couldn't completely close or that they were designed for warm climates like Florida and were highly impractical for Western Maryland, which had five months a year of temperatures often dipping below freezing. Louvres were trendy and therefore marketable.

A succession of articles in Cumberland's three newspapers began in July 1952 announcing that shop facilities were being doubled and bragging about the array of new products and services. I believe these articles were my grandfather's idea. He seems to have been a great promoter, conceiving of free giveaways such as hand mirrors with the company's name and contact information.

The Cumberland newspaper, undoubtedly thrilled with a business that placed as many ads as the Art Glass Company, was only too happy to send a reporter to Cresaptown. One article trumpeted that the company now served customers in six states. Another boasted that $10,000 worth of new glass stock had been added (over $100,000 today) and another that the company had worked on nearly every church in the area. By Halloween, a newspaper photo showed him standing triumphantly in the middle of his almost-completed new building.

He must have had his stroke right around Thanksgiving. Only one ad—already placed before Granddad's illness—appeared in the months after it.

Robert's attack made him reluctantly agree to sell Dad the company's name and materials for about $20,000 (over $230,000 today). Our grandparents had hatched the idea of starting a chicken farm in West Virginia, a notion I heard everyone except them thought hairbrained. Robert was entrepreneurial but not a great financial manager. He underestimated what was required to operate the farm and sold it within a few years before making enough to retire. Then he objected to his son that he had not asked enough for the Art Glass Company and would need to renegotiate terms.

My father could easily have refused; Mom undoubtedly exhorted him to do exactly that. "What the hell is he thinking, Spates? Is he crazy? Just tell him 'no.'" But Robert wanted to fulfill Adeline's new dream of moving to a trailer park in Hollywood, Florida, and Dad had always put his parents' needs before his own. I envision the scene of the four of them negotiating at our metal kitchen dinette table, the two headstrong matriarchs glaring at each other, perhaps exchanging snarky comments, and the two husbands trying to keep them apart and agree on terms.

I was always stunned at what Dad's parents had asked of him and all the things they took, even without asking. The "1925 Kissell incident" was a striking example. Granddad Robert knew that his teenaged son loved his sporty Kissell roadster, which they'd found in bad shape on Maryland's Eastern Shore. They'd restored it and used it to make moonshine deliveries during Prohibition. A 1920s photo showed my father posing in his Kissell, his sly smile suggesting that he felt that this car definitely made him a chick magnet. Not long after that photo, Dad worked a job out of town for a few days, returning to find that his father had cut pieces from the car to patch the furnace.

Even as a teenager in the 1920s, Dad was famously frugal and always managed to save something out of his meagre earnings. One day, Granddad took his son aside. "Servatius, the furnace is about to die, so we're gonna need your money to get a new one." And Dad handed over what he had so painstakingly saved.

How do parents become so selfish and insensitive? Maybe trauma of their own, growing up fearful and driven among the rural poor of our country, with no safety nets like social security in sight? That was a time when children, especially males of lower-class families, had to forego education that might have lifted them out of poverty and become workers who must earn their right to room and board, as my father did.

Until that realization sunk in, I found it perplexing that Dad respected and loved his demanding family, even after what they exacted from him and failed to give him. To me, they seemed more like employers than parents, but maybe Dad saw how they struggled and understood them in a way I never could. My mother would later benefit from Dad's understanding, forgiving nature; with Mom, there was always much to forgive.

Just like when they mangled his Kissell and claimed his savings for a new furnace, Dad's parents' needs were paramount. Dad handed over additional cash for the Art Glass Company, and my grandparents moved to their trailer paradise. I never visited them there and because I never really knew them, I don't remember missing them.

I can just hear my mom huffing, "Good riddance to both of them."

Sometime before Dad left the Celanese, Granddad employed a neighborhood man named Jimmie Kamauf. Jimmie had apprenticed in glass work in Pittsburgh and seemed to believe he would take over the business someday. When Dad took over, Jimmie learned he was not only cut out being a future owner of Art Glass, but he was also out of a job; my father probably could not afford to keep him. Not long after, Jimmie opened another glass company right up the street, bidding against Art Glass whenever there was a big church-window job anywhere in the area. He also undercut prices on local glass work, which forced the Art Glass Company to match his rates. By this time, it's unlikely that my mother understood or cared how all this affected my father's bottom line—or his blood pressure. Dad must have felt as if he had two enemies: one who lived in his neighborhood and threatened his livelihood and one who lived in his house and threatened his sanity.

The deal Dad struck with Granddad included the Art Glass Company buildings, as well as both houses. Soon after, my parents, Cindy, and I moved into my grandparents' house with the French doors in the master bedroom, and my father rented out the larger home where we had been living. My brothers, then about twelve and fifteen, took the two-room space over the glass shop.

The house that my dad helped his father build and had been turned out of when the Depression began is where I remember growing up. There, I witnessed my mother's growing frustration with being a housewife. But even before I came along, Bobby and Fred learned how her frustration could segue into anger and aggression.

Chapter Nine

Growing Up Cresaptown

Monday was Mom's wash day, as it was for most households around the country, so the first of every week I'd see her roll our barrel-shaped Maytag manual washer from the porch into the kitchen, clean it out, and attach its hose to the sink. For years, no one in Cresaptown had an automatic washer—not even Gail's mother. If Mom ever asked for one, Dad would have turned her down, deeming it an unnecessary expense. When Mom ran out of hot tap water, she heated water by the potful, pouring one after the other into the washer tub until she had enough for a load of clothing. After she washed and rinsed the clothes and drained the tub, she used a hand-cranked ringer to squeeze out the remaining water. She cursed as she wrung out my father's long underwear, taking out her frustration on it as though it were her husband.

Once as I stood watching, she stopped laboring over Dad's long johns in the washer, held one up, and carped, "Just look at these disgusting things!" Gazing down at the baggy, yellowing fabric, I saw nothing appealing about the thermal underwear that my father wore for warmth in his unheated shop. I understood her distaste for this clothing, but I was too young to pick up on what she was really saying: that she had little physical attraction for him.

Mom was angry washing the clothes and angry drying them. Weather permitting, she dumped wet clothes and linens from washer to basket, carried them outside, and hung them with clothespins on lines that crisscrossed our backyard. If it was rainy or freezing, she draped everything on racks in the kitchen or carried basketfuls out the back door and down to the basement and pinned them to lines strung there. My mother carried out basket after basket of wet underwear, shirts, pants, dresses, towels, washcloths, sheets. I can see her now in her faded housedress and apron, her teeth clenched and mouth set in a straight line as she grabbed clothespins from her apron pocket and hung each piece, pin after pin, week after week. I didn't think much about it at the time; that was just my mom. Now it seems to me as if she felt her potential, her youth, her life itself was being measured out in those clotheslines and other tasks she hated.

I believe that she burned to realize the potential she was sure she had and longed to break out of the traditional female role of marriage and motherhood and become a professional woman. Fate had conspired against her, forcing her into a life that was terribly wrong for her. There she was, married to a "miser," working as hard as her husband, but unable to spend any of their money as she wanted. Over and over I heard her protest to Dad, "You're making me your slave!"

Mom seemed to have special contempt for her role as cook. As we compared notes about growing up in Cresaptown, Bobby, Fred, and I agreed that Mom's cooking was memorably dreadful. We often sat down to canned beef stew, Chef-Boyardee spaghetti, or single-dish combinations like canned corned beef and cabbage that could be thrown together quickly and cheaply. The worst were created to use up leftovers, though I did develop a fondness for scrambled eggs with leftover corn and peas. If we ever did have chicken or hamburger, she and my father preferred it to be cooked into cardboard to kill off any illness-producing organisms that might be lurking. Sometimes she warmed up milk and butter and threw in oysters for a quick swim before scooping the soup into bowls and throwing oyster crackers on the table. The only seasoning she ever used was salt and lots of it.

Two of Dad's favorites: "shit on a shingle" or gravy made from dried chipped beef and served on white bread, and creamed asparagus on toast using canned asparagus and asparagus juice thickened with milk and flour. I tucked into them or chili, oyster stew, or vegetable soup so often that their flavors are all that linger in my memory of her cooking. I never saw Dad turn up his nose at anything Mom made; he always downed everything gratefully, perhaps recalling his brush with starvation during the Depression.

As much as she loathed preparing main dishes, Mom seemed to relish making desserts. Perhaps in her mind they seemed a distinctly different enterprise from the drudgery of making meals. She may have viewed sweets not only as a fun diversion but also a rare opportunity to show her artistry, like the poems and short stories she crafted with precious free moments.

Sometimes I came home to find her spreading a thick layer of peanut butter on rolled-out confectioners-sugar dough for potato candy or stirring a fragrant pot of dark chocolate fudge made with cocoa powder or caught the aroma of skillet pineapple upside-down cake or, less often, an apple or rhubarb pie. On those days, the tightening at the back of my neck that began whenever I approached the back porch steps of our house relaxed. A dessert signaled she might be in a rare, good mood that evening and there might be no sudden bursts of anger and loud exchanges between red-faced parents. My brothers, who played a part in one dessert-related incident before I was born, seemed to find it hilarious and took pleasure in relating the story to me as Mom looked away, embarrassed.

Mom had an open hostility toward two half-wild, striped cats kept by neighbors two doors down. These felines would kill rabbits and songbirds in our yard, defiling my mother's flower beds with scattered feathers and small dismembered corpses. There was more than one nose-to-nose yelling match between her and the neighbors as she warned, "Keep your mangy beasts in your own yard!"

One breezy spring day while my brothers were at school, she cut up enough apples to make two deep-dish apple pies and, when they were baked a golden brown, placed them on back-porch banisters—a common local practice of removing baked goods from the kitchen's heat to allow the breezes coming across the Potomac valley to cool them—making the whole neighborhood smell like a bakery. The fruit, shortening, sugar, flour, and spices for these pies made them one of the more expensive of her creations and preparing them would have taken most of the entire afternoon. I picture her looking at them proudly as she set them out, humming one of her favorite hymns.

Later that afternoon, my brothers arrived home to find one of the neighbors' striped cats lying dead in the backyard, its body stretched out grotesquely, appearing longer than when alive. They thought it the biggest cat they had ever seen. Running up the back-porch steps, they yelled in the screen door, "Mom, Mom, come look! There's a giant cat dead in the backyard!"

"Oh, shut up and get in here," she growled.

They later learned she had looked out the back window to

witness our neighbor's two rangy felines not only trespassing on her back porch but sticking dirty paws through the top crust of her pies. Seeing the atrocity that the cats were committing on her precious baked goods and blind to the consequences of laying hands on a half-wild animal, she attacked like a savage beast herself. Anger propelled her out the back door and as she grabbed the nearest one, the sound and fury of the battle must have been something to behold. The poor fellow never really had a chance. In her red-eyed rage, she strangled it, stretching out its neck until skull broke free from spine, then flung it out in the backyard before retreating to the house to dispose of her ruined pies and tend to the deep scratches and bites on her bloodied arms. When our bereft neighbors heard what had happened, there was more yelling, though Bobby said they yelled from their porch.

My brothers recounted another family-famous event more than once while an embarrassed grimace on my mother's face signaled she could not dispute its accuracy.

It was only a ten-minute walk through the woods from our house to the Cresaptown School, so like Scout and Jem Finch, my brothers came home for lunch. Our mother was usually in a hurry and overwhelmed, so on one occasion she readied a meal from Campbells dry noodle-soup mix, set the warm bowls down in front of them, and tossed some saltine crackers on the table. Apparently, this was not the lunch Fred had in mind.

"Mom, not noodle soup!" he whined.

Maybe it was the whiny tone, maybe just his lack of recognition of the work she had to rush through to cook them lunch, but it was one complaint too far for my mother. Without a moment's hesitation, she picked up the bowl and dumped the warm soup over Fred's head. I can just see Bobby's wide-eyed stare going from his brother to his mother and back again, trying to anticipate what would come next, and Fred's big, sad eyes as he sat there bewildered and sorrowful, noodles dripping down his ears onto his skinny neck.

"What did you do then?" I once asked my mother.

She waved her hand to dismiss the whole incident. "Oh, I cleaned him up and gave him something else to eat," She seemed only a little sheepish about her angry reaction. Maybe she felt it was an effective lesson because he never complained about the food again.

My brothers always laughed as they told these violent stories, but even then I wondered if they feared Mom as much as I did.

Because Cindy and I were girls, we had to stay closer to home than my brothers and were frequently captive to Mom's moods. Cindy seemed to ignore her, retreating into her own world, but I dealt with it by trying to brighten Mom's mood. When I was with her, I was Consoler-in-Chief. It was a heavy responsibility, so school became my escape.

Few happy visions of home life linger from those early years, but memories of the Cresaptown School are benign ghosts, smiling at me from classrooms and playgrounds. The school year played out as a series of much-anticipated events and holiday celebrations from Halloween Fun Night through May Day. Before the latter was deemed Communistic and temporarily banished from schools across the country, May 1 was a grand time for girls dressing up in white frocks and learning dances that had us weaving brightly colored ribbons around a May Pole. Cresaptown had nine grades, so teachers selected two of the best students from the ninth-grade class to preside as King and Queen of the May. Meritocracy, not democracy, reigned.

When he was a ninth grader in 1956, Fred's photo appeared in *The Cumberland News* along with a girl named Sondra when they were named Cresaptown School's King and Queen of the May. I assumed I would someday be Queen. Already it was clear to me that Mom expected we would all be the best in school, except for Bobby who was bowing out of her plans and going his own way.

In between all the seasonal celebrations, school imparted to me a firm belief that I was smart and capable; I seemed to excel at everything teachers asked of me. I loved language; my mother had been reading and telling stories to me since I could remember, and their themes and cadences seemed to come naturally to me. I read a considerable number of sight words in our *Dick and Jane* readers, and I became proficient in cursive lettering—that antiquated skill that is a curse on modern-day elementary school children and should be made an art class option but has instead become enshrined in many required school curricula as if it were a sacred ritual. I was good at arithmetic because in those days, it was all scrawling numbers and memorizing math facts. No one could beat me at memorizing.

An early raconteur, I once held forth from the front of my classroom. "And then the little dog told the girl he would help her dig for treasure in her back yard." It may have been improvised based on others my mother read to me, but the children were rapt.

Four times a year, we took home a yellow report card booklet roughly the size of a five-by-seven notecard in which teachers wrote descriptions of our progress. In mine, Mrs. Crowe wrote comments like, "Peggy Dale is an excellent little reader, reading very smoothly and understanding what she reads. Peggy has learned many songs and poems and is able to dramatize many stories. I find her a very polite little girl, well-liked by her classmates." Mrs. Crowe meant that my parents had taught me good manners. I was absorbing the principle that well-brought-up little boys were "respectful"; little girls were "polite."

In first grade, our yellow booklets had only rubric check marks on a handful of topics like "reading readiness," along with handwritten descriptive comments about behavior. In second grade, Cresaptown teachers upped the ante, using a one-through-four rating scale for each student's progress on subjects like reading and arithmetic, as well as specific good habits like "Respects the property of others." Like most kids of that age, I was primarily concerned with friendships and play, but it gradually became clear to me that my mother was most interested in the little marks my teachers made in the booklets.

When I brought home my second-grade booklet, my mother pulled me into her lap and went over the little marks with me as I struggled to understand why she considered them so important. She liked some comments but not others, maybe ones like, "Please have Margaret read orally the stories we have in class" (as opposed to those from the *Children's Book of Illustrated Literature*?) and "Margaret is doing very satisfactory work" (rather than "excellent"), and she focused on my Level 2 (rather than Level 1) checkmarks in all subjects. Her gentle prodding for me to excel and her frequent visits to teachers might have been the reason for the gradual rise in my ratings from mostly twos to all ones by the end of the year.

By her account, Mom had been a star during her year at Cresaptown School, her last formal schooling. She had started school in Cumberland, but she and the other Pryor children had to move to Cresaptown's combination elementary-and-junior-high school when Blackjack's debts from drinking and gambling forced him to sell the family's South Cumberland home (which Blanche's mother left her) and rent a place in Potomac

Park. When Phrona was thirteen, she started at Cresaptown School when its new site first opened in 1932, and she used her only year there to show remarkable potential.

Her oft-repeated boast was that she had written the school song, "Oh Cresaptown, My Cresaptown," sung to the tune of "The Marine Hymn," when she was in the ninth grade. The song's lyrics and student-and-teacher co-authors are linked from the school website, but family lore has it that Mom wrote it all herself, and the teacher's name was placed on it later.

Mom related another event that same year when she took a test and made such a high score that someone was sent from Baltimore to retest her. By the 1930s, schools were required to measure IQ and achievement, so her account is possible. Mom's success seemed to have set the bar high for her children. Her stories of achievement drove home to me that she would be most pleased with me if I always brought her the highest marks.

Excelling at school was never a problem for me in primary grades, though I felt school mainly a time set aside for my friends and me to meet at recess and play on the grassy, tree-shaded playground. Lunchtime was a welcome social hour, with the added benefit that food tasted so much better to me than anything I ate at home. The federal government sent schools a variety of fresh products like white bread and butter (not the cheaper margarine we consumed at home), and cafeteria women made from scratch in the school's kitchen everything from peanut-butter-and-jelly sandwiches to vegetable soup and chili. I stuffed myself with everything they offered, but an hour or so after I ate, a terrible, deep ache often gripped my abdomen. On these days, I was in such distress that I lay my little blond head down on my desk and wept, and the school would call my mother to retrieve me.

Once home, I'd lie down on the living room sofa and try to

explain to Mom where and why it hurt. I was such a picky eater at home, overeating school lunches may never have occurred to her. A short while after I stretched out and rested, the pain would subside, and I would be itching to go out to play. At first, my mother seemed to think I was faking it and there was something happening at school to make me not want to stay there, but after questioning me and my teacher, that theory seemed unlikely.

Was that a turning point, a final reason she decided she had to do more than act out in anger at my father? Thinking back to her own childhood trauma, her tormented mind may have turned back to the same logic that made her question me the day she pushed the pillow down on my face. Her mind may never have left the idea that my father had abused me, and she had to have been dwelling on it ever since, letting a strategy to address it take shape in her mind.

Chapter Ten

Small Escapes

In good weather, it was a hard, two-hour drive from Cresaptown on winding West Virginia roads to my mother's kin in Hambleton, not far from Parsons, the Tucker County seat. Mom had no close friends in Cresaptown, ladies she could call up to hang over a fence and gossip with or to sit on front porches commiserating about husbands over knitting. Whenever she decided she merited some down time, Mom would herd my sister and me into the Ford, and we would speed off on a daytrip to see her half-sister Zelda—we called her Aunt Zella—and other relatives on my mother's side who scratched out an existence in that desolate area. Dad couldn't have been thrilled about these little escapes. Gas cost money, and Mom wouldn't be around to help out in the shop and make lunch and dinner. When she gave Cindy a doll and directed me to bring a book, I could count on being dragged to West Virginia, and I always slumped in the back seat beside Cindy, feeling trapped.

In those pre-seatbelt days, Mom drove like she did everything, fast as she could and chin thrust forward toward her goal, with a firm idea of where she was headed, and an energy propelled by her hard-headed will. Her hands gripped the steering wheel tightly, her body bent over it toward the windshield as if she could get more speed out of our old Ford that way. If she had been riding a horse, she would have used spurs and a whip. Out McMullen Highway through Rawlings and past Barton's Dairy, then down through West Virginia through Keyser and Claysville she charged like demons chased her. After Davis and Thomas, it was up and over the Allegheny Mountains on Route 219, the old Seneca Trail. In those days, nearly all rural routes ran to two narrow lanes, and our path wound around treacherous mountain roads with not a guard rail in sight.

On one rainy, overcast trip up Route 219, we were stopped by a local man in faded blue overalls and railroad hat. One hand was raised to halt us and the other motioned a single lane of traffic in the other direction to inch by a parked police car and a pick-up truck that were parked on the side of the road near the edge of a steep drop-off. Woods on that side were so thick with oak trees you couldn't see through them to the bottom. A state trooper stood beside two other men in overalls, the latter with arms crossed, sometimes pulling at scraggly beards. All were glancing over the side of the mountain and occasionally one would say something to the trooper and gesture towards it with a jerk of a thumb. The trooper was scratching his head. As we passed, I looked back out the window to behold the sheer drop unnervingly close to our car and saw amid the thick oak foliage another vehicle hanging by its wheels in the branches. But barring events like this, the drive was so boring that Cindy and I were usually asleep by the time we drove over the Cheat River and turned onto the dirt roads in the hills around Hambleton.

Few poor, rural Hambleton families had phones, but Aunt Zella could get calls through a neighbor's phone down the hill. Even so, Mom didn't always phone ahead early enough to be sure Zella got news of company headed her way. Yet as we bumped up the dirt lane to our aunt's house, she always appeared quickly on her front porch in her faded housedress and apron, her sagging face alight with a wide smile that looked eerily like my mother, except our aunt had far fewer teeth, and many that remained were brown and decayed. By the way Aunt Zella welcomed her half-sister and us girls, I could tell that our visit was a respite for her, as well as for my mother.

The first time we climbed the unpainted wood steps to Aunt Zella's old house, the rickety look and unstable feel of the place frightened me. The linoleum-covered kitchen floor slanted down toward the porch, as if its underpinnings weren't quite sturdy. Though at six or seven, I didn't weigh much, I was afraid it might collapse as I walked over it, and who knew what ghastly things lay below? But the greatest shock was yet to come.

When I whispered, "Mama, I have to wee-wee," she took my hand and led me toward the back of the house, out the back door, and down a short path to a small, unpainted wooden hut. "But I have to go to the bathroom," I whined, prancing about and holding my crotch with both hands.

"Here we are," Mom announced. I looked around, puzzled as she opened the door to the wooden hut. Nothing inside resembled what I had in mind for a bathroom, and when the stench hit me, I began to back away.

"I don't have to go now," I gasped, trying not to inhale.

"Oh, no, Margaret Dale, just march yourself right in here. You'll be peeing in your pants in an hour." She knew I couldn't hold it until we got back home that night, so she pushed me in, made me drop my drawers, and planted me protesting onto the hole in the unpainted boards while flies buzzed around me. It would have made for great comedy in a movie, but it wasn't funny to me. I shed angry, humiliated tears even after exiting the outhouse.

Later we walked down a dusty road to visit Great-Aunt Zernie, who was my Grandmother Floda's sister and whom my mother and Aunt Zella seemed to revere as something of a family matriarch, though she was only in her mid-sixties.

On one Sunday visit to Hambleton, we went with Aunt Zella and Great-Aunt Zernie to a morning church service. I always liked going to the Cresaptown Methodist Church because I got to dress up, and the Sunday School gave us cookies and Kool-Aid and led us in bouncy songs I knew by heart like "Jesus Loves Me" and "Itsy-Bitsy Spider." Methodist church services were boring, with lots of singing from Cokesbury hymnals and monotonous praying, but I liked even that service and its predictable structure. I also looked forward to standing for the hymns and singing along with my mother, and I was even starting to memorize the Apostles' Creed, though I had no idea what it meant.

Aunt Zella's church, though, was backwoods Pentecostal and did not set much store by prescribed liturgy. People behaved in a way I had been taught was completely unacceptable in polite company, let alone in church. After a few preliminaries, they suddenly began yelling and waving their arms about; some clambered into the aisle, got down on their knees, and stretched out supplicating arms, all while shouting and praying. I couldn't figure out what in the world they were saying either; it didn't sound like English.

When I started to freak out, my mother was amused. She may have thought the charismatic behavior would be an interesting cultural experience for me, but when it became clear I was about to bolt, she had to take me outside to decompress. After the service, Aunt Zella gave a near-toothless grin. "This ain't nothin'.

Sometimes services 'round here use snakes." The Hambleton experiences were among the most wretched of my young life, but the scenes I encountered must have been commonplace in my mother's childhood.

Mom's visits to her West Virginia kin seemed to me an escape to what she must have considered her real family: her mother's relatives, her mother's world. Perhaps she was not only still searching for some connection with family and home, but she also wanted me to connect with them. How much she failed at that must have become clear to her when I began asking when we could leave as soon as we got there. All I was interested in was getting back to Cresaptown where things made more sense. After seeing Aunt Zella's church in action, I knew for sure I was a Methodist.

My mother adopted other means of escape besides barreling over the mountains to Hambleton. Always an avid reader, she increasingly immersed her mind in poetry and plays, quoting lines so often, that as a child I assumed that she had made them up until I later ran across them in literature. "They equivocate until they lose the name of action." (A version of this is found in Hamlet's soliloquy.) "The best lack all conviction and the worst are full of passionate intensity" (from William Butler Yeats' poem "The Second Coming"). She doted on the works of Gerard Manley Hopkins, but her delight in Edna St. Vincent Millay may have been as much for the poet's self-determined life as for her work.

Mom also escaped into music, an interest that may have begun when she was a teenager and wrote (or co-wrote) the Cresaptown school song. Perhaps she taught herself to play piano as part of her overall plan to transform herself into the accomplished, educated person she felt she could have been.

After the evening meal was over and dishes were done, she would sometimes repair to the living room and play a hymn or two on our old upright piano. I have no idea how we got the instrument; it didn't sound like Dad to have bought one. Mom got proficient enough to play two-handed and sing the words at the same time, and the sound rings clear in my mind. "Rock of ages, cleft for me, let me hide myself in thee." Or "Leaning, leaning, safe and secure from all alarms. Leaning, leaning, leaning on the everlasting arms."

Were the words of the old hymns her prayers, her pleas for solace, for a path out of the tangle of her tormented mind? I remember how they seemed to calm her, at least for a little while. As I got older, she especially liked it if I joined her on the piano bench and sang along.

Early in 1953, Mom's photo appeared in an ad in the *Cumberland Evening Times*. The caption was, "Phrona Catherine Roblyer, graduate of Catherman's Business School, employed by the Art Glass Company," along with the somewhat misleading brag, "Not an unemployed graduate for eighteen years." How many of their students were like Mom, employed by their own family companies? I think Mom must have convinced Dad that she could help make the Art Glass Company more efficient. That would have been the only reason he would have approved spending money on tuition and all those evening trips into Cumberland.

"Dad told me he was always suspicious that she was frittering with other men in town," Bobby once confided. I think she had another goal in mind, and she raced toward it just as she always sped up those mountains to Hambleton; dalliances with men would only have slowed her down.

Mom seemed to spend every free moment practicing what she was learning at Catherman's. Pencil in hand, she filled page after page with the long curls of the Gregg-style shorthand, a means of writing sentences more quickly as someone dictated a letter or other document; it was once considered de rigueur for secretarial work. "See, Margaret, this curl stands for the whole phrase 'at your earliest convenience.'" I was baffled. Why would anyone use another written symbol system? The one I was learning in school was tricky enough.

Mom had always produced Art Glass Company bills and letters in longhand in beautifully scrolled cursive, but she and my father must have agreed that typewritten documents would make their small business look more professional, and that accounting skills would make recordkeeping more accurate. She had been maintaining the company records for years and grasped company finances as well as Dad, though she never did learn the concept of a home budget.

Catherman's taught Mom typing basics, but her own determination turned her into a fast, accurate typist. Day after day, week after week, she sat straight-backed in front of her Royal typewriter, lasering in on the practice-exercise book propped up on a typing stand beside her, the sound of her determined clacking filling the house. This was the 1950s, but the one I remember was an old 1930s model with round keys, which was probably the cheapest they could find. When I went out to play after lunch one sunny summer day, she sat erect before her machine, her strong hands flying across the stiff keys. She was in the same position when I came in for dinner. She pursued her goal as doggedly as any professional sportsman, working past fatigue, past boredom, past doubt, as though preparing for a big game. I have never seen anyone so focused.

One evening, my mother brought home something new—a sketchbook and drawing materials. I can only guess how Dad reacted. A former art student himself, he may have been envious. I have no idea when she got the desire to draw and paint, but the art class she signed up for when she was downtown, supposedly for business classes, developed into a pastime she loved all her life.

Looking back on those "small escapes," I believe they were the beginning of my mother's taking control of her life, completely reshaping her self-image and building a lifestyle far different from anything she had known. The most important escape, the one that was to remake her future and my own, occurred after I finished third grade, just as summer vacation began.

Second Part

In Flight

Chapter Eleven

Childhood Interruptus

The events in that mid-July week in 1956 must have been simmering and evolving in Mom's mind for years, and her scheme came together neatly and implacably, like a gun being assembled, each piece locking into place until it was ready to fire. I would learn later that guns weren't just a metaphor in Mom's escape plan.

"Mom took one of Dad's guns when we left town," Fred remarked casually as we spoke years later of those remarkable events. "A nickel-plated .45 Automatic Colt Pistol."

I was more than a little incredulous. "But Fred, why would she need a gun? I thought she hated Dad's guns."

"She said she had to have it if Dad came back home early and found out what she'd done." Sometimes, Dad did leave and return earlier than expected, when he realized he had forgotten something he needed for a job. Then I remembered overhearing her accuse him of slinking back to check up on her, but he scoffed, "Oh, woman, I don't care enough to waste my time that way." He would have cared about this.

It's anyone's guess how she planned to use a lethal weapon if he did return. Until I learned about the gun, I wished Dad had caught up with us. But after Fred filled me in on that detail, I suspected that either Mom or Dad would have been dead and the other imprisoned, and what would have become of us? When Mom was sure she had made a clean getaway from Cresaptown, she pulled over just short of a bridge and tossed the gun in the Potomac River. The first step in her clean break from her old life with my father was complete.

Like a murder, what she did had motive, means, and opportunity. In her idiosyncratic turn of logic, she was justified. She believed that if all those years of working like his "slave" weren't enough, there was still the threat she believed he presented to her and her children. She had persuaded Fred that Dad was violent and dangerous, and I don't think she ever trusted my father around her little girls. Unexplained health issues are one indicator a child is being molested, and the stomachaches I had at school may have helped solidify her suspicions. Digestive distress followed me into adulthood, but my father certainly never caused it.

Without knowing it, Bobby helped her with means. His work for Dad had the same arrangement our grandparents had with their own oldest child, our dad—free room and board and some spending money. Bobby had passionate arguments with Dad about the long hours, grueling work, and especially the money, but what made up his mind to do something about it was his passion for a local girl named Mary Ann.

"I had no way to make a living that could support a family, and I wanted to marry that gal in the worst way," Bobby recalled, shaking his head. "My friend Jackie told me he'd just joined the Navy because they'd promised to teach him a trade, and he'd be able to make a good living when he got out. I agreed with him that it sounded like a great idea."

"But Bobby, that doesn't make any sense. In those days, the Navy never told enlisted men exactly what they will train them to do. Anyway, Mary Ann would've had to wait four years until you got out."

"I know, Margaret, but I wasn't thinking with my head."

Bobby was only seventeen and needed parental consent, so my mother accompanied him to the Navy Recruitment Center in Cumberland and signed away her eldest child's future to the caring hands of the military. The Navy made him a communications technician and taught him skills no more useful than how to send and receive messages in Morse Code. His plan to marry his ladylove Mary Ann also disintegrated. At a distance, he was able to recognize qualities that reminded him of his own unpredictable mother. They broke up after his first tour of duty in Adak, Alaska.

Bobby had another great love in his life: his 1950 Pontiac Silver Chief sedan. "I found it on a used car lot in South Cumberland in awful shape—didn't even start up—so I was able to talk the guy down from whatever small price he was asking to something I could afford. I think the lot owner was glad to get rid of it. It took me over a year to refurbish it with whatever materials I could buy or scavenge. When I left for boot camp at Imperial Beach, California, I had to leave it, but Dad promised it would be waiting for me when I got back.

"I was just finishing boot camp when Dad wrote to say Mom had left town with my Pontiac. A few months later I got a letter from Mom demanding the title; she had enclosed a check for $300. That car was worth three times that!"

Years later, as a septuagenarian, Bobby still spoke mournfully of how Mom paid him a pittance for his cherished Pontiac, but he never suggested that she may have encouraged him in his idea to join the Navy because it would free up his car, a key component of her escape plan. If Bobby had been around, I know he would have tried to talk her out of it and probably would have even warned my father. Bobby left at the end of June, and we took off from Cresaptown in the Pontiac a few weeks later.

My father had left for one of his week-long working trips, contacting potential customers or installing stained-glass church windows. I picture him break-necking it around narrow country roads, his hands clenching and unclenching the steering wheel as he thought about how much he could fit into the day before the light faded. That morning, Mom must have waited an agonizingly long time until she was reasonably sure he wasn't coming back—packing, pacing, calculating when it would be safe to leave. Finally, she pulled the trigger by pulling out of the driveway.

I was nine, and Cindy not yet five, but Fred was fifteen, old enough to know that this would not be a usual day. Mom had convinced him we had to escape before Dad killed her. When she instructed Cindy and me to select a toy for a trip, I resigned myself to an overnight in Hambleton. But this time as I was wrenched away from the day of my planned adventures, I was drawn into my mother's anguished dreams, and my father's toughness was tested in new ways.

She hustled us all into Bobby's Pontiac and struck out for Cumberland. Her final stop before leaving town was the bank on Baltimore Street where she and Dad had checking and savings accounts. My father always socked every penny he could into that savings account. We waited in the car while she drained it all, about $19,000 in cash and securities (over $200,000 in today's money). Then she drove off with three children into an uncertain future.

The horror Dad must have felt upon returning home that day still takes my breath away. When Dad was a small child, his parents had once dropped him off with an old couple on a farm out in the country. He never learned the reason they left him with babysitters, but once his parents drove off, the farmers thought to play a little joke on him, one of the cruelest kind. Straight-faced they informed young Spates, "You're our little boy now. Your parents aren't coming back for you." Abandonment must mimic at least some of the same stages of grief as for a death, and he likely spent the week or two before his parents' return enduring that mourning process.

When Dad came home to an empty Cresaptown house, he knew this was no joke, and it would not be short-term. All he had ever wanted was the security of making a good living for a wife and family of his own. Now it was all gone. Knowing Mom, her parting shot would have been leaving a letter ranting about how he drove her to it.

"When I came home from boot camp," Bobby recalled, "Dad was so grief-stricken he could hardly speak. Losing his kids nearly killed him, and he was worried sick about them. I stayed as long as I could, but I didn't have long to visit my friends before I had to report back to the Navy." He shook his head sadly. "I hated leaving him like that."

Just as when he reached the river's edge during the Depression, my father was broken and desolate, rejected by family, alone. He neither drank nor took drugs. We'll never know exactly what kept him going during those first desolate weeks, but I believe it was his determination not to starve to death.

Our journey was south, though it's not clear why. Perhaps Mom was heading toward warmer weather, perhaps toward an ocean, which she may never have seen. I remember little of the trip except that it went on for so many days that Cindy and I were crying and rebellious, and yet my mother kept driving. How many days did we drive? How many motel nights? Did she even have a destination in mind? She wouldn't tell us where we were going. This was scarier and more menacing than anything she had done before. Powerless and angry, I could do nothing to oppose her determined will.

Her wandering path took us down toward the east coast to join Route 17, today's Interstate 95. We drove across Georgia and down the coast, eventually reaching a drawbridge across the St. John's River, named, I later learned, for one of her favorite poets, Georgia native Sidney Lanier. She would have been familiar with his "A Song of the Future," its lines so weirdly evoking her own visions of a future to drown forever a life she hoped to forget.

> Sail fast, sail fast, Ark of my hopes,
> Ark of my dreams;
> Sweep lordly o'er the drowned Past,
> Fly glittering through the sun's strange beams;
> Sail fast, sail fast.

I felt the road slope up sharply as we drove onto the drawbridge, and when we reached the part designed to open for boat passage, it sounded different from a road, not entirely stable. Terror making the back of my neck rigid, I peered over the side and looked down to see what was causing the clattering noise. Beneath us lay a path of metal with holes large enough to view clearly rushing water far below. The noise was so loud that I feared the Pontiac would shake to pieces, embodying all the insecurity of my destabilized life. I closed my eyes and froze, awaiting my doom. *We will fall from this height and drown. Surely, she has brought us here to kill us all. We will die here in this foreign place.*

"For heaven's sake, Margaret Dale, what is wrong with you?" Mom snapped at my whimpering. I was nearly hysterical as we came safely down the other side, but she kept driving, focused only on the road before her. We continued down Route 17, finally arriving in Jacksonville, Florida, the first East Coast Florida city she came to after crossing the Georgia border. As we drove down Main Street, she looked around approvingly. "This looks nice. Should we stay here?"

Lord, yes! Just let me out of this car!

We landed first in a boarding house on North Main Street, a sordid little place that brought down a new plague on us: bedbugs. In one of a long sequence of incredible events of that exile, my fifteen-year-old brother was sent out to locate a furnished apartment to rent.

Chapter Twelve

Bigger World

Mom soon turned tense and panicky. She had willed this new existence into being, and now she alone was responsible for making it work. While we were still in the boarding house, she exploded at Fred when he asked her how you make a pie. "Are you testing me to see whether or not I'm crazy?" she screamed. Did she also view bedbugs as a plague God threw at her to test her resolve?

In the 1950s, Jacksonville was a post-war boomtown, a major banking and insurance center and Florida's second-largest city with a population of about 300,000, nearly ten times larger than Cumberland. Fred found us an apartment house in a quiet neighborhood on Market Street, in the city's metropolitan core. Our landlord was an older couple named Goforth who lived on the floor below us.

My mother focused her considerable energies on two tasks: buying a suitable house and securing a secretarial job. Gone were my friends and our lively games in the predictable, slow cadence of summer days. Here there was no backyard with lovely dirt to make mud pies when it rained, no thick Maryland grass to sit down in or lilacs to smell, and no familiar Cresaptown street to wander. In their place were the Goforths, shabby, barren rooms, and gray, sandy soil that coated skin and clothes simply by wandering through it. But for a few incidents, echoes of loneliness, fear, and boredom are all that resound in my memory of the rest of that summer.

On one of those monotonous days, I found myself with a nickel to buy a soft drink and permission to walk the block or so from our apartment to a small, city-version convenience store: a little of everything and all of it behind a counter. If someone wanted to buy something, they had to ask for it. That resembled no store in my experience, and I was timid and fearful, unsure how to approach the stranger behind the counter in this strange configuration of a store. My gut twisted; I feared being judged a stupid and incompetent child. I had always known just what to say, but in this foreign place, I was sure of nothing.

Without looking at me, the clerk drawled, "Yeah, what y'all want?"

He was probably being matter of fact, but he seemed to me irritated and impatient. "M-m-may I have a tonic?" I managed to stammer, eyes fixed on my bare feet.

The man turned to glower down at me, annoyed. "Well, what kind?" he cross-examined, exasperated. "What kind y'all want?"

He could see I was painfully shy; perhaps he even a little slow and addled, so he gave me some options. "Wild root? Vitalis?"

My head whipped up and I stared up at him, amazed. When I started to back away, he could see a potential sale was ready to run out the door.

"Wait, I ain't seen you 'round here. Where ya'll from?" I somehow managed to convey I was a Yankee fresh from the North. More gently he probed, "So what can I get for ya? Give me an idea of what you want, kid."

"Coke?" I croaked.

His eyes widened, and from beneath the counter, he fished a cold bottle out of a Coke chest of icy water, de-capped it for me, and accepted my nickel. "Okay, kid, here ya go. Next time y'all want a Coke, just say 'soda.' That's what it's called around here, okay? Tonic! Hoo boy, that's a good one," he chuckled. Then, shaking his head, "Yankees." A Coke didn't seem worth the effort, and I never went back on my own.

Not knowing the right way to act made me feel just as adrift as when my mother had questioned me about nonexistent abuse, and I had not known the answer she seemed to feel I should. My desire for a perfection I could not possibly achieve had its roots in the anxiety of earlier days and was fed by fear and uncertainty in my new life. That fear of inadequacy would be a frequent visitor throughout my life.

Fred had no more idea how to take care of Cindy and me than I knew how to negotiate this new environment suffused with strange faces, language, and customs. Because the flyaway sand-dirt filled my shoes when I walked through it, I went barefoot, and Fred took no notice. Soon the skin on my feet developed strange, raised rings that came to my mother's attention because I complained they itched, and Mrs. Goforth educated her on the cause and treatment of ringworm.

Fred had acquired a jackknife that I found quite elegant, and I was amazed at how he used it to sheer the palms off a palmetto branch and sharpen an end to make a play-sword.

"Let me hold the knife?" I begged, "Just for a second." And, indeed, a second was all it took for me to slice off the tip of my thumb. After yelling at my brother, Mom located a doctor who advised taping down the cut-off end with a bandage until it healed and keeping sharp implements out of my reach in future.

One Saturday, my mother took Cindy and me with her to downtown Jacksonville, where I spent much of the day with my mouth agape. Here rose monstrous-tall buildings where traffic like I'd never seen before rushed along wide avenues, and a city park boasted two drinking-water fountains, one labeled "White" and one "Colored." I headed straight for the latter. I wanted to see what colors burst forth from the spigot. Did it have just one or two or had they somehow managed to capture a wet rainbow in this porcelain fixture? My mother figured it out just in time before I made a faux pas of Southern proportions. When I told her what I wanted, she stifled a laugh. She knew that even at nine, I was prickly at being judged stupid or uninformed.

"Oh, no, that's not what it means," she corrected gently. "They mean it's for colored people, Negroes." But that answer made less sense to me than colored water, and she agreed it made no sense to her either.

Freedom wafted through the air that year. My mother's freedom run to Jacksonville came the same time as that city took its own first unwilling steps toward fulfilling some of the basic American rights it had denied its Black residents for so long. In 1955, Rosa Parks took her stand by sitting down on a bus in Alabama, but civil rights took off in Florida cities after May of 1956. That's when two young Black Florida A&M University students planted themselves on a front bench seat beside an amazed white woman and refused the driver's barked order to move to the back. The city-wide bus boycott that followed their arrest awakened both Black and White citizens to the economic power wielded by the Black community, power that neither group had grasped existed until just that year.

My mother was also empowered, able to turn her new

freedoms into realizing the future she wanted. By fall, she had somehow managed to land a good position as a legal secretary with a small but respected Jacksonville law firm. In late October, she filed for divorce, which was granted in December that same year. However, the divorce terms did not include child support. Though my father loved us, I believe he reasoned that she had absconded with enough of his savings to give anyone a good start. The rest was up to her.

Mom enrolled me in fourth grade at Mattie V. Rutherford Elementary School, a short walk from our apartment, and I became immersed in the mysterious recitation of multiplication tables, overseen by the unsmiling, aptly named Ms. Withers, a gray-haired, no-nonsense teacher who no doubt had shepherded hundreds of squirming nine-year-olds through this unforgiving exercise. At first, I had no idea what they were doing. That scared me because my mother expected me to be a high achiever, and I feared disappointing her. Once I recognized it as memorization, I was on solid ground. I could regurgitate facts with the best of them, and I've pondered whether this year, when I was trying harder than ever to please Mom, was when my learning strategies solidified. Memorization served me well enough until high school, when required skills turned to critical thinking and problem solving.

More changes were in store. Before Christmas, my mother found us a stucco duplex on Notter Avenue in the Brentwood neighborhood, about a four-minute drive north of our first apartment. In 1956, Brentwood was a suburban version of the rural neighborhood we had come from—modest, middle class—no white picket fences. About two-and-a-half months into the school year, I transferred from Mattie V. Rutherford to Brentwood Elementary

School. The new house was close to her work, and only a few minutes' walk from both my school and Andrew Jackson High School, which Fred would attend. I was in fourth grade, and Cindy, who was just five, went to a neighbor down the street who was caring for her granddaughters while her daughter worked.

Mom hatched a savvy financial plan. We would live in one side of the duplex and rent out the other. Each side crammed three bedrooms and a bathroom into about eight-hundred square feet, but each had shiny hardwood floors and a shared backyard with a huge pecan tree that showered a bonanza of paper-shell nuts each fall.

Our new home was the site of battles large and small. First came the War of the Roaches. The size of our new adversary's army only became clear the first time we came home after dark and turned on the kitchen lights. I thought it a great Whack-A-Mole game to run around crushing their scurrying forms, but Mom was not so delighted. She called a pest-control company from work the next day to come and drench the place in chemicals.

Then came the fight to find tenants who would pay the rent on time and be good custodians of my mother's real estate investment. One couple began to have loud fights when the husband drank, so Mom added "quiet habits" to her list of criteria for tenants. The more conditions she demanded of renters, the less likely she was to find them, so the other duplex half was sometimes empty for extended periods. Making money was harder than she had thought.

The year was an adaptation for all of us. To my great surprise, many of my Brentwood buddies were more aggressive than my Cresaptown friends; after-school scuffles between boys or girls were viewed as entertainment. "Pssst, Peggy, I hear Judy and Charlene are fighting after school. Let's go watch!" I went along the first time the rumor went around, but I had enough of fighting and wanted things peaceful.

My report cards indicate I remained an excellent student, except for one grading period in March and April of 1957, when I was dragged into another kind of battle.

Mom had agreed to Dad's terms for the divorce: she could keep the $19,000 in cash and securities if she surrendered all claims to the Cresaptown properties. When she left, she had taken the deeds from their safe deposit box—maybe to bug Dad? Mom had been surprised at the costs of supporting herself and three growing kids. She had never before had to concern herself with home budgeting, and unexpected expenses such as pest control, car maintenance, and our visits to doctors and dentists were blowing her finances to bits and keeping her awake at night. She had counted on child support, and my father's refusal must have rankled. Her Cumberland attorney had been holding the property deeds, but at some point, she asked him to return them to her. Her motive is unclear, but I would bet she planned to renegotiate the divorce settlement.

Early in 1957, my father sued his runaway wife. In February, a legal notice in the *Cumberland Evening Times* ordered my mother to turn over the deeds and appear in the Allegany County Circuit Court in person "or by Solicitor" to show cause why she had not complied with the terms of the divorce. Mom was up for the challenge. Once again, she trundled us into the Pontiac, this time headed back to Cumberland. My report card from that time records that I was gone for about two weeks, though she enrolled me in Cumberland's Westside Elementary School so we wouldn't miss any studies—and maybe to keep me busy and out from underfoot. We stayed in some shabby rooms somewhere downtown, but I had high hopes we had returned for good.

"When are we going back to Cresaptown?" Silence.

"Is Dad still there?" She looked away.

"Can I see my friends soon?" I pleaded.

She spat out, "Don't you have homework?"

I let it drop.

My father, focused on keeping the Art Glass Company afloat, let his attorney deal with Mom. He may not have even known we kids were in town until an incident he later related to Bobby. "Dad thought he caught sight of Fred on Mechanic Street, but the boy ran when he called to him." Bobby sighed at the memory of the conversation. "It stabbed Dad through the heart thinking that Mom had turned Fred against him."

After the court appearance, we headed back to Jacksonville with a sullen mother. The trip had not only been fruitless, but expensive, and her mood was dark. She yelled at us about small infractions, and sometimes I heard her crying behind a closed bedroom door. If the door was closed, I did not need to be Consoler-in-Chief.

With Cindy at the babysitter and Mom out looking for work, I became a "latchkey child" after school until Fred came home. I was resigned to being away from Cresaptown, though far from happy about it. Compared to what I was used to, this new neighborhood was humdrum, and I pined for the familiarity and camaraderie of my old life.

Things began looking up when I acquired a new best friend. Suzanne lived a few blocks from our house and her home had many charms mine lacked. To my mother's exasperation, I begged to go there as early as I could each Saturday morning so we could be willing captives to Suzanne's TV, watching the *Howdy Dowdy Show,* the *Mickey Mouse Club*, and cartoons like *Ruff and Ready* and *Huckleberry Hound*. If Mom let me stay into the afternoon, Suzanne's mom would serve us sandwiches and we'd move on to

Fury and *Sky King.*

Mom bought a television later, but TV was only one of the many attractions that drew me to Suzanne's house. Hers was a traditional nuclear family, with a hardworking dad, a homemaker mom, and two daughters—the younger one about my sister's age—and a collie named Sandy that looked like Lassie from TV. They struck me as our neighborhood's own Ozzie and Harriet, a Jacksonville version of my friend Gail's family in Cresaptown. All happiness and no real drama, or so it seemed to me.

My own family was now fatherless. Mom never mentioned him and got angry when I did, so I stopped asking. I learned later from Bobby how Dad grieved losing us, but Mom had left town with all his savings, and he had neither funds nor days off to travel to Florida for a visit. His days must have been full of glass work, lining up more jobs, and laboring over the billing and paperwork Mom had always done. Gradually, he faded away in my consciousness, a memory of a past life.

This strange new environment offered few compensations for what I had lost. At each holiday, I recalled our traditional Cresaptown celebrations and found the Brentwood School versions wanting. Only a few months before, my identity had been clear to me. I was Cresap Park Peggy, Queen of Cresaptown School (or at least, I felt sure I would have been in ninth grade). Now I didn't know who or what I was. I felt hollowed out.

While Florida weather outside my bedroom window rushed from sudden storms to full sunshine, I spent hours listening to songs from the *South Pacific* musical on my record player. When I heard the song "Bali Hai," I closed my eyes and thought of my own shining island in the sun, the Cresaptown paradise that I had lost. Ironic, really, because Jacksonville was closer to *South Pacific*'s tropical setting than Western Maryland.

Our first trip to Jacksonville Beach was the first time I permitted some of Florida's warm light to penetrate my dark view of this new home. One day, Mom grinned at Cindy and me. "You're in for a real treat today. We're going to the beach!" but I had no idea why that would be so great, and I was so bored on the long drive that I fell asleep. A crunching sound beneath the car wheels woke me. In those days, cars could drive and park on the hard-sand part of the beach at low tide, and I was hearing small shells breaking up beneath the Pontiac's tires.

Out the window I beheld such a sensory festival of sights and sounds that it was a full minute of mouth-open wonder before it registered that there were kids of all ages and description (all white, of course), screaming and jumping around in an endless horizon of water and waves. The kettledrum sounds of crashing waves provided dramatic background music. Adults were there, but they did not seem to be in control of any but the smallest toddlers. The rest were in an ecstasy of communion with the roar of waves under a fireball Florida sun. Mom was able to slow me down only long enough for a quick application of sun lotion and a warning to stay close to the car before I was off to join them; little Cindy stayed with her.

After hours of screaming delight and fighting the force of the salty waves, Mom dragged me into the car as I protested that I was *not* exhausted. I was, of course, as well as hungry and dehydrated when Mom pulled into an A&W Root Beer stand. With my first bites of chili-covered hot dog and iced-down root-beer sweetness in a frosted mug, I found the perfect culinary counterpart to the pleasures I had experienced that day.

Jacksonville was no Cresaptown, but it had promise.

Chapter Thirteen

We're Catholics

My usual passive strategies of dealing with my mother—agreeing with her, telling her what she wanted to hear, avoiding any topic that would cause conflict—all fell apart on the day of The Conversation. Until that day, I had no idea she had been consulting a Catholic priest. Cindy was only five, and ever eager to do whatever mother wanted, so now she needed only to deal with me, her opinionated ten-year-old. I had in mind a day's exploring the new neighborhood, but she stood at the front door, blocking it before I could dash out. Then she pulled my squirming, antsy body over to stand in front of her as she sat on the edge of a living room chair. In my memory it was a cold morning, or maybe my mind registers it that way because of the chill that came over me as we spoke.

"Margaret, remember when Mama was a little girl, she met nuns that were so good to her. Remember that?" I nodded.

Mom had once limned a vivid tale of being left for a time at a Catholic orphanage run by Sisters of Mercy after her mother died, though she gave few details. I don't know exactly where Blackjack discarded her or how long she was there. He was not Catholic, so he must have been a bit desperate to go to nuns for help. So many questions remain about how it all happened, but

I can easily conjure the horrors of that day. Did he say they were going downtown for a treat? Did he take her there, tell her he would be right back, and then just leave? Or did he merely drop her off, abandoning her without explanation? I can picture eight-year-old Phrona trying to parse her emotions when she found he had gone. Anguish, relief, guilt.

In the 1920s, an order called the Daughters of Charity ran a local infant orphanage and worked as nurses at Cumberland's Sacred Heart Hospital. Older children went to the DOC orphanage in nearby Emmitsburg, Maryland, so Phrona might have been transferred there. Lay workers at the orphanage told me that a common practice in the 1920s and 1930s when widowers or relatives could not care for their children was to drop them off at a local orphanage and retrieve them later if their circumstances changed.

The garb of the Daughters of Charity at the time my mother was with them included distinctive head coverings called "cornettes" that would appear to non-Catholics to be large, white, winged hats. This cornette was the inspiration for Sally Fields' distinctive—and aerodynamic—head covering in the TV series *The Flying Nun*. My mother had spoken wistfully of her time with the nuns. Their angel-like appearance and gentle treatment of her must have left a deep impression on her anguished and impressionable young mind.

"They were like angels," I mused, not exactly sure even then what these strangely dressed women were or what they did but remembering the imagery in her story.

"That's right, like angels." She seemed relieved she had landed on a good entry point.

"Well, I've been thinking for a long time that I want to be Catholic, like the nuns."

"Mm-hmm." I nodded agreeably, even though I wasn't at all sure how that followed.

"I've been talking with Father O'Farrell at Holy Rosary Catholic Church here in our neighborhood, and that's where I'll be confirmed as soon as I've finished the lessons on how to be a good Catholic."

Nuns, confirmation, lessons? Everything I was hearing was perplexing, and I glanced over at the front door, but Mom turned me to face her. A previous conversation in which she held my arms that way made me shrink from her. Though it had been over five years, I had indelible memories of the pillow she had thrust down over my face, and I stiffened with apprehension.

"Margaret, you and Cindy will be coming with me into the Church. You'll be Catholics, too."

"What? No! NO! I can't! I'm a Methodist," I protested, a little amazed that I was contradicting her out loud. "I can't be Catholic. I won't do it!" I pulled away and backed up, glaring at her.

Her face fell, and she stood. "Well, I can't leave you alone while I go to church. Anyway, I'm your mother, and I know what's best for you. You're going with me into the Catholic Church, and that's all there is to it."

Then something dawned on me. "What about Fred?" I demanded, a slow heat starting behind my eyes. "Can't I stay with him? He could watch me."

"Absolutely not!" She got that look that meant her mind was set. "You'll come with me, you and Cindy. Fred is old enough to choose for himself, but you're not."

I never thought about it until much later, but all the changes in our life probably unsettled Mom as much as they did me. Did her mind turn to the Catholic Church that had rescued her as a child as a way to anchor her and give her solace? I know she was a fan and avid reader of Thomas Merton, himself a spiritual wanderer, who also found his place in the Catholic Church and became a Trappist monk in 1942. *The Seven Storey Mountain*, Merton's 1948 autobiography of his life and his path to conversion, was a great favorite of my mother's.

A foreword written for the 1998 edition by William H. Shannon, Founding President of the Thomas Merton Society, described the church into which Merton and my mother converted.

"The pre-Vatican II church into which Merton was baptized was a church still reacting even three centuries later to the Protestant Reformation of the sixteenth century. Characterized by a siege mentality, wagons circled around doctrinal and moral absolutes, it clung to its past with great tenacity . . . The Church prided itself on the stability and unchangeable character of its teaching in this context of a world in flux. At the time Merton wrote his book, Roman Catholic theology had become a set of pre-packaged responses to any and all questions. Polemical and unapologetic in tone, its aim was to prove that Catholics were right, and all others were wrong."

This in a nutshell was my mother's belief system and reflects the blinkered stance she adopted on so many topics. She settled on an idea and confirmed it in her mind as the only possible stance. After that, she stood immovable. Like Merton, she felt that Catholic Church teachings offered the only true insights on Christianity, and the way Catholics practiced Christianity at that time was the only way to do it.

I never understood why Mom would adopt a belief system that would preclude her remarriage. The Catholic Church frowned on divorce but has no punishment for it because it deems it a legal rather than spiritual concept. Catholic dogma holds that absent a papal annulment, you're married until you die. Remarrying would mean my mother would commit a mortal sin for which she risked excommunication.

And so I was to be a Catholic, forced once more to accompany my mother on a journey I did not want to make. Fred continued down a path I would never know, and I began to resent his autonomy. He joined thespians, band, and other after-school school clubs and was never there to share my misery. Fred had always been my confidant, but as our paths diverged, our relationship frayed, and a gap between us opened that would widen over time. Cindy and I also became distant, though we shared a bedroom. Somehow, I got the impression Mom didn't expect as much of her, but that may only have been that Cindy was quieter and more even-tempered than I and tried to do as Mom directed.

I fought this forced conversion with everything in my preteen arsenal—crying, sullenness, tantrums—but in the end, she had her way, and I became a Catholic. She arranged a rebaptism by a priest, which I still don't know how she managed; rebaptism has been against Catholic dogma since the twelfth century, and I had been baptized as an infant at the Cresaptown Methodist Church.

I got good at acting out the role of a good little Catholic girl, but I was never Catholic like her, an unquestioning believer and active practitioner of all Catholic practices, from nightly rosaries to devotional scapulars. I can still remember us on our knees before the small shrine Mom set up in our hallway, saying the rosary until I imagined I would go crazy from the tedium of counting out those beads, prayer after prayer.

Hail Mary, full of Grace
(Which rosary section is this?)
The Lord is with thee
(God, my knees hurt!)
Blessed art thou among women
(How can I get out of this tomorrow?)
And blessed is the fruit of thy womb Jesus.
(I hate my mother!)

Ironically, the Catholic Church my mother loved for its long-standing traditions was in for a change not long after she joined in 1957. Only two years later, Pope John XXIII surprised the world and his own hierarchy by announcing the first ecumenical council in a century. Pope John recognized that the Church's centuries-old practices were making it feel lifeless and irrelevant to many people, and he wanted to rejuvenate the way the Catholic Church related to the modern world. The council made many changes to traditional practices, notably to the church service, including saying Mass in "vernacular languages" like English instead of Latin. The priest was to face the congregation instead of the altar during Mass, and more modern music and art was permitted. There were fewer "forbiddens." Women no longer had to cover their hair in church and Catholics need not refrain from eating meat on Friday, a practice that earned them the moniker "mackerel snappers." Meatless Fridays are now required only during Lent.

Even as the church changed around her and many of the old traditions she loved fell away, my mother held fast to a pre-Vatican II view of Catholicism. She mourned the loss of her beloved Latin liturgy, and as fewer churches offered it, she sometimes traveled a fair distance to find a church that said Sunday mass in Latin. She was a devotee of the French reactionary Archbishop

Marcel Lefebvre, who continued celebrating the traditional Tridentine mass and was excommunicated in 1988 after defying Pope John Paul and confirming four likeminded bishops.

Like many orders, the Daughters of Charity nuns whom Mom remembered from her childhood changed their distinctive habit in 1964, and she was horrified. "Now they look like every other woman on the street," she mourned, her voice breaking with disappointment and disdain.

How could someone who made such a radical change as leaving her husband and starting over in a new part of the country be so singularly intransigent when it came to so many other adaptations? Do patterns that comforted us in our youth make their way into our psyche, and do we turn to them for comfort as our bodies and the world change around us? Mom wanted new patterns as part of her "rebirth" but apparently wanted ones that would never alter afterwards.

When she became a Catholic, she knew she was at last part of the "unchanging truth" of her church and was confident her daughters would profit from her insight. Did she hope, perhaps, that I would become a nun?

The first time Mom dragged me into Holy Rosary Church, it struck me as resembling a medieval castle with pews, its darkened, gothic interior contrasting sharply with the bright windows and sparse décor of the Cresaptown Methodist Church of my childhood.

Mother wore a black-lace mantilla and a rapturous expression. I was used to her dramatics, but this time she was in costume. When the Mass began, I was completely confused; it was in a foreign language! I missed the familiar cadence of the

Methodist service. I saw a minister—my mother called him a priest—who was doing all these weird things at the altar with his back to us. Most peculiar of all was when he held up a gold metal contraption on a chain and waved it about while gray-white smoke (which I later learned was incense) drifted out. Here was a church nearly as strange as the one we visited with Aunt Zella in West Virginia. I looked up at the ecstatic face of my mother, who seemed unsurprised.

"They'll be going up for communion soon, but we won't be going with them," she whispered. *What? Getting some bread and grape juice at communion was always the best part of a service, and we can't even have that?*

Our meeting with Father O'Farrell to discuss my upcoming transition was brief. "Do you understand that your mother wants you to be confirmed in the Catholic faith?" he boomed. I nodded, looking down at my feet. I was still seething inside, but I wouldn't let it show in front of this black-robed stranger.

I thought him weirdly jolly for the bad news he was delivering. "I know you didn't like the idea at first, but your mother wants what's best for you. I hope you know that." *How little you know of my mother.* I clenched my teeth and, for once, held my tongue. I'm sure Mom was holding her breath.

A year later as I was gradually easing into the foreign land of Being a Catholic, my life convulsed once again when Mom informed me I would be changing schools. The Holy Rosary School was opening that fall, and I was to be in the first wave of new students. Mom was convinced parochial school would give me the preparation I'd need to be confirmed a Catholic, training she could not provide.

In the space of two years, my whole world had shifted on its axis and then continued to wobble. A new place to live and a new school, then another move across town and another school, now a change of religions and yet another new school. No ground was solid, no word could be trusted, no future day was predictable, and it was clear to me who was to blame.

My relationship with my mother became one long, occasionally vicious war of wills. Whether she wanted me to take violin lessons or go to Mass, help her build a backyard patio or say my rosary, everything between us became a battle.

I yearned to break free of my mother, to have some control over my happiness. I was eleven years old, and I wanted out of her world.

Chapter Fourteen

Categories of Sin

School had always been my refuge, an escape to the certainty of order and the calm of predictability. A place, too, where I could impress my friends and earn praise and admiration from teachers. Reconciled to my fate, I looked forward to starting Holy Rosary School, as I had to starting school every fall, ready to wow them all. I wasn't at all prepared for the headlong plunge into the cultural cauldron of parochial school Catholicism.

On the first day of school, I donned the required garb, a navy-blue serge skirt and vest and a white blouse, topped off with a navy-blue beanie and white socks with saddle oxfords. Mom surveyed me with approval. "Now don't you look pretty?" I regarded her sullenly. The uniform never fit me well; I always felt disheveled and out of sorts, as if wearing some weird disguise, playing a part I had not chosen, in a costume that hid the real me.

Mom dropped me off at my classroom and left to deliver Cindy to hers. My teacher was a nun, whom I eyed suspiciously.

"Hello, Margaret," Sister greeted me warmly. "We're glad to have you here."

"My name is Peggy." I needed to set her straight right off.

After a "what I did this summer" show-and-tell, I encountered a topic new to me when Sister passed out thin booklets with red covers: the *Catechism of Christian Doctrine, Prepared and Enjoined by Order of the Third Council of Baltimore*. Based on a compilation of beliefs first drafted in 1614, this was the standard Catholic school text used throughout the country from 1885 and included all the basic prayers, a blow-by-blow listing of the liturgy of the Mass, and a set of thirty-three question-and-answer lessons that we had to memorize.

Learning catechism was a straight-up call-and-response exercise to assure that the other kids and I knew from the get-go our place in the world and exactly what God expected of us. Sister read the question, and we parroted the answer.

Q. What must we do to save our souls?

A. To save our souls, we must worship God by faith, hope, and charity; that is, we must believe in Him, hope in Him, and love Him with all our heart.

Q. How shall we know the things which we are to believe?

A. We shall know the things which we are to believe from the Catholic Church, through which God speaks to us.

God talks to the church, and the church tells everyone what God had to say? I didn't believe a word of it, but Sister directed us to memorize the answers, so I did. I was hell at memorizing.

That year I got a tutorial on sin. Mortal sins could send you straight to hell unless you confessed them before you died; venial sins wouldn't. I could define near occasion of sin, describe the difference between sins of omission and sins of commission, and reel off the seven deadly sins: pride, covetousness, lust, anger, gluttony, envy, and sloth. I became a sin expert.

I also learned dogma that was far different from Methodist beliefs. Purgatory, our catechisms stated, was a kind of holding place for those who weren't quite ready for heaven. Limbo, a place where unbaptized infants went after death, was also in our catechisms, though it was later removed. The idea that babies couldn't enter heaven because they still had the stain of original sin had created an increasing outcry. (In 2007, Limbo would be officially deemed a theological theory, rather than doctrine.) I learned the seven sacraments, from Baptism to Extreme Unction (Last Rites) and memorized the dates of major feast days.

Lunch was cold, Saran-wrapped sandwiches that tasted plastic, and we ate at our desks. This was nothing like the tasty homemade food prepared by Cresaptown School cafeteria women.

One afternoon after recess on a playground that was nothing more than an unshaded stretch of blacktop at the side of the school, Sister was introducing spelling. Suddenly, the whole class leaped to their feet as if they were on springs, and I followed suit. *Fire drill maybe?*

Father O'Farrell had appeared at the classroom door. "Good morning, Father O'Farrell!" the class chanted as he entered. We all stood beside our desks until he said, "You may sit, children." I gathered this was to be repeated when he or any other priest appeared. The strange practices in this place never seemed to end.

I was a star academically, but socially I was labeled The Outsider. Not only did most of my sixth-grade classmates already know each other, either from past schools or church or both, I was the only convert; everyone else had been born into Catholic families and knew exactly what to do and how to act. I was still learning the prayers and the liturgy that was so familiar to them. To top off my Otherness, I was a "Yankee" and talked funny, while they were nearly all southerners who spoke "Rebel." This combination would have been a lot to overcome, but I succeeded in making it so much worse by being a superior student.

My hand always shot up when Sister asked a question, and I aced every spelling test. Regurgitating on demand was my strength, and when we went down the rows of the class, each person reciting an answer in response to a question Sister posed from the catechism, I never missed one. I declaimed the Hail Mary and Gloria Patri enthusiastically, while my classmates' delivery was bored and perfunctory. I out-Catholic-ed all of them. I couldn't have made myself more unpopular if I had come in with a detailed manual on *How to be an Outcast*.

The whole year would have been misery itself were it not for my teacher, Sister Mary Pius. Like all nuns of that time, Sister wore a uniform called a habit, the Catholic equivalent of an Islamic chador. A floor-length dress designed to hide all female characteristics, the black habit of the Sisters of St. Joseph covered everything but face and hands. A crucifix hung below a stiff shoulder-to-shoulder white covering called a guimpe, and another crucifix dangled at her side from the end of her rosary belt. A filmy black veil attached to a white head covering, or coif, framed her face and hung down her back to below her waist. Black stockings and sturdy black shoes completed the outfit.

Sister Mary Pius could not have been older than thirty when I met her, and distinctively, proudly Irish, though we were not permitted to ask about her background before she became a "bride of Christ." She had a broad Irish accent, and I got the impression that she was not long in this country.

I decided that Sister was not pretty, but I found her look appealing, nonetheless. She had lively brown eyes and the clear, glowing skin and sturdy build of an Irish farm-girl. Her substantial dark eyebrows made me think that her white coif hid a wealth of thick brunette hair, or at least what was left of it; nuns were required to keep a boy-short haircut. But there was no hiding Sister's vibrant, fun-loving nature.

"Sister, show us the dance," we'd beg, and she would sometimes grace us with a little Irish jig that could be seen only if she raised her long, black skirts just enough to reveal her black-stockinged feet in a quick-stepping prance. I thought her a marvel.

Though she took her teaching role seriously and had firm control of the classroom, Sister was good-natured, and we loved the sound of her high-pitched, melodic laughter. We also knew she could take a joke.

Sister had a phobia of animals—any kind, large or small. We never learned the source of her fear, but we used it to play a prank on her. One of the girls brought in a bedraggled, stuffed squirrel, ostensibly for show-and-tell, and smuggled it into the metal school-supplies cabinet in the front of the room, situating it on a shelf at her eye level. We held our breath and waited.

As Sister approached the cabinet doors, we nudged each other, barely suppressing giggles. When she opened the doors, looked up, and spotted the poor, scruffy creature, its sightless, shiny eyes staring back at her, Sister squealed, "Jaysus, Mary, and Joseph, help us!" Clutching the crucifix at her breast, she jumped back so fast she almost lost her balance and fell. She took it good-naturedly when the class exploded with laughter, though she demanded that we remove the scraggly thing immediately and banished further appearances. The story of Sister Mary Pius and the Squirrel spread quickly and became the highlight of the school year.

Sister may have been asked to give her convert student special tutoring on what was expected of good little Catholic kids, because she took a special interest in me, quickly realizing I was unhappy there and doing her best to console me. She became my mentor and counselor and probably sent up countless prayers on my behalf, but the attention she focused on me served only to get me labeled Teacher's Pet and the target of more than the usual middle-school malice.

Sister Mary Pius was also the school's choir director, a job she took seriously. We practiced the hallelujah she taught us so often that it may be the last memory to die in my brain. I just knew Mom was in ecstasy that my voice was part of the children's choir-song she heard floating down from the loft during special masses.

I have vivid memories of Sister Mary Pius in the loft after we had finished singing, kneeling at the railing with her dark-veiled head bent so far over her folded hands that they almost touched. Her pose worried me. Did it betray some interior turmoil or deep anguish usually hidden from us under her exuberant demeanor? Was she praying for guidance, for courage, for wisdom? Or did she merely have a long prayer list that perhaps included one of her young charges she sensed had a long, hard road ahead? My fellow choir members assured me she was okay, but I was sure they didn't know enough about anguish to spot it. I certainly did.

Penance was one of the sacraments I'd learned about in catechism, but nothing could have prepared me for what that entailed, namely, the torments of the confessional. But if Cindy and I were to achieve the Catholic benchmarks of First Communion and Confirmation, I had to endure a ritual that took shape in the Dark Ages.

Protestants confess directly to God (or alternately to their therapist or bartender). The theory behind the Catholic priest as intermediary is that he acts as *in persona Christi*; he stands in and acts for Christ, who is the only one who can forgive sins. It's like sending a Western Union message to The Lord. There is still a sender and receiver, but someone else is handling the transmission.

Sister Mary Pius taught me what to expect, and though I was terrified of entering the dark confessional, my first attempt went without a hitch. Mom was euphoric, but I hated it and resolved to confess as little as possible.

"How was it, Peggy," she inquired eagerly, a sweet smile on her rosy face.

"Not too bad," I white-lied. "Makes me nervous though."

"It's good for you," she asserted solemnly. "Clears your mind."

We were supposed to go to confession every week but claiming you had nothing to confess usually gave you a pass. Certainly, I should have confessed hating my mother more every week, but I had little interest in searching my soul and painting a more accurate picture to some guy I hardly knew.

One morning, Sister met me at the classroom door. "You're in luck!" she announced brightly, as if I had won the Irish lottery. "Father Murphy is coming to hear confession at the school next week. You can practice more then." Had she found out I hadn't been to confession in weeks? I certainly didn't feel lucky.

Traditional church confessional booths of that time had a partially obscured opening between priest and confessor providing a degree of anonymity. But Father Murphy sat behind a table in a brightly lit auditorium, one hand up against his brow to block his peripheral sight. Sister practically had to push me through the door. I sat across the table from him, our chairs arranged so we faced in opposite directions.

I began to recite, "Bless me, Father, for I have sinned. It has been three weeks since my last confession . . ."

"Shhh-sh-sh, not so loud, not so loud," he snapped, irritated. "Keep your voice down. Everyone can hear you."

Completely flustered, I forgot what to say next. After a few seconds of silence, he hissed, "Well, what are you waiting for? Tell me your sins?"

I pictured my classmates waiting outside the room, smirking over my stupidity. *What are my sins? What ARE my sins. What are SINS?* My carefully prepared short list vanished from my brain.

Sensing my panic, Father Murphy sighed and began to coach me. "Have you uttered any curse words? Disobeyed your parents?"

Suddenly, my list reappeared in my brain, and my voice came to me. "I was mean to my sister twice," I whispered, relieved, "And I ..."

"What?" he leaned towards me, "Now I can't hear you." Clearly no tone of voice was acceptable to this guy. I wanted to grab him by the cassock and shout, "What do you want? I'm doing my best here!" I somehow got through my torment, and he bestowed the words of absolution I had been waiting for. "Ego te absolvo a peccatis tuis, in nomine Patris, et Filii, et Spiritus Sancti. Okay, your penance is to say three Hail Mary's and do a good Act of Contrition." And with that, I was released.

After leaving the room, I began the Act grudgingly. "O my God, I am heartily sorry for having offended Thee . . ." *And O my God, I REALLY hate confession! Oh, no, another sin!*

A confusion of doubt and guilt preyed on my mind. I wanted to please Sister and Mom, but I remained skeptical of some of the Church's basic doctrine. I couldn't see how the Catholicism could be "the One True Church" to the exclusion of all others. What about Methodism? It had always been good enough for me before I got to Jacksonville. And I never got why I had to bare my soul to some guy I either barely knew or hadn't even met before.

Despite my misgivings, the Church's trademark guilt was beginning to sink in.

I found it a constant challenge to remember all the rules. Once, I peered into the refrigerator and grabbed a leftover chicken leg, chowing down on it before realizing it was a Friday, letting the last bite fall from my lips.

Oh, God, was that a venial or a mortal sin?

In my child's brain, becoming Catholic was a whim my mother had indulged in because she was selfish and thought only of herself. I conflated it with all her other capricious acts and even at twelve years old, yearned for the time I would be free to make my own choices. Her demand that I change my religion had burdened me with a host of new problems and a profound weight of helpless guilt that would only grow with events later in the school year.

Chapter Fifteen

Parochial Guilt

Small pleasures began to surface in the otherwise barren landscape of my social life at my new school. Pop Beads were big in 1958, and it was a status symbol to collect as many colors as possible and combine them in new ways. Hula hoops also made their appearance that year, and for a time their electric-green and electric-pink plastic circles brightened up the playground. I was a fast runner and gained a wary respect among the boys by beating most of them in footraces, so recess often found me with them. Most of the girls didn't like me; I was excluded from birthday parties and suffered the occasional snide comment when I got my usual 100% on spelling tests. I ignored them or went crying to Sister, which made them hate me even more.

A stringy-haired, bespectacled girl named Kathy took it on herself to be the point of the spear. Larger and taller than the rest of us, with a bulky build and close-set eyes, Kathy was a less-than-stellar student and may have been so much taller than we were because she had been held back a grade. The contrast between her school achievement and mine must have rankled, as did the special attention I got from the school's favorite teacher. And, of course, there was my extreme Otherness, how blatantly different I was. Yet I was somehow unaware of just how much sentiment was building against me.

One crisp January day, as Cindy and I started out from school for home, I was suddenly conscious of whispered voices behind us and glanced back to find Kathy and two of her cronies following us. When we turned the corner that put the school out of sight, Kathy began to jeer.

"Hey, you!" she yelled. "New girl!"

Such creative epithets. Is that all you've got?

Cindy looked back apprehensively, then up at me, and fear prickled up my neck, but I kept walking. Suddenly Kathy and her pals closed the gap, and I turned to face them. One of Kathy's friends was holding her glasses.

"Go home, Kathy," I sneered, my face reflecting my disgust for them. I turned and whispered to Cindy, "Keep walking." I took her hand, and we quickened our pace toward home. I reasoned that if we could reach our block, Kathy wouldn't dare pursue me in sight of my house.

Turning my back on her must have made her wild, and Kathy hustled up behind me and shoved me. "Turn around and fight, you coward!" she screeched.

One of the seven deadly sins flamed inside me.

"Coward! You're too chicken to fight!" she yelled again.

Kathy wasn't used to moving her girth so quickly, and the exertion made her round face sweaty and red-blotched. She shoved me again on one shoulder, and the force of it nearly sent me to the ground. Cindy dropped my hand and began to cry and glance about, uncertain what she should do. I whirled to face my attacker, and the black look on my face must have given Kathy pause. She glanced over at her two friends.

"Get away from me!" I cried. "Leave me alone!"

"Sister's pet! Where is Sister now? Fight me, Sissy!"

I had never had a physical fight with anyone before. I never saw it happen at Cresaptown, though it was common enough at Brentwood School. At four-and-a-half feet tall and seventy pounds or so, I was at least a head shorter and maybe twenty pounds lighter than my opponent, but when she came at me to hit me, I rushed at her like a shot cannonball, focusing on Kathy all the pent-up passion and resentment I had been fostering for so long. I forgot all the sins, mortal and venial. I hated her and all her friends. I hated my life. I hated my mother for taking me away from all my old friends and the places and customs I loved and bringing me there and making me Catholic and putting me through all of this.

We fought as only little girls can, scratching, slapping, hair-pulling, clothes-tearing. I was dimly aware of Kathy's friends bellowing, "Get her! Get her, Kathy!"

I had learned only a few actual curse words, but I pelted her with what I had. "Damn you! Damn you, damned devil!" I shrieked. "I hate you, hate you!"

Kathy seemed more than a little surprised by the fight this short, skinny kid had in her, and after only fifteen-or-twenty seconds of battle, she pushed me away and stepped back. I was crying and scarlet-faced, and my uniform blouse was torn and half off me, but my teeth and fists were clenched, ready to answer whatever she had. We glared at each other, panting. Kathy's hair and blouse were as disheveled as mine, and though her friends were still egging her on, she hesitated. Then it happened.

A car slowed in the street and came to a stop beside us, and a woman rolled down her window and yelled, "Hey you! Big girl! Quit picking on that little girl!"

The stranger may not have accurately gauged what was happening at that point. I think Kathy sensed I had the rage needed to beat her and, more importantly, realized she had been spotted by someone who might report to the nuns that Holy Rosary girls had been seen fighting on the sidewalk. Kathy might have to admit she'd committed a mortal sin. Suddenly, she spun and walked away quickly, her minions following, glancing back at me then up at her, surprise registering on their round faces.

I was left with the grim task of explaining to my mother the scratches on my body and my torn uniform. She blamed me. "You must have antagonized them," she declared. "You got what was coming to you, didn't you? Why can't you just learn to get along?" *Ah, the guilt!*

The next day, Kathy was quite friendly. "Hi, Peggy," she greeted me warmly, an expression of respect in her small, bespectacled eyes. Did she think I might tell Sister? I didn't, but the murderous look I threw her backed her away, and she kept her distance after that.

A photo taken the following spring shows Cindy and me in white First Communion dresses and veils; my mother had achieved her goal. I was well and truly Catholic in every way but in my mind. Tuition funds may have begun weighing on Mom's mind, and my constant carping about the school had to have worn on her nerves. She also knew that one elderly nun, perhaps a substitute teacher, had been cruel to my sister, hitting her head with a ruler for God knows what infraction; Cindy was certainly among the most shy and obedient of children. Though we weren't that close, I was protective of my little sister and hated what was happening to her. Suddenly Mom announced that we would not be returning to Brentwood School that fall. *God truly does hear prayers!*

At the time, I was blind to the comfort and structure the

church offered my mother's anguished and distracted mind, as it did for Thomas Merton and does for millions around the world. Even I found myself comforted by some of the Church's customs. I would sometimes drop by Holy Rosary Church on my way home from school to light a candle or sit in its dim light and say a prayer. The Virgin Mary and I became friends. When I wanted something or was afraid or troubled, I knelt before her statue and breathed a Hail Mary or two as a kind of request line to heaven. I relished the belief that a woman could intercede for me and carry my appeals to her son and his dad. Some of the comfort of the church still flows back to me in the sound of Gregorian chant or the Latin mantra "*ora pro nobis.*" The 1985 pop song "Kyrie Eleison," now heard mainly as "grocery store music," makes me smile like one with secret knowledge. How many non-Catholics know it is a plea to God to have mercy on us?

Still when the opportunity came, I left the Catholic Church with no regrets save one. I came to see Sister Mary Pius. I loved her too much to lie to her. Not telling her would have been a sin of omission. "Sister," I mumbled, looking down at my sandals, "I'm sorry, but I've decided to leave the Church."

She looked crushed, and I wanted to hug her, to console her and tell her I would be okay, even though I would be Methodist. She asked me to wait and swished long black skirts into her classroom. When she returned, she handed me a note and embraced me quickly. I felt her stiff guimpe cool against my cheek. Then she turned, closed the door quietly, and disappeared from my life. She had written:

Dear Peggy,

Be good and you will always be very happy.

Stay sweet and stay good. Keep your pretty smile. It will make you many friends. Please pray for me as I always do for you. God bless you 'cause I do.

Sister Mary Pius

Ah, the guilt!

One blustery day decades after I left the Catholic church, a friend and I arrived at the Saint Benedict Abbey in Saint-Benoît-du-Lac, Quebec, Canada, just before Vespers. The cloistered Benedictine monks who lived and worked there sang Gregorian chant, which we had never heard in person. This was the first Catholic service I attended since my return to Methodism. We slipped into a pew in the back a few minutes before dark-robed figures filed in quietly and took seats in pews facing each other on either side of the altar. As their voices rose, trees with dark, bare, branches outside the window behind the altar whipped and swayed frantically in the wind, the storm outside contrasting with the sanctuary's quiet tranquility. Sister would have glowed thinking of me there, and I have no doubt it was her prayers that got me through the tempests that arrived in my life soon after I left Holy Rosary.

Chapter Sixteen

Close Encounters with Sin

Holy Rosary schooled me in the names and categories of sins, a nomenclature for iniquities. I had become an expert on the jargon of evil, but I never really understood what it was all about until the summer after I turned twelve.

By the time we moved to Notter Avenue, Mom was working full-time as a legal secretary and had to confront a problem she never had before: childcare. I was starting fifth grade that fall, but Cindy had not yet begun first grade because she wouldn't turn six until November. Mrs. Parks, a neighbor in the next block, was hired to keep Cindy all day until Fred came home from school. Mom then expected him to keep track of Cindy and me. He was never a very attentive babysitter and could be counted on even less as his extracurricular activities accumulated.

Cindy stayed with Mrs. Parks until Mom came home from work, and I was often free to wander. I suppose I should be flattered that my mother felt that I was capable enough at the age of ten to permit me such freedom, or maybe she perceived this neighborhood had that safe-Cresaptown vibe. Anyway, dangers that could befall children left to ramble a neighborhood on their own weren't as publicized a concern in the 1950s, though they were no less a hazard.

Sometimes I'd drop by Mrs. Parks' house in the afternoon to enjoy Kool-Aid and cookies and play with her older granddaughter, who was about my age. But Mom's arrangement with Mrs. Parks came to an abrupt halt the day my mother happened to pick up Cindy and me when Ms. Parks' daughter was there collecting her children. Mom talked with the daughter as we played outside and looked irritated on our walk home.

"You won't be going back to that woman's house," she growled as we neared our house. That familiar tone in her voice told me that arguing was useless, but I had to know the reason she suddenly didn't like Mrs. Parks.

"Why not?" I whined. Mrs. Parks' granddaughter was a fun playmate, and I had grown quite fond of afternoon Kool-Aid and cookies.

"That woman told me she works as a 'B-girl,'" Mom spat out. "I don't want you near that house again." I had no clue what a B-girl was, but I assumed it was something unsavory. Much later I learned it was short for "bar girl," a woman who works in a bar or nightclub to encourage male customers to buy more drinks. Deserved or not, B-girl became synonymous with prostitute.

After Fred graduated from high school and moved on to Florida Southern College in Lakeland, Mom placed both Cindy and me with Sarah. I recall her as a round, older lady with fly-away red hair tinged with gray, who laughed a lot and stirred butter and syrup together to spread it on warm biscuits—the most mouthwatering thing I had tasted since we came south.

The summer before I began seventh grade, once again at Brentwood, my mother suddenly decided to move us again to a new babysitter. I never knew for sure why Sarah wasn't good enough, but our safety and well-being were always foremost in Mom's mind. I assume she kept searching for what she felt would be the ideal childcare situation.

Cindy and I began staying with a white-haired woman and her husband who lived not far from us in a large frame house with a big front porch and swing and a huge kitchen and dining room. The place was old and dark and reminded me of Great-Aunt Zernie's clapboard house in Hambleton, West Virginia, only a lot larger. We were to head home around the time Mom would be home from work.

I don't remember the couple's name; let's call them the Guhls. Mrs. Guhl was an even better cook than Sarah. Lunch always seemed to feature either Southern-fried chicken or pork with heavy, rich gravy, along with bowls of fluffy white rice, and okra or bacon-flavored greens. It was all served up with biscuits or cornbread and sweet tea from cut-glass pitchers. This was lunch! I can't image what they had for dinner—probably leftovers.

The Guhls had an adult son whom I'll call Earl, who dropped by his parents' house occasionally, but I don't remember him saying two words to me until a day when Mrs. Guhl was not around.

I was sitting on the front porch swing musing on Southern-fried chicken when Earl opened the screen door. He was smiling.

"Peggy, come inside a minute," he ordered, looking first at me, then past me, his gaze sweeping around the street past the porch.

My response was automatic. An adult had given me a command. I jumped off the swing and followed him to the dining room. When we were well out of sight of the front door, he stopped and began toying with my long, blond locks, his other hand on my shoulder. "You have such pretty hair, Peggy," he sweet-talked, smiling down at me. "I really like you, you know?" Stroking my head, he leaned over and whispered in my ear, "Do you like me?"

Uncomfortable, I murmured something like "Sure" and

turned back toward the front porch. It seemed a long way away.

Still holding my shoulder and smiling, he urged, "Come here for a minute, baby. I want to talk to you," and he pulled me into the kitchen, farther back in the house. Only then did I realize the other Guhls were nowhere around. Then he leaned his back against the refrigerator and, taking me by both shoulders, pulled me towards him. His voice was honeyed, coaxing.

"I'd sure like to get to get to know you better, Peggy. Maybe when you come here, we could spend time together, hmmm?" I tried to pull away from him, but he drew me back, holding me in place against him, his arms wrapped firmly around my waist

Too late I realized I was in trouble, and my mind raced. *How could I have given him the idea that I wanted him to be so familiar with me?* I went back over the last few minutes. *I should not have gone with him when he asked me to come in the house. I should have told him "No" when he asked if I liked him. I should have, I should have . . . this was all my fault. Mom will say I made him do this.*

My eyes were downcast as I struggled to remain calm and figure out how to get out of his grasp. Putting a finger under my chin, he tilted my head up and brushed his lips against mine, murmuring how pretty I was and how good I felt.

By then I was physically off-balance, afraid, and repulsed. Though his tone was soft and cajoling, I sensed the menace in his hands and knew that I should not antagonize him, or things might turn even worse. I dropped my head again to avoid his lips, but his right hand dropped down to my buttocks, letting a finger fall between my thighs, and he squeezed. My eyes flew open, and my head jerked up to meet his eyes.

He was grinning broadly. "Do you like that?"

I was terrified, yet somehow, I kept my cool and nodded. "Mm-hmm. But it's time for me to go home now."

He seemed surprised and the smile vanished, but he loosened his hold a little. "Well, I'll see you tomorrow then?" His tone had changed; now it was almost pleading. I smiled and nodded agreeably, then pulled away, regaining my balance, and headed out of the kitchen.

"Cindy," I sang out calmly, trying to camouflage my fear and panic. I had to take her with me. God knows what he might do to her. Was he following me? I dared not look back. "Come on, time to go home!" I fast-walked toward the front door, willing myself not to run.

She emerged from one of the side rooms where she had been playing, and I took her hand. "Let's go home now," I ordered, pulling her toward the front door, but like me, she had a mind of her own, and at first, she resisted, pulling away from me. We weren't supposed to walk home until later, but perhaps she could see the fear and urgency in my eyes because she didn't object when I whispered, "We need to go *now*." Once we were well away from the house, I described what Earl had done.

"Did he ever do anything like that to you?" I asked. She started crying, so I dropped it.

We had calmed down by the time Mom came home, but my stomach churned as I considered the problem I faced. I had long ago learned to say nothing that would upset her, but I wasn't going back to Mrs. Guhl's. I was also afraid I would get blamed, so at first, I just mentioned casually that we didn't like Mrs. Guhl and didn't want to go to her house anymore. Mom's eyes narrowed. Then it became a game of twenty questions with few answers while I fidgeted.

"Why? What happened?"

"Nothing."

"Did she do something to you?"

"No."

"Well, why don't you like her?"

Silence.

When she became frustrated with the lack of information, I finally blurted out that I was afraid of Mrs. Guhl's son, and she made the leap to what she was inclined to think of all men anyway and dropped her probe. Maybe she was afraid of hearing details. Mom promised me we wouldn't have to return, but she must have decided then and there what she needed to do.

That Sunday as we walked to church, she took Cindy in one hand and me in the other and detoured us down the street to the dreaded Guhl house. I refused to get near the front porch, so Mom went inside for a few minutes, then emerged to join us on the sidewalk. When a worried-looking Mr. and Mrs. Guhl also emerged on the front porch, Mom began to berate them.

"You didn't tell me you had a son living there," she yelled. "You should be ashamed, ashamed!"

Then Earl appeared at the screen door and looked straight at me. I backed away, ready to run as he emerged. Shaking with rage, Mom shrieked at him, "Shame on you! Shame, you, you monster!" Pointing a shaking finger at him, she screeched, "What kind of person does that to babies!" As Mrs. Guhl turned to look at her son, I tugged at my mother's arm to get her to leave. She finally stalked off, leaving the three Guhls on the porch staring at each other and our retreating figures.

How ironic it seems to me now that with each move we made as my mother searched for better babysitting, the more at-risk we became. After the horror story with the Guhls, we had no more babysitters. Instead, we were on our own most days after school. Maybe Mom felt I had shown I could handle myself and keep both Cindy and me safe. She found day camps for us during summer.

❧

Mom had tried her best to protect us from evils like sex abuse and had to admit she had failed. What she didn't know is that the incident made my thoughts turn to sex, though I never have called it that. In fact, I never named it anything. Though innocent as an Easter lily, I sensed that what Earl Guhl had done was somehow related to what Mom and the Holy Rosary sisters were so worried about. Where to go for authoritative information was the problem that perplexed me.

Chapter Seventeen

Sex and Other Evils

I never told any of my friends about the Guhls, but some Brentwood School girlfriends claimed to know a great deal about kissing and boys. Our talk drifted inexorably to the subject of sex, though of course, the term itself had not yet entered our vocabulary. Male and female physiology and how babies got made were biology topics of mystery and misinformation to us all; alas, the Florida curriculum meticulously avoided the topic of sex education.

My mother had given birth to four children and had acquired a boyfriend named Willy in Jacksonville, whom I now know was her lover. Yet like most of our mothers, she was singularly unqualified to deliver sex education and never sat me down for "The Talk." When she saw a pregnant woman walking down the street, she would snicker, "I don't know who she is, but I know what she's been doing" and laugh uproariously, but I never got the joke.

One of my friends saw a boy write "f-u-c-k" on the wall outside the school, and she and the other girls rolled their eyes and looked disgusted.

I was puzzled. "What's that mean?" They looked at me as though I were dimwitted.

"It's how you get pregnant," one declared in a teacher's

authoritative tone. That brought up the mechanics of sex and pregnancy. Another girl guessed you had only to be in the same bed with a guy to get pregnant.

"What, just lie up close to him?" I pictured something hopping from one body to the other. They laughed, but it turned out no one knew the correct answer. The first girl offered she had heard that it required putting the boy's thing into the girl's orifice down below.

Incredulous, I scoffed, "That's the most disgusting thing I ever heard. Where on earth did you hear that?"

The authoritative source was my friend's older sister, who had added that a baby came out from the same place as where you went to the bathroom. I had heard that the baby was inside the woman before birth and had to come out somehow, so that seemed plausible.

"Which hole?" I queried. No one knew that either, but we all hoped it was the one where pee came out.

To be the One in the Know with my other thirteen-year-old friends, I reluctantly went to my mother. She was in the kitchen, pushing clothes into the top of the Maytag washer.

I posed the question to her. "How does somebody get pregnant?"

Her eyes widened and she looked stricken and frantic. I started backing away even before she replied. After looking to the washing and then the ceiling and finding no help either place as she tried to work out how to answer me, she suddenly demanded, "Who have you been talking to?"

"One of my friends, but never mind," I threw over my shoulder as I exited. "I don't really want to know anyway," and quickly left the room. I had no desire to upset her. After a minute, Mom called me back. "You know what you asked me? Come here." As I approached, she gestured toward the lid on the top of the round washer, which had a gasket-ringed hole in which to place a tube to fill the tub with water.

"A man goes like this," she instructed, pointing to the hole. She looked triumphant, as if she had landed on just the right analogy.

I looked down at it, horrified and repulsed. "Okay," I muttered, backing away. "That's all I needed to know."

What she described didn't really answer my question, and I was so embarrassed by her coarse explanation that I no longer asked for her insight on anything about the female body, including what exactly was going on when I started getting my period later that year. She merely handed me some Kotex pads and said, "Do you have any questions?" I didn't even know what to ask. At the time most girls need their mothers to fill them in on the Facts of Life, I had no one to ask about such things, no one I felt I could count on for authoritative advice.

The following year, I brought the intense drive for perfection I had learned so long ago to Kirby Smith Junior High School, where I made straight As every term. Cindy was still at Brentwood and inhabited her own world of church and friends. Fred might as well have moved to Mars when he left for Florida Southern in Lakeland. I heard little about his time there. My best friend Suzanne became immersed in a family tragedy when her little sister was diagnosed with leukemia; I saw her less after that, but I made other fast friends and endured my first crush on a dark-haired looker named George. My real love, though, became grammar, whose reliably hard-and-fast syntax rules I could count on not to change. I gravitated to school topics I could master with memory.

At Mom's insistence, I had taken private violin lessons at Brentwood from Mr. Kochelny, a strange little man with bushy salt-and-pepper eyebrows, wild gray hair, and a thick German accent. Marvin Von Deck, the music teacher at Kirby Smith, had too many violinists and somehow convinced my mother that I should switch to the bass viol. What a comedy I must have made: a little girl struggling to get an instrument twice my size on a city bus. I was steaming every time I had to pick it up, but I got to be in the school orchestra, fulfilling yet another of my mother's dreams she could never realize for herself.

Neither our achievements nor the comforts of the Catholic Church were enough to calm my mother's growing fears and anxieties. I was too caught up in my own pursuits to register the combination of pressures working to strain Mom's always-fragile coping abilities. I just knew that her mood was darkening by the day, and her behavior was becoming increasingly bizarre.

Mom was always drove at a gallop pace, and Fred recalled once when she began passing a car on a two-lane road, realizing too late that another vehicle was coming straight at us.

"She yelled at you and Cindy to get down on the floor because she saw we were about to crash. The only reason we're alive today is because the oncoming car ran off on the narrow shoulder to avoid hitting us. I still remember the whooshing sound as we passed within inches of it."

A slammed door or a pot banging in the kitchen sink signaled the start of one of Mom's unpredictable tantrums, and I'd brace for what would follow. She screamed, she yowled, she wept and cursed. She rolled around on the floor. Once I heard her wail, "If they killed Christ, what will they do to me?" She directed it to no one in particular, yet I believed I should have an answer for her.

Coaxing her down from her high hysterics always seemed to fall on my shoulders. I had to reassure her that she still had us, that we loved her. Though I was Consoler-in-Chief, calming her was a tall order and seemed to work less often.

Bobby, dropping by while on leave from the Navy one day, was treated to one of her fits. Like Fred and me, he perceived it as a tantrum but reacted differently.

"Stop that bullshit right now," he bellowed, fists clenched at his sides. "Or I'll go out and get shit-faced drunk, and then we'll see who acts more stupid."

She clammed up immediately and it didn't escape me that she never acted that way around him again.

One afternoon I came home from school to find my mother under her bed, moaning and gibbering, "Evil, evil all around me! Devils everywhere!"

Fred stood at the bedroom door shaking his head. "C'mon, Mom." He was unable to hide his disgust. "Stop that now." We both viewed her behavior as histrionics.

That only made her squall louder, so he threw up his hands and exited the room. I got down on my knees and elbows and peered under the bed. "Please, Mom, please come out," I pleaded. But I, too, failed to persuade her so I followed Fred's lead and left. She finally emerged, her face puffy and red. With no audience, her drama ended quickly.

The worst part for me was the caprice of her moods. One day she would be fine, coming home from work smiling and joking. The next she arrived silent and angry, banging around dishes and pots and pans and going on a long crying jag about all the ways her life had gone wrong.

One evening after dinner, I wandered into the kitchen looking for something to eat. My teenage hunger never seemed to abate. Mom was at the sink washing dishes. I opened the refrigerator and remarked absentmindedly, “I’m still hungry, Mom. What else is there to eat?”

She hurled a spaghetti-sauce-coated dinner plate to the floor and as it crashed, my hands flew to my ears as I braced for the coming tirade. “Yes, I know, I know, I’m no good at anything!” she wailed. “No good in the office, no good as a mother, no good giving you anything you need. Not a good wife or even . . .” Her voice trailed off into a moan, and her shoulders shook with sobs.

I worked out later that she had expected her boyfriend, Willy, would marry her someday, but he turned out to be a two-timer, after only sex and her money. He apparently got some of both before she caught on. The Catholic Church would have considered remarriage after divorce a mortal sin and left her open to excommunication, so I guess she was more interested in getting remarried than being Catholic.

Medical mishaps also wore on my mother’s nerves—and finances. Cutting off the tip of my thumb with Fred’s switchblade when we first arrived in Jacksonville was the first in a series of expensive medical incidents. Etched in my memory most vividly was my surgery for an ingrown toenail.

I had recurring infections in the nail of my big toe and finally found myself sitting on the doctor’s exam table with white tissue paper covering my lap as the nurse prepared me for surgery. I insisted on sitting up and watching as the doctor injected needle after needle in and around my toe to numb it before cutting out the side of my toenail. Mom was also watching, her arms crossed and her back against the wall behind me. When the cutting started to get bloody, I lost my nerve and lay back on the table. My mother made not a sound throughout it all.

“All done?” she inquired quietly as the doctor stood back to let the nurse bandage the toe and foot.

"Yes, all done!" He snapped off his gloves, appearing very pleased with his work.

"That's good," breathed my mother, then slid down the wall and sat on the floor in a faint as the doctor and nurse rushed to revive her.

I think now that my mother must have been watching everything that she had ever wanted slide gradually out of her reach, one thing and one person after another, like a slow motion French movie. Cindy reached the age I was when we first moved to Florida and had her own friends and interests, and Fred was at college and home very little. I began acting like a thirteen-year-old, talking back to her and saying things I knew would sting her, like how much I hated being Catholic. Like most teenagers everywhere and throughout time, I began defining myself in my own terms, rather than as an extension of my parents, but unlike most teens, I began yearning for a day I would never have to see her again.

Mom ran out of money for Fred to attend college out of town, so he transferred to Jacksonville University and moved home. When his Thespian Club performed part of a play based on Thomas Wolfe's novel *Look Homeward, Angel,* Fred had a small role. Mom, Cindy, and I attended, which is when I had a moment of bright crystal clarity. As I watched the battling Gant family characters on stage, I realized that, like Eugene Gant, my life and happiness lay far away from my mother. My mental distance from Mom expanded; I would not be her consoler and ally anymore.

Nearly five years after our exodus from Cresaptown, the money

Mom had absconded with was dwindling due to all the expenses she didn't anticipate and her complete lack of money management skills. She traded in Bobby's Pontiac for a lilac Austin Cambridge she thought would be cheaper to run, but it turned out to be a British lemon, often in the shop for expensive repairs.

Too late she discovered that relinquishing her role as our full-time caregiver had exposed Cindy and me to dangers like the Guhls, and she had no idea how to deal with problems like how to handle burgeoning sexual awareness in a rebellious teenage girl. Balancing work and family pressures was constantly on her mind, and she wasn't sleeping much, but what may have shifted her from anxiety into existential crisis was what was going on ninety miles off Florida's Key West.

One overcast day in 1961, I was idling at the bus stop after school when Army troop trucks rumbled down Jacksonville's North Main Street headed south.

I turned to a girl next to me. "Where are they going?" She merely shrugged.

"Not real sure, but I visited my cousin in Miami last week, and he told me saw tanks and trucks on trains. He didn't know where they were headed either."

Fidel Castro had toppled Cuba's authoritarian leader in 1959 and Cuba fell under a communist regime. When John F. Kennedy, the first Catholic president, was elected in 1960, my mother—with characteristic drama—dropped to her knees and gave thanks. But even before he took office in 1961, President Eisenhower severed diplomatic relations with Cuba. The failed Bay of Pigs invasion followed in April.

The Cuban Missile Crisis would not happen until the following year, but military movements through Jacksonville were all the talk. My friends and I giggled under our desks during "duck-and-cover" drills that were to protect us in case of nuclear attack, but I'll bet our teachers were not amused. Now the Cold War screamed from front pages of Florida newspapers. As she read the headlines, Mom must have understood that she had brought us from the relative safety of Western Maryland to a place closer to a communist threat than nearly anywhere else in the United States.

Mom gradually slipped into a deep despair from which she did not seem able to rebound. I believe she felt that God was punishing her for all the sins that she had committed in the years since her decision to leave Cresaptown: pride at believing she could make it on her own, lust for her involvement with Willy, and an adamant, intransigent anger with my father. I would soon learn the penance that would be required.

Third Part

Flying Backwards

Chapter Eighteen

Leaving Paradise

As I strolled slowly home from Kirby Smith one warm evening in the spring of 1961, I turned the corner and spotted our elderly neighbor Edna in front of our house, wringing her hands. She glimpsed me at the same moment and motioned for me to hurry.

"Come fast as you can, Margaret," she cried, worry drawing down even further the deep creases on her face. "Your mother is very sick. Henry and I are driving her to the hospital."

"What happened?" I called out, running by then.

"She's in so much pain; we aren't sure but, well, she may be having a heart attack." Edna broke down, weeping into her hands. I had never seen someone other than Mom act so emotionally, so I could tell she was serious, and I also began to tear up.

We poured Mom into the car, and by the end of our drive to the hospital, with Mom moaning and sobbing Hail Mary after Hail Mary all the way, it was poor Henry and Edna who nearly had heart attacks. Mom, though, was merely having a panic attack and was home the next morning. The whole emotional episode must have been grueling for our elderly neighbors, who no longer spoke to us.

After this, I think Mom's decision to appeal to my father for help was inevitable. She had no one left to rely on. Her flight to freedom had ended in an ignominious fall to earth.

A few weeks after my mother's false alarm, my father suddenly appeared, wearing Sunday clothes that looked to me like a foreign costume. A brown suit with a fedora and wide tie replaced his usual flannel shirt and denim overalls, but the worried look on his weathered face was familiar. When Mom called Cindy and me from our bedroom and we found him standing in the living room, I hesitated, glancing over to see what Mom wanted me to do, but Cindy ran and threw her arms around his waist.

My mother's jaw was set, and her voice sounded flat and weary. "Well, Margaret, look who's here. Aren't you going to say hello to your father?"

Then I joined Cindy to hug him. Dad seemed startled as much by how much we had grown as by our show of affection. He was there, I think, to discuss the terms of Mom's surrender.

Not long after Dad's visit, Mom announced that we were leaving Jacksonville, and no amount of begging or crying would move her once she had decided. My Florida world that had finally replaced Cresaptown as my real home was lost to me. Mom had also lost her shot at paradise. In all our five years in Florida, she never did get a piano on which to pick out her hymns, and she was so busy making a living she had no time for art or writing. She couldn't become the person she thought she could, even with her husband out of the way.

Mom quit her job and packed up our belongings, and we journeyed back to Cresaptown once again, a disappointing anticlimax to the wandering odyssey she had begun almost exactly five years before. She and Dad must have negotiated that she could keep the duplex and its income. Our Notter Avenue house was all that remained of her dream of independence.

Perhaps five years of single parenthood had made her forget the reasons she left, or maybe she willed herself into amnesia. She might have thought her relationship with my dad would be better than before, that now he would finally understand what had driven them apart and would treat her differently. She appeared to feel that the danger she had convinced Fred our father presented—the jeopardy that she claimed had driven her to desperate measures—had now dissipated. I truly believe her plan was to re-marry Dad and recover financial stability, but my father wasn't stupid, and his memory was intact.

One morning after we returned, I climbed the Art Glass Company's outside stairs to Dad's office in search of a stamp for one of the dozens of letters I began to write to Suzanne and other Jacksonville friends. Hearing a murmur of low voices from the one-room apartment behind the office, I stuck in my head to see who it was. To my amazement, my parents were lying on the bed, locked in a fully clothed embrace. A Cheshire grin came over my mother's face, but Dad just looked embarrassed. Quickly, I backed away into the office, and a red-faced Dad joined me a moment later. Mom came out next looking surly and kept that mood the rest of the day. I figured that my sudden entrance spoiled her plan to get Dad to remarry her.

Now she had to live across the driveway from the man she hated and had tried so hard to leave. She was once again "slaving" for her ex-husband, seeing him every day, cooking for him. Perhaps the only way her life was better than before she left was that she didn't have to sleep with him. Everything else was worse.

In our absence, Dad had rented out the larger of the two houses and was living in the smaller one we had all lived in before leaving for Florida. Cindy, Mom, and I took his place in the small house, and he was banished to the floor above the shop, just across the driveway from all that hate. Whenever Mom railed at Dad, he could stalk back to his apartment. He didn't have to sleep with her either.

One day soon after we arrived back in Cresaptown, we pulled into the driveway to see our neighbor across the street seated on her front porch. Mom waved merrily and hollered, "Hellooo, Mrs. Ward, I'm back!" But Mrs. Ward rose, turned, and marched into her house without a word.

Mom now had no friends in the neighborhood. They all knew what had happened, and as far as I could tell, they were all on her ex-husband's side. Maybe they viewed her as the arrogant ex-wife who thought she could make it on her own and had been taught better. Now even her across-the-street neighbor wouldn't speak to her. Mom's world seemed drained of hope, the absence of flight, the silence that follows song. All her plans thwarted and nothing to look forward to, she seemed to hate Dad even more. He was again Filthy Old Man.

Mother and I began to clash almost immediately after returning from Florida, not only because I was an angry teenager who wanted my own way, but because I resented all she had put me through in the last five years. My behavior seemed to be like an essay she was grading with a rubric I didn't understand—and I was always failing.

The topic of my reputation was an ongoing theme. The week we returned, I noticed some Cresaptown teenagers who looked about my age communing in front of the corner drugstore, and a couple looked familiar. I was eager to reconnect with the local social scene, so one warm afternoon, I put on a clean shirt and some pedal pushers and headed out the back door.

She called out from the kitchen, "Where are you going?" My change of attire had not been lost on her.

I jumped off the back porch steps, and tossed back over my shoulder, "Just over to the drugstore to see some friends. I won't be long."

She practically broke the screen door coming out to stop me. "You can just march yourself back in here now," she yelled. "No daughter of mine is going to hang out with that worthless trash in front of the Rexall!"

The volatility of her reaction took me by surprise, and though I tried to protest that I had recognized at least some of these kids and they weren't "trash," I could not persuade her. I came to understand that she felt if I went over there, my reputation would be sullied forever. My Aunts Bee and Gay had been known hell-raisers, and she didn't want anyone thinking it ran in the family. The white picket fence syndrome manifested itself once again.

We also clashed on how I should dress, though my preferences were anything but provocative. I was fourteen, but she still envisioned me as a little girl. When I found a light-blue chiffon dress lying on my bed, its ruched front dotted with tiny applique flowers and no waist, I could see it was a perfect style to hide a teenage girl's figure. A neighbor whose daughter had outgrown it had offered it to Mom. When I was nine, I would have killed to have a dress like this. At fourteen, with teenage haute couture running to tailored Villager shirtdresses and Ladybug A-line skirts, appearing in it would have killed me socially. I hung it in the back of the closet. Whenever she begged, "Let's see you in that pretty 'new' dress," I would emerge dressed in something else.

Then I returned home to find ashes among the gas burners on top of the stove. An acrid smell hung in the air.

"What happened here?" I queried, poking at the ashes.

"The dress. You didn't like it, so I got rid of it."

I was incredulous. "Couldn't you have given it to Cindy?" I stared at the gray flakes on the stove.

"I got it for you," she snapped. I think she was trying to make me feel guilty, but it didn't work. I just thought she was acting nutty, as usual.

I had told Mom I didn't believe in Catholic dogma, but she seemed startled by my announcement. "I'm going back to the Methodist Church—this weekend." She had stolen so much from me—my innocence and peace of mind, both my beloved homes—even my spiritual support system. Now was my time to begin taking my life back.

When she tried to make me continue attending Sunday masses with her, I flatly refused, feeling my new power to reject her demands and control my fate. She did lure me into accompanying her to card parties at the St. Ambrose Catholic Church. I found the card-party culture amusing and somehow comforting; the protocols and language for a bidding game called 500 never changed, and there were often six or seven tables made up of three-to-four middle-aged and elderly Catholic ladies, all vying for the top prizes of a homemade cake or set of embroidered dish towels.

At first, Mom and I went together, but one night, she waved me off, saying I should go by myself. For that I had permission. Mom apparently felt that at least I was on St. Ambrose grounds, and it might, just might, be a way to get me back into her beloved faith. I never won the cake, and I never went back to being a Catholic either.

One night at home after a card party, I remarked that Mrs. Harper had won the cake again. The ladies all joked that she grew the cards she needed in her hands. "Well, it's a poor scorekeeper who can't win for his own team," Mom remarked sourly. I think she was implying that the ladies decided who would win top prizes based on who they liked, and they didn't like my mother. Cheating like that would be difficult to do, but I didn't say anything. Then I remembered she had made the remark at one of the card parties, and the ladies glanced at each other unsmiling. This was serious stuff to them, and they didn't appreciate snide insinuations from this newcomer.

Mom had never been popular in Cresaptown even before we left for Florida. She once groused that none of the women from her Cresaptown Methodist Church Sunday School class sent so much as a card when she was in the hospital undergoing a hysterectomy, though class protocol dictated visiting or sending flowers when a member was sick. I learned from Fred that before we left town, Mom made a bid for a committee chair position at Cresaptown Methodist, and when she lost out to a more popular lady, she never returned to church until she became Catholic.

Ironically, my own prospects increased as I transitioned from the big-city world of Jacksonville to small-town Cresaptown. After a brief settling-in, I discovered a place where I could not only escape Mom's tight control but also have more fun than I ever thought possible within walking distance, a place where my Florida tan would serve me well.

Chapter Nineteen

Drama Down at the Pool

Gail and I resumed our friendship as if I'd never left, and it was she who clued me in to where the real Cresaptown action was. Even now I am astonished that the same mother who freaked out when I wanted to fraternize with adolescents outside a drugstore allowed me to consort unchaperoned with a confederation of scantily clad, hormonal young teens at the Celanese pool. Gail and I occupied ourselves with studying the latest swim fashions, sizing up possible crushes, and gossiping with girlfriends. What we wore increasingly signaled who we were; it became a costume drama. What boy was about to ask out which girl? Who was about to invite someone to go steady? What pair was fighting and breaking up and why? The pool was headquarters for all of Cresaptown's juiciest teen news.

At first, Gail was my only pool-mate, but it didn't take long to form new friendships and get reacquainted with some former Cresaptown schoolmates. Those breezy summer days, with all the naiveté of the uninformed, restored some of the lightness my life had been lacking.

I woke smiling on days I could finish my chores and head off to the pool. Mom sometimes looked worried but gave grudging permission as she could usually think of nothing else for me to do. I went trotting off down the road and through the woods and blackberry bushes with my towel and swimsuit to arrive as soon as possible after it opened, and I stayed until late afternoon or when friends started to leave.

In July, the water was tropical from lying for weeks in full sun. Bleachers stood on either side of the pool opposite the pool house and behind them grassy banks where we could brown in the sun on blankets and towels. The loudspeaker blared a local radio station of background music, all the current rock-and-roll tunes we knew we would be hearing at school dances but didn't realize would serve as the 1960s soundtrack playing in our heads for the rest of our lives. "Run-run-run-run-runawaaaay," "Blue moooon," "The name of the game is I like it like that," we warbled, we wailed, we chanted. Rock and roll will never die, so long as memories like those live on.

One late July afternoon, I joined Mary, a new friend from down the street, to lounge on bath towels in front of the bleachers and discuss the Cresaptown social scene. As we surveyed the boys and girls cavorting in the pool and lolling on the other side, the discussion took a new turn.

"You're really lucky, you know," Mary opined, glancing sideways at me. "You could have your pick of these guys." She waved her hand in the direction of the boys frolicking in the water.

"Sure," I laughed. Then I saw she was serious. "Why would you say that?" I sat up. *What if it were true?*

"You're pretty and blond and you're 'the new girl.' Everyone is talking about how you came from Florida." Only fourteen and she was already grasping the unique romantic allure of the unknown. She turned and propped on an elbow to face me. "So, who do you think is cute?"

The boys were playing a water-beachball game, splashing just a little so they didn't get the lifeguard's whistle, and now I studied them in a new way. It didn't take me long to spot him: stocky, blond hair, round open face, and dimpled smile—not exactly Hollywood film-star handsome, but character-actor appealing.

"What about him?" I asked Linda, "The one smiling." Now it was her turn to sit up.

"Randy? Gosh, I never really thought about him, but yeah, he's a nice boy and pretty smart like you. He's a year older than you are, so he'll be going to Allegany this fall. Want me to let his cousin know you like him?" Bless Mary. A born matchmaker. Before long, Randy was spending time on a towel next to ours.

Free time was often spent writing to Florida friends, mostly Suzanne in Jacksonville. Seventy-five missives from 1961 through 1965 came her way, sometimes every two weeks, until we both became too busy with college. (Suzanne kept every letter anyone ever wrote her, so when we reconnected years later, she sent them back to me—a memoirist's treasure trove.) My letters were lengthy and detailed, a time capsule of my thoughts and feelings I unknowingly created for myself. Each was an epistle on the happenings of the previous weeks, an intensive commentary on my life, my soul open and raw.

The letters rage with a teenager's central conflict of how to segue from childhood to adulthood and forge an identity separate from family. Underlying them all was anguish peculiar to someone marinated in years of anxiety, someone whose family has provided no moral or cultural base and who yearns to be somewhere and someone else. In my view, I could completely trust and rely on no one around me, not even Gail, so Suzanne became my long-distance confidant and therapist, and she tried her best with a difficult client.

My mother was still working hard to keep me simmering in a stew of Catholic guilt to keep me out of trouble and focused on my education. "Stay away from this worthless trash around here," she harped ad nauseum. "They don't have your brains or talent. Focus on your future!" My first and most mortal-sin-level commandment was to be a Good Girl.

One morning, I sidled into the kitchen where Mom was washing out her hose and announced, "Randy asked me to a party." I was proud I was already becoming popular, that teenage obsession.

She whipped around and fixed me with a look that nearly cut me in half. "Who is Randy?" she hissed.

"He's from Rawlings. I met him at the pool."

"You are most certainly not going to any party! Didn't I tell you to stay away from this local trash?" She pointed an accusing finger at me.

"But he's a nice boy, Mom," I objected, tears starting. "Gail and Mary know him."

"Where is your head, girl? Don't you know what he wants? He doesn't want a good girl; I can tell you that!"

The diatribe confused me and made me back away, but the die was already cast. His smile stirred something warm in me. I was attracted to him with the intensity only a fourteen-year-old can feel. My desire to be around him convinced me to do something I would have considered unthinkable before: I kept our meetings secret from Mom. By fall, I wrote Suzanne: "We keep in contact through Mary and see each other at the pool." How easily desire overcame guilt.

One weekend I told my mother I was visiting Karen at her house, a calculated subterfuge; I did not tell her Karen was

Randy's cousin. I described the scene to Suzanne.

> Randy and I took a walk, kicking leaves. We just walked along, looking at the colored trees and talking. Later that evening, I joined him on the porch swing in the back of the house. It was freezing cold, and I was shivering like anything, so he put his arm around me. Suzanne, suddenly that breeze wasn't cold anymore! We talked for two solid hours. Oh, that full moon and the slow music from inside the house."

The first amorous encounter of my young life merited a romance-novel description.

I never told Mom about meeting Randy, but she needn't have worried. We never ventured beyond just sitting close to each other and talking. I was smitten with Randy and in love with the idea of romance, but I had no operational definition of what Good Girls did and did not do. The way I felt about him seemed somehow outside Good Girl parameters. Certainly, lying to my mother about him was, and a terrible conflict invaded my mind. I craved being with him, but how could I be a Good Girl and keep seeing him?

Randy was from a far different social culture than the one I had been steeped in during the last half-decade of my life, first by my mother, then at Holy Rosary School, then more by my mother. I described to Suzanne my moral outrage on hearing Gail describe behaviors that were the social norm in Cresaptown: "Suzanne, you won't believe this when I tell you, but these kids have 'kissing parties.' They actually neck at these parties and don't think there is anything wrong with them. I just hope that my standards won't be lower by being here."

I believed that only people who were in love and intending to marry should be kissing each other. Through Gail, I discovered that at these parties, my sweet Randy actually kissed girls—several of them! If he kissed me now, what would it mean? In today's world, my Southern friends would laugh, shake their heads, and say of that prissy little girl, "Bless her heart!"

Hearing about Randy's kissing-party behavior gave me the shove I needed into Good Girl status. *Mom was right after all. He's not a nice boy.* A profound guilt filled me for liking the feeling of his arm around me, the warm closeness of him, but I pushed aside those feelings and let our liaison die. In this way, my first romantic relationship was wrenched away, and shame took its place. Round one for Mom and Sister Mary Pius, but there were many more rounds to go.

Chapter Twenty

Shades of Despair

The first fall we were back, I was the suntanned blonde from the Sunshine State, and my Cresaptown School classmates buzzed around me like bees to Florida honey. Everyone wanted to hear more about the tropical paradise where I'd lived, and I was only too glad to gush about the wide beaches, fragrant trees, and my beloved Kirby Smith Junior High. As much as I hated Jacksonville when I first got there, now it consumed my thoughts. Pretty soon, their "Tell me more" requests segued to sighs of "Yeah, we've heard. Florida was so much better than here." Pronouncements like, "Kissing parties are disgusting and immoral," sealed my fate, and in a few months, I went from being the new kid everyone wanted to get to know to a pariah with few friends. Like the Martian-raised earthling in Heinlein's novel *Stranger in a Strange Land,* which had just been published earlier that year, my native land was an alien landscape to me.

I missed every opportunity for acceptance in my new/old Cresaptown School. I had always hated physical education, and this year's class began with basketball, which I had never played. As we practiced exchanging two-handed pushes from the chest our first day on the court, I caught a ball squarely on the end of my left index finger, shooting an excruciating pain through it. An x-ray diagnosed a hairline fracture, requiring that I sit out six weeks of basketball. While my classmates bonded over a team sport, I did math and science homework on the sidelines, excluded again.

Over the year, I gradually lost the assured, confident-Peggy voice that drew friends and could hold a classroom rapt with stories. In class, I focused on trying to show off how intelligent I was—another sure-fire way of driving kids away—and most faces in my class turned away or looked down at their desks whenever I spoke.

One sweet girl named Marianne tried to draw me into her circle. Smiling, she asked, "Peggy, we're learning the twist. What dances were you doing in your other school?" But my Kirby Smith friends weren't dancing yet, so I just shrugged. I wasn't invited to any of those Cresaptown kissing parties; I had made my opinion of those quite clear to everyone.

By December, the Christmas holidays that only five years before had been a sparkling and magical time that I anticipated all year only put me more in touch with how adrift I was. To Suzanne, I lamented, "Seems like these kids really hate me."

As things worsened at school, I left my daily reality and daydreamed myself into another body that flew to other places where a sea of accepting faces greeted me. Taking solace in letters to Suzanne, I moaned to her of memories about Jacksonville.

> Oh, to hear that roaring sound that means Jacksonville Beach. My poor little Rebel heart is aching to see my adopted state again! I can picture it all in my mind. Notter Avenue, the summer scent of mimosa and crepe myrtle, that baking heat, those warm nights, the breeze that came in just as you thought you couldn't stand it any longer, sitting on the steps in the warm dark and listening to the Florida sounds. All that, I left for this barbarous place!

Had I been more self-aware, I would have grasped the irony of my own history. I had longed to return to "barbarous" Cresaptown as much as I now wanted to get back to Jacksonville. Something about Cresaptown felt so familiar, and I wanted desperately to fit in, yet at the same time, my head was filled with memories of the place where I had learned to be happy and the life I had built in Florida. An early winter letter captured my ambivalence.

> At night, it started again. I went out on the porch and watched it come down. It fell in big flakes on the ground, silently, as though not to waken a sleeping world. As it came down, I couldn't help saying to the old place, "It's been a long time, a long, long time." Five years to be exact. Five years in Florida. I'm torn between two places! I still love Florida and I'm dying to get back there once more. But when I see the snow come down in the dark, it brings back memories of a past, long gone and never to return except when it snows like that.

Fred and Cindy seemed to be adjusting to their new Cresaptown circles, which only compounded my gloom. *What is wrong with me?*

Florida Governor Lawton ("Walkin' Lawton") Chiles, who suffered all his life from depression, wrote that he got "the blacks," an even deeper kind of gloom than "the blues." That school year, "the blacks" crept in and took hold of me. I hated going to school and hated being at home. I developed migraines and my back ached. An early-spring letter mentioned that my favorite poem was "Crossing the Bar," Tennyson's elegy for himself, which he directed be placed in all editions of his poems. It ended with,

> For tho' from out our bourne of Time and Place
> The flood may bear me far,
> I hope to see my Pilot face to face

When I have crost the bar.

My mother, concerned about me but incredulous I would waste worry on what she felt were ignorant yokels, sneered, "You're better than all of them. Why do you even care what they think about anything?" But she could see that guidance wasn't helping, so she threw up her hands and stalked off, tossing back, "Just fill someone up with love of themselves, and what spills over is yours."

Her transactional take on how to make friends was "make people feel good about themselves, and in exchange they'll feel good about you." Through her sarcastic tone, I heard, "No one ever likes anyone for themselves; you have to fool them into it." I perceived that someone who never had any friends wasn't a qualified counselor, so I quickly filed her advice under "Motherisms" and ignored her.

My mother's own bouts of depression weren't helping my mood, but where my wretchedness was silent, brooding, and inward, hers was the loud, unpredictable, "Woe is me" lamentation I remembered from our last year in Jacksonville. She once wailed, "I may as well kill myself. That would solve my problems." With a shock, I realized that if she were gone, maybe I could be free; maybe everything would get better. I hated myself for thinking it, but my mind kept going there. *Maybe I wouldn't have to escape. Maybe she would die. Then I could be happy.*

As my anger grew, her depression began to annoy me. I had quit my "job" of Consoler-in-Chief during her moaning sessions. Cindy and Fred had nearly always ignored her until she stopped; now we all did. On one occasion, she began to speak of her own mother, Floda Mae, perhaps to reconnect with the beloved daughter she had longed for and whom she felt was now pulling away from her.

Her face tightened into the grief she still carried after all those years. "My mother was an angel," Mom murmured as her gaze turned faraway, focusing on that sweet face in her memory. "Too good for this world." Her voice lowered, and she turned toward me, whispering, "He killed her. That devil killed her." Was she thinking of her mother or perhaps herself, the girl she might have become? Only that once did she reference Blackjack's crimes, and she gave no details.

I think she wanted to tell me about the life her father took away from her with his abuse, as well as from Floda Mae, but she saw I had no ears to hear or mind to comprehend. I was a teenager and angry about everything, how she had wrenched me away from all the people and things I loved, not once but twice, how she always seemed to think only of herself, her own pain. She could have tied me down and shouted in my ear, and I wouldn't have listened. All I heard from her was the same sneering disgust toward all men she always had, the same contempt she had for my father. Anyway, I hadn't the experience then to understand the violation she had experienced, and maybe she looked into my eyes and saw it would not help to tell me.

Like Mom, I also took out my anguish on my father, dismissing him as she did. One evening when Mom was at a church meeting, Dad was in his workshop next door and could see that I was watching TV, so he came into the house to join me.

It made me uncomfortable to have him there, and after a couple of minutes, I snapped, "Can't you go back and watch your own TV?"

He rose, and his face reddened. I thought he would hit me. Instead he came nearly to tears. As he left, he muttered, "Someday you'll regret saying that."

He was right about so many things, but especially about regret. Before it was all done, we would both have much to regret.

Dad was perhaps the only one who noticed how so many small things bruised me. An offhand comment, an exclusion from a school activity, or a less-than-stellar grade dissolved me into a hot flow of tears. "You've got to get tough in this world, Peggy Dale," Dad would sigh as he regarded me with those worried eyes.

I believe now that the pain and regret of his life had found yet another source in my unhappiness. He had seen me begin life strong and capable like he was when he started out, but now I exuded the weakness Mom had wrought in me. I think it tore the heart from him to see me as fragile as glass, unable to make myself into a person who could withstand the pressures of everyday life.

Then one day my teenage insolence went too far. I don't even remember what I said, probably something like, "Sure, old man. What would you know about anything?"

Dad started up from the kitchen chair, grasping his heavy, ceramic coffee mug. I had never seen anyone look at me with such rage, and I ran into the living room to escape. I don't think Mom guessed what he was about to do. He had never been violent with any of us. The mug hit me about nine inches below my neck, and I fell to my knees, stunned, my back throbbing.

My mother screamed, "My God, Spates, what have you done?"

He rushed to me, and I cringed and hid my face, convinced he was there to finish me off with his "fists of steel," as Bobby had called them. Instead, my father began to rub my back, saying over and over, "Oh no, Peggy Dale, oh no, I'm so sorry. Oh, no!"

But his hand rubbing the bruise just made it worse, and I arched away from him.

"Get away from her, Spates," my mother cried. "Haven't you done enough?"

His violent act seemed to hurt him far more than it had

me. He apologized so many times for losing his temper with me, and yet I don't remember ever saying to him I was sorry for my thoughtless words. Later it would become clear to me how much my father loved me, loved me despite how I was becoming another Catherine, the woman who had hurt and rejected him and tore his family apart.

"You've got to get tough in this world." How often he warned me! Decades later, I dwelled on my father's frequent exhortations. Was he thinking of how he had endured endless days and nights of walking in the desolate landscape of the Depression-era South until he came close to starving? And were images flashing before his eyes of how he came home to find that his wife had left with his children and his life savings? Was he thinking, too, of how he had forced himself on to the next step, refusing to surrender, calling on all his reserves of toughness for moments like those?

My father had learned a lot about being tough, and he was trying to counsel me to be strong no matter what life might throw at me. He also knew I had no experience of the destitution or despair he had known and that I would not have listened if he tried to explain, so he spoke to me only that one brief sentence. Perhaps he repeated it more to himself than to me.

"You've got to get tough in this world."

He would say it so many times, yet all I remember thinking was, *Right, Pop. How could you know what I'm feeling?* I could not comprehend where the sentiment came from, so I did not value his words. If I had any idea then how much he had endured, it might have softened my view of him and given us a bond as parent and child, something on which to build a real relationship. Whether that bond might have developed if Mom had been out of the picture, I'll never know, but he was right. I really did need to get tough to endure all that was to come.

Chapter Twenty-One

Civil Commitment

Other than in letters to Suzanne, I never shared my problems with anyone outside the family, until one school day as I lingered after class with my English teacher Miss True, and she noticed my ashen face. "Peggy, are you ill, honey? Is there anything I can do to help?" Living up to her name, Miss True had spotted the truth of me, the pain inside my successful-student shell. I presumed that no matter how anguished I became, no one besides my parents ever really noticed, but here was someone who not only saw, but offered help, and it caught be off guard. I burst into tears and would not stop crying.

"Everything is all wrong," I blubbered in a nearly incoherent unburdening. "I can't do any-th-th-thing right. Everyone h-h-hates me. I hate myself!" I immediately wanted to tear my face off, embarrassed that I had displayed my visceral emotions in front of non-family members.

"Sweetheart, everyone likes you." Miss True' large, brown eyes filled with empathy and disbelief. "You're such a lovely girl and so capable. You're doing A+ work in my class, and I know you're doing just as well in your other classes."

"I can't stand it! W-w-why did my mother ever bring me to this h-h-hell hole?" I stammered between clenched teeth.

Miss True quickly apprehended that she was out of her league in this situation, so she led me gently down the hall to the principal, who called in the school counselor. We all sat, and they leaned toward me to learn the source of my problem. I'm sure they thought they'd heard it all from past students: abuse, neglect, violence, suicide.

When I cried out what I'd heard Mom say, "If they killed Christ, what will they do to me?" the two women exchanged worried glances and hugged me, first one and then the other. Mr. Chaney, the principal, laughed and sat back, perhaps believing I was dramatizing for attention. That was partly true; I did want someone to notice. Miss True held my hand in her soft, plump ones while the school counselor got me a glass of water.

After they calmed me down and sent me to my next class, Miss True huddled with the principal and the guidance counselor and decided that the gentle Miss True should do a home visit to talk with my parents. However, no one informed me. I came home the next day to find Mom, Dad, and Fred in the kitchen, looking nervous.

The instant I entered the door, Mom blurted, "Margaret, what exactly happened at school?"

When I learned Miss True was coming in a few minutes to meet with them, I froze in horror. The shame of a teacher talking with my family about me! Did everyone at school know? If things were bad before . . . I can still remember Miss True's big, brown eyes and gentle voice as she sat at our kitchen table describing the scene in the principal's office.

Suddenly, Mom turned to Dad and exploded. "This is all your fault, you contemptible, filthy old man! If you hadn't been such a miser, we'd still be in Jacksonville where she was happy. You've ruined her. You've ruined all of us, you worthless SOB!"

Miss True's plump face reddened and her jaw dropped as Mom demonstrated the real source of my unhappiness. Later Miss True confided in me in hushed tones, "Your mother is not normal; she needs help." As if I had any control over that situation.

Not long after, Dad informed me that doctors were coming to take Mom to a hospital to get her help, and it would be better if Cindy and I weren't around when she left. Relief flooded over me like a curing balm. At last, an end to turmoil lay in sight!

I don't know where Cindy was sent that day, but I had spotted my friend Mary and her little brother playing in the backyard of their house a block away, and I ran over to join them. Mary's house sat on a small hill, and her backyard with its gently sloping bank offered a clear vista of my house and driveway. We climbed their backyard tree, and I glanced down to my house occasionally to see if I could glimpse the ambulance from the hospital. I didn't tell Mary about the family drama playing out there. When a state police car appeared in the driveway, I was shocked, yet I remained outside, even after the late afternoon breeze turned the March air even cooler and Mary's mom called her children inside. Shivering, I lingered in Mary's yard, waiting for the police car to leave. Finally, I climbed the tree and saw the driveway was empty.

I sneaked in the back door, half expecting Mom to be there, ranting and accusing, but the kitchen was vacant and silent. When Dad finally showed up later to make himself a cup of coffee, he looked unsteady, so I waited for Fred to arrive.

"Why was a police car here? I thought doctors would come in an ambulance."

"As a precaution," was Fred's terse explanation. He didn't seem inclined to say more. Had it been a surprise for him, too?

Studying the facts of the time, I pondered how Mom could have been involuntarily committed to "Sykesville," the place everyone called the Springfield Mental Hospital in Sykesville, Maryland. Despite her histrionics, I never agreed with my brothers that Mom was "crazy."

Sykesville opened in 1896 and grew to a population of over 4,000 by 1950, devolving into a rundown dump for warehousing the state's unwanted. In 1949, the *Baltimore Sun* published a series of exposés called "Maryland's Shame," reporting horrors that ranged from moldy, insect-infested rooms to rape. Conditions improved to some degree by the time Mom was tossed in there, but I don't think spending time there did her any good.

In 1962, it was still all too easy to make a case for involuntary civil commitment—incarcerating people against their will for the crime of being depressed or different. Only a few years after Mom was held in Sykesville, a movement began to "deinstitutionalize" mental health patients and send them home for outpatient treatment.

In 1975, the Supreme Court's *O'Connor v. Donaldson* decision set a standard for civil commitment. Under the court's "dangerousness" criteria (immediate threat of suicide or homicide), Mom could not have been sent away. Fred and Dad must have known that Mom would not get much in the way of evaluation or treatment, but Fred had a ready answer when I asked how he and Dad had decided to commit her.

"Margaret, after that meeting with Miss True, Mom threatened to take Cindy and leave. We had to stop her."

"Where would they have gone? She didn't have much money."

"Who knows? Mom was crazy! Maybe she would have headed back down to Florida, maybe to West Virginia, or maybe she didn't even know where she'd go. She'd just take off like she did before. We couldn't let her take little Cindy. She was only ten."

After Mom was sent to Sykesville, I was filled with hope, and my whole body felt lighter. Even my attitude toward my father brightened.

Bobby, stationed at Joint Base Andrews outside Washington, DC, got word that Mom was in Sykesville, about an hour away from him. His reaction was far different than mine. He persuaded his Navy Chaplain to square it with his command so he could go to her.

When he arrived at Sykesville, he couldn't find her in her ward, so he searched for her in the adjacent courtyard. She came out of the shadows, shuffling like a zombie, looked up at him, and moaned, "Oh, Bobby, are you here, too?" She had to have been highly medicated; antipsychotic medications like Thorazine had come into vogue. Bobby later described how pitiful she looked, her hospital gown hanging on her emaciated figure; it was all he could do to hold himself together until he could complete her discharge paperwork. Just as easily as she had been committed, Mom was released. I guess she wasn't that crazy after all.

Bobby drove her back to his apartment in Cheltenham, Maryland, to live with him, but she stayed there only a couple days before she was demanding that Fred and Dad come and get her and bring her back to Cresaptown. When I heard that she was returning after only three weeks, all I could do was hang my head and quote one of Randy's favorite sayings. "That's life." To me, it meant, "Who knows why things happen the way they do? They just happen. Get used to it, babe!" I should have recalled Dad's advice. "You have to get tough in this world."

The next time I saw Bobby, I asked, "Why on earth did you go get her out of Sykesville?" I still believed what Fred and Dad told me, that doctors were helping her.

"Margaret, that place was a hell hole. Mom shouldn't have been there. Dad would never have come up with that idea on his own. Fred probably convinced Dad to do it." At the time I wished that Bobby had asked me what I thought about it, but now I know he was right. We were all just offloading our problem to Maryland's derisory mental health system.

After Sykesville, Dad recognized that his ex-wife needed to be cared for as if she were a troubled child, and that he would always have to support her financially and even emotionally. He didn't have to, of course, but that was Dad. Deeply ingrained in him and Bobby was the belief that family was the most important thing, even if they were bitter and toxic, angry and raving, demanding and unpredictable. Mom was all those things, and I became some of them, but he always forgave us and treated us both more gently than we deserved.

Upon her return from Sykesville, Mom seemed chastened. Her tantrum rages were replaced by sullen anger, her resentment of my father simmering beneath bad moods. "Did you know they were planning to send me away?" she quizzed me.

"No," I lied. "They didn't tell me anything."

"Honey, did you miss me a lot when I was gone?"

I hesitated before lying again. "Sure, Mom." My hesitation confirmed her fears; I had sided with her husband against her.

For a while, she reminded me frequently of my betrayal, then seemed to set it aside, though I know she never forgot. She probably realized by then that she could no longer count on my allegiance in her war with Dad, and as my value to her shrank, she never again treated me as lovingly as she once did. I was no longer Margaret the Pearl.

Summer brought relief from "the blacks." The worst seemed behind me, and I was determined that the life changes that lay ahead would be more of my own choosing, rather than my mother's.

In Muriel Spark's novel, *The Prime of Miss Jean Brodie*, released the year I returned to Cresaptown, the eponymous main character asserts, "Give me a girl at an impressionable age, and she is mine for life." My mother had me since I was born, and though I didn't know it then, she had already had considerable influence on my behavior. But was it a life sentence? Would I be hers, doomed to be just like her, for life?

I knew there was no chance of escaping her hold on me until I could be on my own. In education, I saw a path toward achieving that goal, and my focus became fixed on the path ahead, my passageway to freedom.

Chapter Twenty-Two

A New Voice

After Mom returned from Sykesville, I finalized my "divorce" from the Catholic Church by attending Cresaptown Methodist Church once more. At my Sunday school class, revealing that I had been a Catholic for the past four years elicited gasps from some, eye rolls from others. "Catholics aren't even Christians, you know," was the starch remark from one girl. Though I yearned to be accepted in my new/old setting, I couldn't let that go unchallenged.

"Of course, they are!" I insisted. Now it was my turn to roll my eyes. "They were actually the first organized Christian church after Christ died. Where did you hear a thing like that?"

"My mom and dad." My new friend's eyes narrowed as she beheld me, a former heathen.

Everyone knew that it was never good policy to challenge a parent's information, yet I persisted. "Whoever told them that just doesn't know anything."

"It's true; Catholics aren't Christian!" objected another girl. "They worship idols! My cousin was in a Catholic church once for a wedding, and he saw them." She crossed her arms to signal that was that.

The irony washed over me. Everyone seems to think "my

religion" is the one with the received word. As a Catholic, I had learned that I was a member of the One True Church, the only Christian religion to have the revealed truth of doctrine and practice. All other religions were wannabes, pretenders. As a 1960s Methodist, I was asked to believe that Catholics weren't even Christians; they were one step above Jews who as non-Christians were going right to hell.

A distance of years gave me insight on how that time drained me of the comfort of a spiritual life while giving me a perspective on just how counterproductive differing dogmas can be. I see now how much stands between us and God, how many of our beliefs are playing out customs from another place and time. How many of them hang an opaque curtain between us and the insights we yearn for? *Who are we? Why are we here? What happens after we die?* At the time, I was confused about who I was, what I was. I wasn't a Catholic, but I certainly wasn't the kind of Methodist my new friends were.

Many years later Elaine Pagel's books would help me understand how long ago this dense curtain was woven. "From the first century (CE) to the fourth, Christian leaders began to divide 'the saved' from 'the damned' less in terms of how they act and whether they accept a certain set of doctrines and participate—or don't—in specific religious communities."

Interactions with those at home and church unsettled me, and I began writing poetry as a way of coping with my conflicting emotions. Like Mom, my favorite theme was myself, a poet in constant self-analytical mode. Many poems were about Randy as I tried to make sense of what I felt for him and why I kept wanting him after pushing him away.

I sought solace in books, especially stories with tough female characters like Margaret Mitchell's *Gone with the Wind* and Edna Ferber's *So Big*. Mom pushed me to read Trappist monk Thomas Merton's *Seven Storey Mountain*, but I threw it aside after a couple of chapters, finding it tedious and preachy. To me it sounded like an advertisement for Catholicism, and I suspected it was her sneaky means of re-indoctrination. My own experience made me applaud A. J. Cronin's priest who resisted classifying people by creed in *The Keys of the Kingdom*.

Haunting elegies like "Crossing the Bar" continued to captivate me, but I also became intrigued with poetry that made me feel good, like e e cummings with his playful treatment of language and punctuation. My mother introduced me to Dorothy Parker, a new favorite of hers, and I wrote one in her style that made Mom laugh:

Once I fell in love, as some may say.
Now fallen out of love, I'm there to stay.

At the same time, Mom wrote my favorite of all her poems, "First Cause" which struck me as if she were breaking down mid-verse in a keening cry for her own lost, never-to-be-recovered freedom. The first verse read:

Freedom is the word!
Guard it well you patriots, musing by the fire
Freedom is the burning wish
The heart's desire.
Ah, well you then might weep and beat your breast
And lay your dearest dreams to bitter rest
For Freedom's name is God
And once abandoned comes no more.

Bobby returned from his Navy tour in Germany with a wife. Placid, sweet-tempered Ingrid wowed us with dishes we had never tasted like warm German potato salad and hamburger tacos and spoke a delightfully idiosyncratic, German-flavored English. "Oh, look at dat, Bobby, a squir eating wenchtables." We found her adorable, and my father was especially charmed. He felt Bobby was lucky to have won her. I thought, *Welcome to America's looniest family*, but after so many long, melancholy months, the lightness Bobby's family brought on their visits felt good.

In the 1960s, Allegany High School offered Grades 7 through 12, but because I had completed Grade 9 in Cresaptown, I started Allegany as a sophomore. It began to dawn on me that Cresaptown was a commoner to Cumberland's Queen City, where kids from outlying areas like Cresaptown attended high school but would never be part of its teenage-royalty class, the moneyed, professional people—families of doctors, layers, and merchants—who lived in or close to Cumberland. All that mattered to me was that my life suddenly improved socially, and my outlook brightened. A September letter to Suzanne was giddy:

> Allegany is the most terrific school I have ever known (even Kirby). I am working hard and loving it. I am taking French now and that is just a ball. We French students go around chattering in broken (or rather shattered) French whenever possible. I'm eating it all up, like French pastry!

The week I arrived at Allegany, one of my tenth-grade colleagues who had started Allegany in seventh grade was curious about my first name. "Some of your Cresaptown friends call you 'Peggy,' but the teachers call you 'Margaret.' What do you like to be called?"

Good question. Who am I now?

"Actually," I reflected, "I've been thinking I'd like to try something new. I've always liked the sound of 'Margie.'"

"Why not!" she urged. "You're a new student here. It's a new beginning, so why not pick the name you want?"

After that, she sang out, "Hi, Margie!" whenever she saw me. Eventually I decided I preferred my old nickname "Peggy," but she had been so supportive, I hadn't the heart to tell her I had changed my mind. To me, just as important as choosing the name I wanted was sensing the importance of her words "new beginning." A fresh start was exactly what I needed.

As a sophomore, I decided on my own to join the school orchestra because it meant I would play for the senior classes' productions of *The Music Man* and *Bye, Bye, Birdie*. I began finding my own voice—through music and articulating my opinions—but on one occasion in my junior year, I took a stand by not saying a word. Mr. Sykes was leading our practice in the orchestra pit of our school auditorium when an announcement crackled over the school P. A. system. The President had been shot while riding in a motorcade in Dallas and had died in a nearby hospital. I was so shocked I had to ask someone if I had heard correctly. President Kennedy was an almost mythical figure in our house. "Our first Catholic president," Mom frequently intoned reverently.

Mr. Sykes barely acknowledged what had just happened. When he prepared to start practice again, I put down my bass and took a seat in one of the front rows, glaring at him. Only then did he finally say something.

"I remember when FDR died," he mused, still holding up his baton. "Everyone was so upset." *FDR, really? Is that it?*

The other students looked from him to me and then at each other, wondering what they should do. A few of them put down their instruments. Mr. Sykes tried to resume practice but finally gave up. We all sat quietly until the bell rang. I had led a silent revolt.

In my junior year, another news item left me nearly as shocked, but this one arrived in whispers among the Cresaptown girls. One of my friends from childhood was pregnant. Later another whisper began. She had given birth and had requested to return to school. I admired such a gutsy move, but in the 1960s, any girl who got pregnant out of wedlock was deemed a shameless hussy. Principal Ardell Haines decided she should be kept away from decent girls and boys and blocked her return.

When I heard of this, I went straight to his office to challenge the ruling and lodge my protest. I was an Honor Society student and had never been called before him, so I was warmly welcomed into his office. He probably thought I wanted a college recommendation letter. His smile faded when he learned my real mission.

He shook his head in disbelief. Did he perhaps think I shared my friend's "immoral" tendencies? "That won't be possible," he sniffed. "We can't have her here strutting her stuff."

"Strutting. Her. Stuff?" I spaced out my words to communicate my disdain for his ignorance. "Strutting her stuff! She just wants to get an education. Everyone needs an education." I regarded him frostily. That stopped him only a few seconds before he reiterated his decision. It seemed that I had become a feminist version of my mother, defiant in the face of masculine power.

My anti-establishment phase climaxed when seniors were invited to present proposals to select the senior class musical. Previous senior classes had wowed with *The Music Man* and *Bye, Bye, Birdie*, and our class leaders had proposed other theatricals like *South Pacific* and *Brigadoon*. I had in mind a different production.

Anyone who wanted to propose a title was invited to deliver a ten-minute pitch to the senior assembly from the auditorium stage, so I prepared my talk about *The Mikado*, a hilarious Gilbert and Sullivan operetta I had seen Fred's Thespian Club perform at Andrew Jackson High School in Jacksonville. Standing in front of the senior class, I described the plot and suggested we cast our six-foot-seven-inch star basketball player Steve Vandenberg as the Japanese ruler, the Mikado, who appears at the end of the play to exclaim, "Bless my soul! My son!"

The laughter and applause that erupted among the students startled me. *Someone likes my idea!* The rank-and-file of the student body seemed enchanted with the idea of us all wearing kimonos in a Japanese village with characters named Nanki-poo and Yum Yum, and when I had presented the idea of the school's basketball hero in the title role, they were sold.

After some preliminary paper voting, the two semi-finalists were announced, and to my delight, *The Mikado* was one of them. A big-wig faction down in the front-center of the auditorium wanted *Brigadoon*, and the rest of us decided we didn't. Shouting began between the "rich kids" and the other 99%, who seemed to catch on that this was a proxy fight they could identify with. A triumphant roar went up when the votes were tallied and the results announced. *The Mikado* had won.

I exulted in this triumph, but, alas, my moment of political power was short-lived. The teacher who was to serve as the play's director shot straight to Ardell's office and made her own pitch, and the final verdict was announced: *West Side Story*. If the school held this exercise to teach us the democratic process, we learned instead about the nature of life under authoritarianism.

From choosing my own religion to taking a stand on school

issues, my voice grew stronger, and bits of my confidence returned. "The Blacks" diluted to moodiness and anxiety, following me like tenebrous shadows. My constant agonizing was not lost on Mom, who trotted out another entry from her fat file of "Motherisms." "The will to succeed is equally as strong as the will to fail."

I was usually inclined to ignore her advice, but this piece stuck with me. *Maybe I really am in a one-person race. I just have to believe I can win.* I wasn't aware that just as the race was getting harder, I was erecting my own hurdles.

Chapter Twenty-Three

Prizefighter and Passerine

My consistently glowing report cards always seemed a bright spot amid Mom's many disappointments. I once heard her crow to Edna and Henry, our Jacksonville neighbors, "Margaret Dale made honor roll again. I think she's probably the brightest kid in her class." Her applause was welcome, but it was my dread of her disapproval that made me "keep up the good work" despite all the hell she made in our home. Even then I kept my small-child fear of her power over me. My ninth-grade standardized scores on the California Achievement Test had been in the top ranges, which puffed Mom up even more.

My friend Gail remarked, "Did you really have college-level scores on the CAT?"

I cringed inside. "Who told you that?" Great grades and test scores never won me any friends.

"My mom did. I guess she heard it from your mom." *I'll just bet she did.*

Mom had high expectations for me, but she never attended high school, a fact she neglected to mention. In 1933, when Cresaptown School students completed Grade 9, the highest it offered, the school held a graduation ceremony. Many 1930s

Cresaptown students considered it their final graduation and felt nine years of education was enough. The Great Depression saw less enforcement of the mandatory attendance laws; children were often needed to work and supplement family income.

My mother's hunger for knowledge and her belief that schooling meant escape from the kind of life she had known made it unlikely she felt a ninth-grade education was "enough," but two obstacles might have stood in her way.

One was transportation. For my high school years 1962 through 1965, rain or shine, I hoofed the half-mile from my house to Warner's Restaurant at the McMullen Highway where I caught the school bus into Allegany High School in Cumberland. However, free school bus service from where Mom lived in Potomac Park to Allegany High School did not begin until a few years after she left Cresaptown School.

Family funds were likely a more urgent reason Mom never made it to Allegany. Blackjack was a poor provider in the best of times, and I would wager that when the Depression's economic impact began hitting home, it had the same life-changing impact on Mom's family as it had on Dad's. In 1930, my father's parents had told young Spates he couldn't live with them unless he brought in an income to help the family survive. When Mom finished ninth grade at Cresaptown in 1933, Blackjack probably sat her down and delivered the same type of message to her.

I can hear her begging, "Please let me, please, Daddy! I can walk five miles, and I can work after school every day. I know I can do it! I know I can!" and I can see Blackjack shaking his head. "Phrona, you know how expensive high school is, all those fees, and you'd be wanting new clothes. You'd need winter boots, too. We can't afford all that. You should work full-time to support the family. Anyway, you're just a girl. Why would you need more schoolin'?"

And I can picture her rage when she knew she would not be getting further education. "It's not my family, it's yours—yours and hers. I hate you, you stupid, nasty man. You can't even get a full-time job! I hate you both, you and Blanche!"

She must have believed she had no control over her destiny. Now I had to make up for the opportunity she had been denied. *No pressure; just excel in high school as well as Mom thinks she could have.*

By the time I reached high school, I needed no motivation from Mom to study hard. I knew that good grades paved my way to college and my path to freedom from her. Academics were paramount, but Allegany was also an opportunity to study what "normal" looked like socially. I began to feel the pull of teenage hormones and the social pressure to be seen going out with boys. Today's teens often hang out in groups or socialize online, but in the 1960s, if you weren't seen at the movies, ball games, or dances with a partner of the opposite sex, you weren't considered popular.

I felt unattractive and awkward around boys other than Randy, and though I had given him the cold shoulder in Cresaptown, at Allegany I sensed he was my best chance for dates. I also longed for what he gave me: acceptance and—though I was unaware then what to name it—a burgeoning sexual desire. When I flashed him a warm smile on my way to homeroom one day, he did a double take and nearly dropped his books. Randy had to be wary of trusting me again, but he took the bait.

At Methodist Youth Fellowship hayrides, roller skating parties, and dances at Cresaptown's premiere local hangout, Cuffy's Corner, Randy and I became an item. Luckily, my mother's firm position on my seeing boys had softened by then. She must have realized she had inoculated me sufficiently on the need to be a Good Girl. But she knew that so long as I viewed it as sinful to even kiss a boy outside marriage, I would never be happy in my new social milieu, let alone find a mate later. Her encouragement broadened at last my definition of Good Girl.

One obstacle to any normal boy-girl relationship was my fixation on Nick Prescott. In my miserable first post-Jacksonville year, I became a skilled daydreamer, fantasizing about meeting Hollywood stars who would think me charming and find my sincerity and intelligence more alluring than the frivolous starlets they were gadding about with. I conjured my Ideal Guy, whom I named Nick Prescott—the man I would someday meet and marry. He resembled real-life heartthrob, actor Montgomery Clift—slender, sensitive, and dark-eyed, with an easy laugh and so popular that all the girls would yearn for him. (Years later, Clift would come out as gay.) In my imagination, Nick Prescott would be a great kisser, but he'd be even taller than the five-foot-nine Monty and would gaze down at me with dark, adoring eyes.

I'm not sure why I singled out blond, stocky Randy from the pool crowd; he couldn't compete with my imagined ideal, but few others ever asked me out until late in my junior year. Being seen with Randy in so many settings might have given everyone the impression we were exclusive. Just when he might have thought he was getting somewhere, I cold-shouldered him all over again. My letters to Suzanne say I deemed him not ambitious or brainy enough for me, but the real reasons were as complicated as my teenage mind—part hormones, part trying to figure myself out—and a large helping of my mortal fear of not being a Good Girl.

I was flabbergasted when Randy joined me on the way to my World History class; I had been ignoring him for weeks.

"Wanna go to Turkey Day?" was his nonchalant invitation. His offer meant that I had a date to one of the area's two annual signature events of the 1960s, the other being the prom in May. Unlike many schools today, Allegany never had a prom king and queen. Instead, each November students elected a homecoming court, and on Thanksgiving Day, each school played its biggest rival, in our case, Fort Hill High School. The Turkey Day court of each school paraded around the field during halftime, resplendent in formal attire and crowns, regally waving to us peasants in the stands. Many families in our area celebrated Thanksgiving by going to the Turkey Day game before heading off to dinner.

Even now, I can close my eyes, and I am there. The cool silk of the late-autumn air brushing my face, the smell of the new-mown turf on the football field, the fragrant, yellow "mum" corsage the girls all wore—so big it seemed to cover half the chest. I can feel, rather than hear, the band's rata-tat-tat, boom ba-BOOM that shook the ground, stirring something primal inside me. Who won the game? Who cares? I was there to play my part in the pageantry.

Thanksgiving with Randy was a full day of firsts for me. After the game, Randy's parents, aunt, and uncle took us to Thanksgiving dinner at Moon's, a family-style restaurant in Cumberland. Though I didn't mention it for fear they would learn how strange my family was, this was my first Thanksgiving dinner, as well as the first meal in a restaurant with people waiting on me. In Jacksonville, we had gone to the A&W Root Beer take-away stand and, on rare occasions, Morrison's Cafeteria, but this more formal setting was a novel experience. Waitresses brought bowls of food and hovered over tables inquiring if patrons wanted more. I was nearly too overwhelmed to eat.

My family may have had Thanksgiving dinners, but neither

Fred nor I recall one. My mother was not inclined to cook a big, celebratory dinner; she hated cooking anyway and probably felt she had little cause to celebrate. Thanksgiving was a holiday for normal families, not my peculiar one. Though some families went out to eat for Thanksgiving, my parents never went to restaurants on any day. In Dad's Depression-era thinking, they were as frivolous a use of family funds as building a fence around the yard. In my time with Randy and his family, I relished this opportunity to learn how normal families behaved, and I yearned to be like them. I was just beginning to glimpse what "normal" looked like.

In December, Randy and I were sitting in my driveway in his car, as usual taking forever to say goodbye because we didn't want to, when suddenly he pulled me close and kissed me. He had waited nearly three years to do it, and it seemed as if I had waited all my life for the experience. I was sixteen. That night I began to see what all the fuss was about. Teenage urges were kicking in, and I gushed to Suzanne, "There are times when we feel like two people in love." Kisses accelerated to necking over spring and summer, but after Randy started our local state college in Frostburg, he inexplicably vanished from my life. Maybe he wanted to see if he could do better than me in college. After a whole year of nothing from him, I told Suzanne, "Suddenly last week, who but Randy asked a friend of mine to find out if I'd date him again. I told her I would. I've simply got to go to our Senior Prom."

I had dated other boys that year, but no one had asked me to my Senior Prom. Randy seemed flattered to accompany me, and I had a prom date, so it worked out all around. Though I still viewed Randy and I as mismatched, my outlook on the future turned slightly more optimistic. To Suzanne, I wrote, "Doors have been opening for me. Randy is a beginning, just one of the doors."

Despite spending lots of time thinking about boys and barely surviving a mind-bending experimental chemistry curriculum called Chemical Bond Analysis (CBA), I managed to graduate in the top 5 percent of Allegany's largest-ever class of baby boomers. I was so confident that I popped into the office of guidance counselor Mr. Cuba and announced, "I need a scholarship." He looked doubtful and muttered he'd look into it, but I could never get a formal meeting with him. I dropped by so often I was certain he was hiding out from me. Maybe he had seen one too many pretty girls get college scholarships only to win nothing more than an MRS degree, or maybe he felt the world had enough English majors.

Neither Mom nor Dad supported my going to college anywhere but Frostburg, so while my classmates went on to what I considered exotic locales ranging from the University of Maryland to the California Polytechnic Institute, I gritted my teeth and resigned myself to living at home another year and starting higher education a half-hour drive from home.

Summer took an unexpected turn when Mom threw me a gala backyard graduation barbeque—a first. Toni, one of my high school buddies, arrived with a date named Eric, who was visiting his sister in Cumberland for the summer. A junior at City College of New York, Eric had emigrated from Poland with his Jewish family when he was three years old. Toni's family often took her on out-of-town trips that summer to look at potential colleges, which allowed Eric and me time to find we shared many interests. He taught me to play bridge, and my letters to Suzanne brimmed with talk of our card parties and discussions.

After Randy listened to me gush about Eric one night on the phone, he grumbled, "Sounds like you're in love with him."

"Don't be silly," I scoffed. "Eric's not my type, and besides, he's Toni's boyfriend." All that was true. Though well-rounded intellectually, Eric was also round-faced and paunchy, with dark-rimmed glasses. Anyway, I'd have felt rotten going after Toni's boyfriend. Randy nonetheless began showing up at all our card games.

Eric and I, bonding over bridge, became friends, and he invited me to his sister's home where they fed me borsht and I pumped them for more information about Jewish culture and Eric's New York home. Here at last was a chance to feed my growing hunger for the big world outside my small hometown.

Meanwhile, I learned that Randy failed freshman courses at Frostburg and had to attend summer school; playing cards to spy on Eric and me may have cut way back on his study time. I began comparing Randy to a successful Chemistry major at City College. My teenage body craved Randy's warmth, but I was sure that somewhere out there was a better match for me. After some especially passionate kissing at a drive-in movie in mid-July, I grew afraid of these new, intense desires. I had wanted to know what normal people did, but I sensed the "normal" outcome for this was something I didn't want, at least not with him.

"Randy, we should stop dating." I sprang it on him as we headed home. He never said a word, just drove me home so fast I was afraid he meant to crash the car. He soon found a Frostburg girl and married her within a year of our breakup, then joined the Army as a second lieutenant and left town. In retrospect, I know poor Randy deserved a handful of Purple Hearts for the wounds I inflicted on him, as well as a special award for bravery for trying to make our relationship work despite my ambivalence.

Before we left Jacksonville, I had felt as powerful as a prizefighter.

I had successfully transitioned from my small Cresaptown world to big-city Jacksonville and fought menaces from a classroom bully to a pedophile while never viewing myself as a victim. In Florida I had begun to find ways to create a bright Florida life despite Mom's gloomy outlook. Yet only one traumatic first year back in Cresaptown had inflicted emotional wounds that refused to heal. I was no longer able to "get tough in this world." I had become not strong but increasingly fragile, even as I maintained Dad's never-give-up tenacity.

Pretty Cindy had a busy social life, and Fred was finishing undergraduate work at Frostburg State College (now Frostburg State University) where he had a steady girlfriend named Phyllis. I made few friends at Allegany, and small distresses shook any confidence I gained there. Fred delivered one such injury to my fragile self-esteem. He informed me that Phyllis needed a subject to analyze for a psychology class project, and without my permission, he had offered me up, a clear violation of my privacy rights. This was years before universities were required to set up Institutional Review Boards to protect human subjects.

"Want to read her report? I'm so proud of her; she's such a good writer," Fred gushed, handing me Phyllis' writeup.

My eyes fell on sentences like, "Peggy is often hostile and moody," and I burst into tears. "Why, Fred?" I wailed, "Why did you let her do this?"

Fred shrugged, "Why are you so upset? It's just a stupid college paper."

My letters to Suzanne painted a high-school life brimming with boys, dances, engaging schoolwork, and football and basketball games. To impress her, I wrote myself into the kind of life

I wanted, but I never regained the self-confidence and sense of belonging I had at Kirby Smith. Despite my focus on learning what "normal" was, I never felt anything close to normal. Instead, I remember high school as a long period of pretense as I waited for better days to arrive. Turned into a creature as delicate as a bird that any small blow might crush, I kept flying on, a migratory passerine en route to a destination I sensed rather than saw.

When I started Frostburg State College as a day student, I viewed it as the first leg of my flight out of Cresaptown. As I fought my way out of Mom's influence, my learning curve angled sharply upward in my first year of college, and I soon learned first-hand the challenges that had faced Randy.

Fourth Part

Flying Forward by Degrees

Chapter Twenty-Four

Higher Education

Frostburg State College was only fifteen miles up McMullen Highway from Cresaptown, but when I was on campus, home seemed farther away. Most kids heading off for college anticipate excitement, new faces, and fresh vistas of learning and accomplishment. For me, it was nearly enough that I was away from Mom. I still had to live at home, but I spent as much time away from it as possible, leaving early in the morning and not returning until after dinnertime. I never forgot how Fred had spied on Bobby and reported to Mom, and I was relieved that I wouldn't have to fear Big Brother surveillance at Frostburg. Fred had graduated from Frostburg and was teaching near DC.

Dad had traded in Mom's "lilac lemon" for a used, stick-shift, Army-green Rambler station wagon. Not much to look at, but in good working order. To attend Frostburg, I had to learn to drive it; I had never taken driver's education. In fact, I remember learning little in my high school curriculum that was ever of much practical use. I even eschewed typing class in favor of orchestra, a decision I came to regret when I had to prepare college papers.

Mom taught me to drive, a draining experience for us both. Using the clutch on the steepest part of Cresaptown's Van Meter's Hill, I froze and she had to pull up the emergency brake and sprint around the car to slide into the driver's seat as I moved over, sweating and shaking. I passed the driver's test on my first try, and though Mom remained leery of my driving on my own, she knew she couldn't keep chauffeuring me back and forth to Frostburg. College, even one only fifteen miles away, brought me an autonomy she had more cause to fear.

I suppose I had thought that because it wasn't New York's City College or the University of Maryland, Frostburg would be like Allegany High School North, and I quickly learned my error. My professor for freshman English was a slender, swarthy young Armenian American I'll call Mr. Gevorgyan. He had black hair, a thick mustache, and a menacing smile. We virginal 18-year-old girls thought him very glamorous and possibly dangerous. He liked to taunt his inexperienced rural teens by reading us D. H. Lawrence poems with vivid sexual metaphors.

One fine fall day as golden leaves swirled by the window, Mr. Gevorgyan, lecturing from his perch on his desk, began, "Here Lawrence is comparing sexual acts to violence." He leaned toward us with narrowed eyes sparkling and one hand clenched in a fist before him. "Because sex is a violent act, isn't it?"

If he intended to shock us, it worked. It must have amused him when the girls in the front row looked stunned and shifted back in their seats while the boys glanced at each other, smiling nervously. It was the first time I had ever heard anyone other than my high school biology teacher Mrs. Buckley even utter the word "sex." I was even more shocked with the C+ on my first composition assignment. Mr. Gevorgyan terrified me, and when I visited his office asking for help, a smile spread across his mustachioed countenance as he eyed me up and down like metaphorical lunch. "Ah, Miss Roblyer." That predatory look so intimidated me that I nearly bolted.

I took no chances on subsequent papers and worked as hard on them as anything I'd ever done in school. Thc improved grades I made in English were an enormous relief. Not only did I not have to seek further help from wolfish instructors, I'd also have caught holy hell from Mom if I'd made a C in English.

The Frostburg social scene proved even more challenging to me than college coursework. Cindy had always seemed effortlessly at ease around boys since we set foot back in Cresaptown, and as I struggled socially in college, her popularity only seemed to grow in high school. Sometimes I questioned how Cindy and I had the same parents. I always felt that part of the reason she was so laid back was because she was born after me, and Mom never seemed to weigh her down with the same kinds of demands and anxieties she did me. I have no doubt that was an oversimplified view; Mom left her Jean-Brodie imprint on all her children, but especially us girls.

For most Cresaptown females, marriage was their best path out of their parents' house, but it could never be for me. My mother's example was a spectral figure blocking that exit. I resolved I would never find myself like her, dependent on a man, trapped without options. How often had she reminded me that being able to support myself was a precious freedom, though she didn't realize that it was her control I was working so diligently to be free of. One young man I met at a Ridgeley Fire Hall dance tested my determination.

Ridgely lay just across the Maryland state line in West Virginia, a few minutes from downtown Cumberland. You could buy beer at the Ridgely Fire Hall—the legal drinking age in West Virginia was eighteen and in Maryland twenty-one—and it hosted a Friday night hop, which made it a popular destination for teenagers. One night, a dark-eyed charmer named Richard asked me to dance. He seemed intelligent and articulate, but not haughty about it, cosmopolitan and sophisticated, yet approachable. "He's a dreamboat," I later gushed to Gail. Richard bought us Cokes, and we repaired to one of the tables around the dance floor and talked until closing time.

"My family in Connecticut has money, but I can't seem to do anything they like," he grumbled. "I'm not going begging to them for college tuition. When I muster out of the Navy, I'll have my own college money."

I thought he was more suave than anyone I had met, except possibly Eric, so I had to know. "What are you doing in this dead-end town?"

"I'm heading off to Japan for my first tour, so I'm spending my leave staying with the family of a guy I met in boot camp. I don't need to go back home; I'm on my own now." In the space of one Ridgely evening, I was hooked.

We went out every night for a week before he told me he loved me. After some especially passionate necking at his local friend's house, he pulled back and held me by the shoulders, considering me carefully. Perhaps he thought he knew just what I wanted to hear.

"Peggy, I love you," he murmured, gazing into my eyes. "What I should do is take you across the state line to West Virginia and marry you tonight."

I beheld those dark eyes for a few seconds while the reality of his remark sank in. *Oh my God, he's proposing.* My mother screaming in my head, my reply was firm. "No, I have to get an education first." Only later did it hit me how the trajectory of my life would have changed had I accepted. After that, I resolved that no man would ever make me forget the path I was on. Richard left for Japan, and our affair carried on through torrid letters for a few months until I met another guy who vowed he loved me.

I wrote Suzanne, "I've been reading some Thomas Wolfe. I find him fascinating but kind of frightening. I saw the *Look Homeward, Angel* play at J.U. one night. It was so good I hated it for its truthfulness." Wolfe's story was frightening to me because the plan I was formulating for escaping to my future away from family was risky and full of unknowns. Without telling my parents, I applied to the University of Maryland, determined to pay my own way so I wouldn't have to request support from Dad. I wanted to be a writer but needed to be able to land a job immediately upon graduation. Being self-supporting was key to escaping that house.

The University of Maryland, like Frostburg State, educated the state's teachers and dangled a juicy carrot before teacher education majors. If they agreed to teach at least two years in the State of Maryland after graduation, tuition would be covered. *Free tuition!* was all I heard. I decided to become a teacher—for two years. I'd figure out how to become a writer after that.

I also learned how I could cover UM living expenses. The same 1950s space-race paranoia that yielded my dreaded high school CBA chemistry curriculum also delivered the National Defense Education Act of 1958 to fortify the nation's defense programs and prepare educated workers for the space age. I applied for an NDEA loan.

Mom's scowling disappointment was palpable when I didn't make Dean's List at Frostburg, but with a solid B as my annual GPA, I was confident I could succeed at UM. *If I could only get accepted, I'd show them—mostly Mom—I could make it in the big city*. While I waited on decisions about both applications, I focused on getting a job to make a little college spending money, ideally one outside Cresaptown.

⁂

"I'm going to be a waitress at the Bedford Springs Resort," I announced to my startled mother. I had never so much as laid eyes on the place, though it was only thirty miles west of Cumberland and a familiar enough name in our community. A popular golf resort, it had hosted more than a dozen U. S. Presidents from Zachary Taylor to George W. Bush, and stories about other famous visitors frequently appeared in the *Cumberland Times*.

She shook her head. "Your father will never let you drive the Rambler there every day."

"Oh, no, I don't need a car; they don't let waitresses off the grounds at night. They have a dormitory. Sally got a job there; you can ask her Mom about it." Sally was one of my high school friends, but Mom didn't know her well and had never even spoken to her mother. She nodded, but I was confident she wouldn't make the call. She'd have to admit to a total stranger that she didn't trust her own nineteen-year-old daughter. However, my plan to earn big money as a Bedford Spring waitress was cut short when Sally called to deliver disappointing news. They had stopped hiring for the summer.

I had just about resigned myself to making a pittance as a salesclerk at Rosenbaum's Department Store in Cumberland when I spotted an ad for the Glen Haven, a resort north of Frostburg overlooking Deep Creek Lake and so far out in the Western Maryland woods that it included free motel rooms in its employment package. A $70-a-week salary plus tips and free lodging for waitresses at the bar/restaurant meant I wouldn't have to be in Cresaptown for the entire summer, after which—fingers crossed—I would be leaving for College Park. Applicants had to be twenty-one, but I was sure I could "be" twenty-one if I had to.

Mom would never have let me work at a bar, so I sold it as being just like the Bedford Springs Hotel, complete with a girls' dormitory. She had never heard of the Glen Haven, and I could see she was doubtful, but in the end, she agreed to inform Dad I was working at Deep Creek Lake. She and I both knew he would focus on the fact I was working.

A friend gave me a ride to make the forty-mile trip for the interview. I bought a pair of nonprescription eyeglasses to make me look older and tried not to giggle nervously like the immature teenager I was when owner Anne Delligatti, the wealthy ex-wife of Jim Delligatti (an early McDonald's franchisee who created the "Big Mac") interviewed me.

"And you are twenty-one?" My slight build and five-foot-four-inch frame made me a very young-looking nineteen, even with my fake glasses.

"Of course." I held my breath, but she never checked my driver's license. I burbled to Suzanne, "It's a new experience for me to be serving liquor—I don't drink at all. I hope I can get through the summer without being caught."

And so, my magical season began. I went to work at 6:00 p.m. and got off at 2:00 a.m., which was usually when my social life got underway. I met people from all over, from locals to Anne's wealthy international friends. A group of Army reserve parachutists came to the bar frequently to relax during their annual summer exercises, which they called their "prop blast." I was as in awe of their macho look and behavior as they were of the pretty blond waitress saving money for college; they vied with each other to impress me.

One of the officers taught me how to water ski, and another introduced me to a form of poetry he had learned about in Japan. After their summer training ended, a book was waiting for me with the bartender, a slim collection of Japanese haiku I still treasure. In the front, he had inscribed, "Dear Peggy. This is the best (only) one I could find. I hope you will recall the Green Beret 'invasion' fondly. Many of us will remember your sweet smile. Harrington, COE, 19th SFGA."

In my first year of college, my romantic education included advanced courses in necking, but my perceptions of sex had always come from whispers and rumors from girlfriends and steamy movie scenes. I had formed a hazy image of a Nick Prescott-type lover and a sequence akin to something out of a cheesy romance novel. *He looked deep into my fearful eyes and slowly drew me to him, holding me close until my fears melted away like spring snows in sun. Passion welled in me as our bodies warmed to each other, and when we kissed, no fear remained. His lovemaking, sensual and slow, drove up my desire until my whole body screamed for him to quench my burning need.*

Right. My actual first sexual encounter that summer was as different from what I had envisioned as frost from flame. The experience was more akin to an incident that took place thirty years after that when Fred, who was by then twice married and living in Annapolis, invited my husband and me to join his family there for the Fourth of July.

For its annual Independence Day celebration, Annapolis sets off a pyrotechnical display from a barge in the middle of Chesapeake Bay. To get the best spot for viewing the show, we all drove onto the Naval Academy base after dinner. We claimed a spot on the green overlooking the Bay, laid down blankets, and tried to amuse ourselves until it got dark enough for the display to begin.

After a forever wait, the first fireworks appeared in the sky over the water and we settled in for several minutes of "ohhhh" and "ahhhh." But then came a ba-BOOM, followed by something that sounded like the crackle of sparklers. After that, silence. We could make out a thin column of smoke rising in the night air over the barge. We waited another half hour until word filtered through the crowd; an accident on the barge killed a worker and canceled the pyrotechnics show.

And that's what my first sexual experience was like. After breathless anticipation, no fireworks. After a couple months of disappointing sex, my desire for him was dead.

For sexual fireworks, I had to wait until the end of the summer, just before the Glen Haven fired me when they found out I was only nineteen. I fell hard for a guy named Jay who was at home on leave from the Army and staying with family in nearby Oakland, Maryland.

Jay was tall and thin with the lean-muscled shape that military duty gives young men, but it was his heavy-lidded grey eyes that mesmerized me. He was just back from Vietnam with a Purple Heart and a ticket-home foot wound from stepping on a Vietnamese booby-trap called a punji stick. He was scheduled to muster out of the Army the following year and major in pre-law at UM. Unlike me, he knew he would have free tuition, courtesy of the U. S. Army.

I asked him what Vietnam was like; we were just beginning to hear about the carnage, and a fresh-faced boy from my high school had come home in a body bag. In his honey-smooth deep voice, Jay drawled, "Just a lot of jungle patrols, but kind of excitin'—like huntin'. If I'd been wounded over there and couldn't have kids, like some guys I heard about, I wouldn't mind goin' back and makin' a career of the Army." He was cluing me in that marriage and children were his priority. They certainly weren't for me, but I was too captivated by those grey eyes to notice.

Chapter Twenty-Five

Away with Me

I was still at the Glen Haven Bar when the fat envelope bearing the University of Maryland logo arrived in Cresaptown. I relished the idea of Mom standing in the kitchen, openmouthed as she dialed the phone to call and read it to me. "I am pleased to inform you of your acceptance to the University of Maryland." The same letter announced I had been approved for the NDEA loan. I believe she thought I was incapable of doing anything so momentous without her help, and I reveled in the astonishment in her voice that I was accepted. A new act in the play was about to begin.

By the time I made it back home, she had already bought into the idea, but we had to sell it to Dad, who sensed an impending drain on his funds.

"How're you paying for that?" he rumbled warily.

"I've got loans, Pop!"

"Loans! Loans!" he huffed. "You have to pay those back, you know." He never bought on credit.

I assured him I would work part-time to make ends meet and would pay off the debt after I graduated and got a teaching job, but he continued to resist. He was not only a Depression-era parent, he also knew what I did not: College Park had one of

Maryland's highest costs of living.

"Why can't you just stay here for free and go to Frostburg like your friends?" he protested, his face growing red with frustration. I understood his logic and even predicted his reaction. Mom had called him a miser so often that I assumed he could probably afford to pay my way to UM so I wouldn't have needed loans, but it would never have occurred to me to ask. Now I can see his point. If I flunked out, I'd spend years paying off debt from the short time I was there. Staying at Frostburg was logical, risk-free. When you're young, I realize now, you never think of the things that could go wrong. When you're older, it's all you can think of.

I could never explain why I had to leave or why getting out of that house was worth the risk; he and I had never talked about anything. And how could I communicate to him how long I had hated Mom and how desperate I was to get away from her? Even if he understood, he probably would have repeated his old mantra that I should "get tough in this world."

At nineteen, I didn't really need their approval to go to UM, but my mother became an unexpected ally. "She's capable of better things than Frostburg, Spates! Let her go." Perhaps Mom saw the status involved. It was the white picket fence all over again, minus the destruction. Seeing it was useless to fight two hardheaded women, he gave up and stomped out. To Suzanne I announced, "You are now writing to a student of the University of Maryland!"

I had applied too late for a dormitory room, but Fred was living in Annapolis, so Mom convinced him to truck me around College Park to possible rentals. The first we saw was a Hyattsville apartment on a direct bus line to the central campus. Three girls were sharing two bedrooms and wanted a fourth to share a room with one of them. Fred looked around and made a quick decision it would be just right for me, and when I emerged from checking out the bedroom, he had left without saying goodbye. The girls were chagrined he had dumped me there before they agreed that I would be a compatible roommate but finally decided I would have to do.

In 1966, everyone registered for college classes in person, and at UM it was in a steamy field house that smelled like old socks and sweaty jocks. The huge gym was packed with people, more than I had ever seen in one place, and the din was incredible. Frenetic teenagers jostled to join long lines at tables where bored-looking UM employees handed out punched computer cards, each card representing a section of a course. The longest lines were for the popular classes, and choice times in required subjects always went first; no one wanted 8:00 a.m. classes.

Sometimes a class would fill up before you got to the front of the line, or the only time left would conflict with something already on your schedule. Then came the calculus of whether to grab that class and try to change the other one that conflicted to another time or just select another course. Each move required us to join another long line, as we sweated and hoped that class wouldn't close before we reached the front. At the end of the day, a thin stack of punched cards held my college life for that semester.

Walking the UM campus for the first time, I was awed by the immense scale of the place. Every structure loomed before me majestically; I felt like Gulliver in Brobdingnag. I could circumnavigate the entire Frostburg campus in the space of twenty minutes, but locating the building for each of my UM classes was like finding my way around an entire town. For the first time since I started college, I was genuinely excited about my courses. Here at last was the cosmopolitan milieu I found lacking at Frostburg.

To relax back at the apartment, I watched episodes of *Star Trek*, which had just premiered that fall. Gene Roddenberry taught all of us viewers a basic course in science fiction that year, but one episode also gave me a memorable lesson in self-assertion. That was the evening I hustled home from class and ran up the stairs to our apartment just in time, I thought, for the opening credits: "Space, the final frontier . . ." As I burst in the door out of breath, a half dozen pairs of male eyes turned toward me. The television was already on, but on the screen was not the deck of the Enterprise or a new and hostile planet the crew was exploring, but sweaty basketball players dribbling and jostling. On the living room floor sat six guys; I had never seen five of them before.

Chagrined, I questioned my roommate's boyfriend, "What's going on here, Ted?"

"Basketball," he replied, turning back to the screen. Five other pairs of eyes turned back, too. "Melody okayed us to watch the game here."

This was the sixties, and I'm sure the expected response from a female was "Oh, fine" or maybe, "Would you like some snacks?"

I had another reply ready. "Yeah? Well, I pay rent here, and I'm watching *Star Trek*."

I dropped my books on the sofa, marched over, and turned the dial to the channel where Captain Kirk sat center-stage on the main deck of the Enterprise, musing on some command decision. There were loud protests and an appeal to Melody, who was in the bedroom studying. I plopped into a chair in front of the TV, prepared for battle with anyone who made a move for the dial.

"Quiet down, guys. I can't hear Mr. Spock."

They huffed out the door, throwing black looks at me and probably thinking it was all Betty Friedan's fault. I savored that small victory; I had exerted newfound power.

Home for the holidays, I found that my mother had started taking her own college courses at the local community college. She left her Fall grade report on the kitchen table so I would be sure to see her A in the single course she took. Of my first-semester B average taking six courses at the University of Maryland, she uttered not a word. I was also doing my share of housework at the apartment and had a part-time job at Hecht's Department Store in the King of Prussia Mall, as well as struggling through German and geology. She had always had some comment on my grades, even when she was disappointed in them. What was she saying by saying nothing at all? I would know soon enough.

"Sleeping together" would not be an accurate description of what Jay and I had been doing, unless it covers occasional car-sex in parking lots or back roads while keeping one eye open for police, a less-than-romantic experience, if you've never done it. Nor would I recommend going at it while driving down the highway at night, a feat I still can't believe we accomplished. What I wanted from him was all about fireworks sex, never about commitment. In the course of five years, I had morphed from a prissy, better-than-everyone schoolgirl who eschewed kissing parties into a fully sexualized, orgasm-craving woman. Had my mother known, she'd have judged that her worst fears had come true. I had become like my "hellraising aunts." I would not realize until later that I was in solidarity with them and many other women of our time, discarding our parents' morality and choosing our own path.

I met Jay in the 1960s, the apex of the sexual revolution and the women's liberation movement, but I had not yet availed myself of a key invention that enabled both these radical social changes: the pill.

When Jay invited me to stay at his parents' house and attend New Year's Eve revelries in Oakland, "meeting the parents" didn't land on my consciousness as significant, though it should have. I was just focused on the "party" idea and that we might occasionally have access to a real bed. It was also a great way to get away from my own parents.

Jay and I slept in separate rooms, but the night of the big party in downtown Oakland, we stayed behind long enough to grab some alone time in his childhood bedroom. Once we arrived at the party, he kept ordering Old Fashioneds and got completely legless. His brother Kevin persuaded him to leave just after midnight, and after we guided him wobbling into the house, Jay focused bleary eyes on me, wrapped limp arms around me, and laid his head on my shoulder.

"I love you, Peggy; I love you soooo much," he moaned. I stood there incredulous as Kevin peeled him off my shoulder and dragged him off to bed. Jay wailed down the hall to his room, "I looove you, Peggy."

Spring semester found me immersed in the nuances of two languages: German and the Czech-inflected English dialect spoken by the graduate student teaching my sophomore mathematics class. When my "curse" did not appear on schedule, the idea I might be pregnant did not even register; Jay had always used protection. In one of our phone conversations, I mentioned my lateness to him and how bloated and icky I felt, which must have rendered him dry-mouthed. Only after my "curse" came did Jay confess over the phone that on New Year's Eve, he had had an "equipment failure" with the condom. I was furious.

"How could you let this happen? When were you going to tell me?" I raged.

"Why worry you for nothing? Anyway, I would have married you."

I tried not to think about my lost freedom and shattered future. Even now I wonder if Jay really had an accident or if he did what he felt he needed to do to get me to marry him.

Our romance lasted longer than most of my infatuations, but the fireworks faded, the inevitable victim of conflicting goals. Jay was laser-focused on getting married and starting a family right away, and he finally figured out that I was not even going to consider marriage until I had my degree and maybe not ever with him; we broke up in March. I ran into him on the UM campus just six months later, and he was married with a baby on the way. I remember my disappointment that he wouldn't wait for me so I would have a handy, on-campus sex partner. For me, the excitement of the 1960's went downhill after that.

Now I try to imagine who this self-centered woman was and what made her. Maybe she lacked role models for empathy and love in practice, or maybe she started out independent and her youthful experiences turned her self-absorbed, even narcissistic. Whatever made her, I believe she ceased to exist when Bill's suitcase appeared.

When I made it home for the summer at the end of my first UM year, my mother had plenty to say, this time not about grades. Now she had other issues to litigate. As we stood in the front yard admiring her roses, she turned to me with a familiar disapproving look.

"I heard from one of your friends you are smoking Mary Joo-ana," she sniffed, giving the word her unique phonetic spin. Then she watched me closely for signs of my guilty mind. Neither I nor any of my friends even knew anyone who used any drugs, let alone tried them ourselves. I had never so much as smelled pot.

I quickly pegged it as some kind of test. "Who could have told you that?"

"Oh, one of your friends here." She tried to look convincing while lying through her teeth.

"How would one of my friends here know anything about UM?" I scoffed. "In any case, it's not true. I've never done anything like that. And why would you believe such a thing?"

She harrumphed off, still unconvinced I was not a pothead. Dad offered neither comment nor question on my college career, only gazed at me occasionally with what I believe was a mixture of pride, amazement, and relief. I think he had half-expected I would flunk out of UM, and because I was underaged, he would be stuck with paying off my loans.

While on the prowl at the Ridgely Fire Hall that summer, I spotted a guy who reminded me of Jay, fit-looking and clean-cut. His name was Don, and though he had also been in the Army, he somehow managed to avoid Vietnam. He was vague on details, refusing to talk about it. I didn't care. After all, I wasn't looking for a mate, just a good time. Don was good-natured and had a silly sense of humor that kept me in a good mood. He also had a hot car, a 1966 green Mustang ragtop that attracted admiring looks in the Ridgely Fire Hall parking lot.

Don was summering with his brother at his family's country getaway home outside Bedford, about thirty miles from

Cumberland. After his father died, his mother had moved to State College, Pennsylvania, to be near his sisters, and she was paying Don and his brother Sid to look after the Bedford place while she decided what to do with it. I didn't ask for details. Don seemed incredulous that I was interested in him, and I had to pursue him until he asked me out. We saw each other as often as he could get down from Bedford.

Don eventually confessed he had flunked out of Penn State, got drafted, and gone AWOL after two weeks at an Alabama boot camp. His mother managed to convince him to throw himself on the mercy of his commanding officer. Don could have been court-martialed for desertion during wartime, but the uncommonly understanding Sergeant Faircloth somehow arranged a general discharge for him, which may have saved Don's life. At the time, his shady background seemed irrelevant. I had someone to date who had a sweet ride.

When my Spring semester grades arrived, I was first to open them, and this time, I was the one who left a grade sheet out on the table. By choosing the University of Maryland, I had overcome an array of complex obstacles and made my way in a difficult new environment with little support, yet I had earned a solid B average for the year. I might have earned better grades if I had not been focused so much on socializing, but I didn't care about that either. Negotiating new settings and figuring out how "normal people" interacted was part of why I made the move.

That grade sheet buoyed my confidence. There I was, little Cresaptown Peggy, a successful college student at UM, thriving in the wide world. My self-worth swelled, and my grade report gave me the confidence I would be able to make it on my own.

One evening after Don took me home from our date, we moseyed through the back door in search of a snack. My mother came out of the living room and, seeing us together, looked pained and turned on her heel.

"Mom, did you see my grades?" I called after her.

"Yeah," she tossed off, not even looking back as she walked. "Think what you could have done if you had tried."

I was so embarrassed that I wanted to drop through the floor. Something in me snapped into place, a long overdue decision.

Chapter Twenty-Six

The Knowledge of Alternatives

Our house had no suitcases. I had a dilapidated, round "hat-box traveler" that I took to college, but the lid fell off from all the back-and-forth trips. Maybe my father hid or disposed of the others to make it a little more difficult for Mom if she got any more harebrained ideas about lighting out on her own again. I was in a hurry and didn't have that much to pack anyway, so I found an empty cardboard box and threw in a few clothes and some underwear, my other pair of shoes, a hairbrush.

When Mom saw what I was doing, she regarded me suspiciously, hands on hips. "Just where are you going with that?"

"Away from you," I muttered. Fear snaked up my neck as I dragged the box to the back door. I was twenty, and most of my friends had already left home, but the idea took hold of me that if she figured out what I meant to do, she might fight me physically or enlist Dad's help to block my plan.

Realization seemed to come over her like a spiritual awakening. "But when will I see you again? Will I see you again?" She was suddenly supplicating, her voice rising.

"I'll let you know," I threw over my shoulder as I let the box in my arms push open the screen door. Don, parked in the driveway in his green Mustang, jumped out and opened his trunk. I shoved in my box and threw myself into the front seat.

"Let's go now," I implored. "Before she figures out a way to stop me."

Just like that, it was done. I crashed through a barrier I had spent half my life chasing. I had eluded her pincer grip on my self-esteem and shown her I didn't care what she thought of me. Now I would have to endure no more waking to her black moods, no more fearing the new suspicions and criticisms a day with her would bring.

I would never be the incarnation she wanted, the version of herself she was sure she could have been had men not stood in her way. I believe she felt I had denied my birthright. In her eyes, I was a failure, which made her a twice-over failure. She had tried to make me share her disappointment, but I would no longer suffer it. I wanted out from under the sheer weight of her misery.

My plan had always been to live in the house of my childhood between semesters until I got my teaching degree and could afford my own place. But Don's offer to stay with him for the summer offered me another choice. I didn't know exactly how it all would work, but I had found my way around a university the size of Cumberland; I would find a way to do this, too.

I was keenly aware of being at an inflection point in my life's path, and that it was past time to go. Maya Angelou wrote, "We would all have to be born again, and born with the knowledge of alternatives." My rebirth came when I realized I no longer had to continue playing my mother's toxic game. I had alternatives.

How ironic, I think now. All my life she modeled for me the

kind of strength I needed to stand up to her. From her, I learned how to leave my old life behind.

"Think what you could have done if you had tried." So I showed her what I could do.

Chapter Twenty-Seven

Advanced Problem Solving

When a friend from Cumberland begged me to share a dorm room with her in our junior year, I jumped at the chance, only to realize not long after I moved in that our compatibility was limited to our love of sleeping late. After a particularly nasty dispute during which she called in dormmates to take sides, I phoned my only friend who had an apartment. That evening occasioned the year's most educational event.

"Sure, come on over," Jeff purred, spider-to-the-fly fashion. "My roommates and I are hosting a party tonight."

"Wish I could, but I have homework. I just need a place to concentrate so I can finish it and crash for the night. I have an early class; I'll be out first thing."

"Oh, well, just let yourself in then. Door'll be open." I didn't care if he was annoyed that I wasn't coming for fun and games. I just needed a temporary getaway; I'd figure out later what to do about alternative living arrangements.

When I arrived, the apartment was dark except for a low light coming from the living room, and I groped my way towards it to the wailing of "Louie, Louie" on the record player. An unfamiliar odor wafted toward me, growing stronger as I neared the dozen or so jovial young people lolling on pillows in a circle. The red light was a candle inside a red-painted skull, glowing like the fires of hell from the floor in the middle of their circle.

Jeff waved me over to join him. "He-e-e-y, Peggy! Help yourself to the cherry cola and Fritos!"

Hunger overcame me, and I sat behind him outside the circle, making a dinner of the chips as the party people passed around something. That's when it hit me what kind of bash this was. When the toke came to Jeff, he sucked on it, held in the essence for a few seconds, exhaled, then leaned back with glazed-over eyes and offered it to me. I shook my head and whispered, "Homework. Where'll I be tonight?" He fell to his elbows, threw back his head, and laughed before struggling to his feet. Ignoring the gaiety emanating from the living room, I completed my homework and drifted off to an uneasy sleep.

Mom would never hear about my first—and only—college pot party and probably wouldn't have believed I had not jumped at the chance to smoke "Mary Joo-ana." I knew I had enough to worry about without becoming a pothead.

Short-lease rooms in or around College Park were plentiful for UM students, so negotiating other living arrangements during the school year turned out to be the least of my problems. My first year at UM was such a success that I was sure I had made the right choice to risk everything by moving to College Park. I realize now that I learned as much during breaks as I did in classes.

The summer before my senior year, I wanted to stay as far from Cresaptown as possible, so Don and I agreed to share an apartment in State College, Pennsylvania, where his family lived. The only job Don could find was driving a cab, but my blond hair and bouncy personality landed me a spot at the Dutch Pantry Restaurant, a plum position in area waitstaff circles. The tips were rumored to be good and the work not too onerous; the menu was small and so was the restaurant.

The restaurant styled us as Mennonite girls in blue-and-white printed aprons over white uniforms and white caps that we pinned into our hair. We purchased our own uniforms and the restaurant supplied aprons and caps. I fancied myself spiffy as I skipped out the door to work.

LeeLee, one of the girls I waitressed with that summer of 1968, told me that the commotion I made two weeks into starting work there made quite an impression on her. I never meant to make an impression, let alone a commotion, just a little cash to carry me through my senior year at UM. I definitely never counted on getting a civics lesson from a temporary waitress job.

When I strolled into the restaurant one Monday, LeeLee pulled me aside. "Did you hear about the new requirement?" she whispered anxiously. "Frank is making us wear girdles starting next week!" Frank was our manager, and the waitresses agreed with LeeLee that he was "constipated," meaning he had a sour disposition.

A familiar resentment flooded my brain. Once again I was encountering someone with a deep need to lasso others into their blinkered worldview. A memory from high school stirred when I had crossed swords with the principal who refused to allow one of my friends, a new mother, to return and complete her graduation credits. As I considered Frank's new regulation, I began to wonder if these scenes signaled more such battles to come.

I thought for a minute. "How'll he force us? He doesn't know what we have on under these uniforms."

LeeLee's round face lit up. "I guess you're right. We could just lie." The plan might have worked, but she blabbed it to everyone, and it got back to Frank by way of Jean, another Dutch Pantry waitress with designs on rising to management.

The first day the new edict went into effect, Frank ordered me into his office and, towering over me, began the interrogation. "Are you wearing your girdle?"

I nodded and forced a smile. "Sure, Frank, sure I am."

He eyed my skinny butt. "Jean will go with you to the restroom to check."

I did a quick calculus. Was keeping my job worth letting a restaurant tell me what to wear under my uniform? Teeth clenched, hands on hips, I took my stand. "No. Jean won't. My underwear is my own business, not hers—and certainly not yours."

"Get a girdle on or you're fired!" he barked.

"Forget it; I quit." Other waitresses had gathered to watch the scene, and mouths flew open as I ripped off my blue-and-white apron and threw it at his feet. The little white hat followed.

I was proud of myself for standing up to an adult bully, just as I had a teenage one at Holy Rosary. At the time, I thought I was coming out from the shadow of my mother, becoming my own person. Now I know I was becoming more like her, emulating defiant behavior to masculine authority I had seen modeled all my life.

Within weeks, LeeLee called, excited with the news. Frank was gone. The girdle requirement was not a Dutch Pantry policy, but Frank's whim, and Jean, sensing a career-making opportunity, snitched to the chain's headquarters.

The company was offering a "please-don't-sue-us" payment to anyone who had been forced to quit over Frank's girdle requirement. The windfall was welcome, but I felt I had also been gifted something more valuable: a seminar on the rights of individuals in a free society. Later that summer, the whole country got a course on the same topic at the Democratic National Convention in Chicago.

No one I knew in State College ever heard what happened to Frank, and I wonder if he learned anything at all from being fired for his fixation on girdled butts. I like to think he ended up selling women's unmentionables.

I arrived in State College during Penn State's glory days, before a dark curtain of scandal fell. Football was king and some called head coach Joe Paterno the Pope of Penn State. Don's family—his widowed mom Dorothy, his brother Sid, and sisters Laura and Audrey—lived in town. Laura was an unmarried nurse, but Audrey had a large family with her husband, an assistant football coach at the university. Naturally, all of them were rabid Nittany Lion fans. The first time Don and I attended a game, the animalistic roar that arose from the stands when the team took the field stunned me, but before long, I became as zealous as they were, a convert to their raucous football religion.

When I was not focused on football, I got to know—and fall in love with—Don's family. Don and Sid had long ago worked out comedy routines centered around growing up with their domineering dad and would reenact them just to crack each other up. They seemed happiest when making each other laugh.

Dorothy bought Sid's cigarettes, cooked him mouthwatering chicken paprikash, and waited for him to meet a girl who would motivate him to return to Penn State and complete the couple of courses he needed to finish his theatre degree. I was convinced that was never going to happen. Sid once bragged to me, "My ambition is to smoke cigs and piss on the flowers." Still, Dorothy laughed at all his jokes, even those at her expense.

One Mother's Day morning, Sid brought a greeting card to the apartment his mom shared with Laura. As he walked past Dorothy's bedroom, he glanced in, and seeing her sleeping, he continued down the hall to the kitchen where Laura was reading the newspaper at the table.

Dropping down in a chair, he idly inquired, "Mom sleeping?"

"No, she's dead" Laura deadpanned.

Sid threw the card in the air. "Well, that's thirty-five cents down the drain."

As Laura and Sid rocked the kitchen with laughter, Dorothy woke and padded down the hall rubbing her eyes to learn the cause of the commotion. When she heard the joke, she laughed so hard she had to sit down and dab her eyes with her handkerchief.

Their whole family vibrated with optimism and good humor, and Don and Sid were an ongoing improv show. This was a marked contrast from the moody, volatile environment I had grown up with, and I loved being part of it and the entire Penn State community. Don's mother was the most nurturing person I've ever known, the mother I had always wanted, and I believe she loved me like a daughter. In all the time I knew her, I never saw her angry. Best of all, her eyes always lit up when she saw me.

Don and I couldn't afford to eat out, so during Spring Break, when he suddenly said, "Let's drive down to Warner's for dinner," I knew something was up. If a local boy wanted to impress his date, he'd take her to Warner's German Restaurant, Cresaptown's only dining establishment, buy a crock of Mateus Rosé, and order wiener schnitzel and Bee Sting Cake. We certainly couldn't afford all that, and neither of us drank anyway, but pizza and Cokes were indulgence enough. We had discussed marriage, and graduation was only weeks away, so I anticipated what was coming. As he pulled the small box from his pocket and opened it, I suddenly couldn't breathe.

Diamonds from his mom's wedding set sparkled from a brand-new gold setting. He said nothing at all, just sat there smiling awkwardly with the ring still in the box in his hand.

"Is that what I think it is?"

"Well, what else would it be?"

My follow-up question should have been, "Is this really what we both want?" Instead, I smiled and held out my left hand so Don could slip the ring on my finger. I was that eager to have a recognized place in Don's family. As Don's wife, I would be daughter-in-law and sister-in-law, and all the rest would work out.

Don and I agreed that after we married, he would find a way to return to PSU's good graces and obtain his accounting degree. We also concurred that children were not in the picture. His dad had been a brutish bully, and neither of us had growing-up images of a happy family life. Personally, I had always viewed kids as superfluous to my vision of a successful future, and Don shared my opinion.

Dorothy, overjoyed, confided, "If it weren't for you, Peggy, I don't know what would have become of Don." She loved him, and I think she loved me for saving him. My mother-in-law and I formed a close bond, and the parents of my tortured childhood slid quietly away in my memory. My alienation from my parents had orphaned me, and now I was adopted by a loving family.

Not long after my engagement, I answered the phone in State College and heard a familiar voice. "Hello, Peggy. Remember me?" Memories flooded back of the dark-eyed charmer who had three years earlier proposed that we flee across the state line to West Virginia and marry. I wondered why he had called; I had "Dear Johned" him within six months of his deployment in Japan.

"Richard, so good to hear from you," I lied. "But I should tell you I'm engaged."

"So your mom said." His voice was ice-edged. He had called the Cresaptown house, and Mom gave him my number. "I hope it's what you want."

I began babbling excitedly about my upcoming graduation and my teaching plans, until he suddenly interrupted, "You're different," he observed in the same cold tone. "You sound—not like I remember."

So much had happened to me between his proposal and Don's that I apparently even sounded different. Certainly, I had grown more self-assured, and now that I would possess the door-opening power of a degree, I was not the biddable little girl Richard thought could be swept off her feet. If my voice was different, it was because I was moving fast toward transforming myself into the person I wanted to be. Now I was confident that marriage to Don was really what I wanted. Or was it?

When I entered UM as a sophomore, I had such a high opinion of myself for managing my getaway that I thought I just might take the place by storm and become the straight-A student my mother was sure I could be. One year in, UM had taken me by the ear and spun me around until I no longer knew what to expect. Courses like psychology, Shakespeare, biographical writing, and German captivated me. Even an 8:00 a.m. start time didn't deter me from making every class on time and soaking up every second. But I never could have predicted what I would learn in the final semester of my senior year.

UM couldn't have been the only major university in those days that was clueless on how to prepare schoolteachers, but I've always felt they should have known it would be a mistake to wait until a student's last semester in college to put them in front of a public-school classroom. That spring, I "shadowed" a teacher and was permitted to do tasks like taking attendance and answering students' questions about assignments. I also babysat the class if the teacher had to dash out for a few minutes.

Question: How does a 5-foot-4-inch skinny, blond twenty-year-old student teacher stem the rising tide of the pandemonium of thirty-five students laughing and yelling when the teacher leaves the room?

Answer: She doesn't.

When the teacher dashed back in, the tide went out again just like that. The students all knew I had no authority over them and would be gone in two weeks.

Six weeks of practice teaching at Wheaton High School in Silver Spring, Maryland, came next. My supervising teacher was a single, fortyish dark-haired woman who used to be pretty and made sure I knew she had once been an airline stewardess. Her favorite pastime seemed to be flirting in the hallway with male teachers (married and unmarried) and laughing in the back of the room with the female students while I was laboring through my delivery of a carefully prepared lesson. "You need to learn how to connect more with the students," she sniffed. "Your lesson plans are fine, but you don't hold their attention." *I wonder why?*

Midway through my final semester, I was sure I didn't want to be a teacher.

In June of 1969, Cindy graduated from high school, UM awarded me a Bachelor of Arts with Honors in English and Secondary Education, and Don and I married in the Cresaptown Methodist Church. I was afraid if Dad gave me away, Mom would have a meltdown during the ceremony, so I asked Fred to do the honors. The guilt that hit me later when I realized how I had hurt Dad could not compare with his pain when I took his rightful role away from him. He didn't show up at the wedding.

My mother was clearly unimpressed by my education degree, but a teaching certificate allayed the fear she had instilled in me of being trapped by marriage and left without options. I was confident that if things fell apart between Don and me, I could support myself. I wrapped in tissue my dream of becoming a writer, laid it away, and turned to the business of earning a living.

Chapter Twenty-Eight

Hard Lessons

In the years after I left college, the strength of will I inherited from my parents was tested in new ways. My tuition-remission agreement with Maryland required me to teach in the state for a minimum of two years, but student teaching in Silver Springs had not only left me with doubts about a teaching career but also a horror of big-city schools. Jobs were certainly more plentiful there because students were unruly, hard to motivate, and much more worldly than I was at their age. One of the tall troublemakers liked to sidle up to the desk, supposedly with a question, but really to stare down my blouse.

One of the few high-performing students, a soft-spoken ninth grader named Ben, suddenly disappeared from class.

"Ben's been out since last week," I mused aloud as I took roll.

"Oh, he won't be back this year," chirped a know-it-all girl from the front row. Everyone else looked down and blushed or stared at her disdainfully.

"Why not?"

"He got arrested." She mouthed, "Marijuana."

I had other reasons to look for work outside the Metro area besides my nightmares of fighting through what I was sure would be two drug-and-crime-riddled years in an inner-city Baltimore classroom. Penn State had notified Don that to get back into a degree program, he'd have to make A or B grades in a year's worth of PSU coursework, which he could take at branch campuses or by correspondence—the kind where you snail-mailed your professor long, handwritten assignments and wondered how much of them he read. Cumberland was commuting distance from the Altoona, Pennsylvania, branch campus, and Don found work as a low-paid clerk at a Cumberland PPG paint store. I was suddenly under pressure to find a teaching job in Allegany County.

A snag quickly surfaced. Allegany County had no open English teaching positions. After a frantic search, I managed to find a middle-school English teaching position within driving distance of Cumberland. Accident, a small town in Garrett County, was at the highest elevation in Maryland and an hour's drive from Cumberland on two-lane roads—unless it snowed.

The State of Maryland anointed me a teacher, but kid behavior always bewildered me. Student teaching showed me I had no idea how to relate to them, let alone manage a classroom of them, but I was determined to get tuition remission. I sweated through a year of teaching squirmy middle schoolers English and—surprise!—two sections of social studies. Lucky for me, the county called a record number of snow days during the worst winter in a hundred years. By spring, I had chest pains that earned me a week-long hospital stay and a battery of testing. The diagnosis? Anxiety.

As usual, Mom added to my burden. In one phone call, she jeered. "Why are you working at that worthless, do-nothing job anyway? You could have gotten a degree in anything you want. You could do anything, be anything. Why have you never tried living up to your potential?"

I reached for the sharpest barb I could think of, one sure to wound her. "Oh, and you have?" And I hung up.

Dad called me back, and I could hear her raving in the background as he exclaimed, "What did you say to her?" He was clearly anguished I had hurt her feelings. "Take it back, Peggy Dale," he pleaded. "She's your mother!"

Now I marvel that after all she had done to him and to his children, he defended her. So often I asked myself what gave him such depths of compassion to forgive his parents, to forgive his wife, to forgive me, over and over again? Could someone else have taught it to him, perhaps a poor fisherman by the river who took pity on starving strangers?

Dad knew I would someday regret despising her for all the injuries she had inflicted on me, and though he didn't know the whole story, he was right, as usual. As I began to see the pattern of her life, respect for the strength that allowed her to survive it all—her painful childhood, the loss of her dream of freedom, even her family sending her to Sykesville—restored some of my regard for her. "Hurt people hurt people," the saying goes. Yet even when I understood how the past had scarred her, forgiveness would be longer coming, after she could no longer hurt me with an unexpected barb or sharp look.

The following year I managed to land a teaching position in Cumberland, but those two years of school teaching convinced me I wasn't cut out for that kind of work. I would have to find another livelihood.

Don began Penn State's correspondence courses and drove through a record-snowfall winter to in-person classes at Altoona's branch campus. Amazed at this burst of determination after years of nonchalant interest in his future, I began to feel he just might turn out to be as ambitious as me. Maybe—just maybe—this could work after all.

❧

My mother began learning the essential skill of stifling her criticism of me, and a wary warmth took shape between us. I hadn't felt anything for her but fear and anger since I was small in that long-ago time when I viewed her as my protective goddess. I could tolerate her now in small doses, and anyway, I had my own place to retreat to if she got snarky. Dad was always working, as usual, so I saw him even less. I never realized the change that had come over him until one night at Ingrid's house.

Though hard work and sheer strength of will that still takes my breath away, Dad came back from Mom-induced near-bankruptcy and had gradually begun buying up small rental houses. He paid cash for one not far from Cresaptown in the Fairgo. When Bobby was on tour in Alaska, Dad allowed Bobby's wife and kids to live there rent-free. That didn't sound like the Dad I had grown up thinking a miser, but he had a soft heart for Ingrid. Maybe he saw her working hard to raise Bobby's kids while Bobby toiled in faraway places with the Navy.

Sometimes Ingrid announced a Taco Night, and the whole family flocked to her Fairgo house for a convivial evening of homemade tacos, ice cream, and poker. Don and I looked forward to those evenings as a break from our grind. Even Fred and his first wife, Phyllis, still childless then, would occasionally drive in from Annapolis for a Taco Night. Don and I had no other social life. I had lost touch with all my local friends, and a big night out for us was springing for an all-you-can-eat fried-clam dinner at Howard Johnson's Restaurant in La Vale, a short drive from our third-story walk-up in downtown Cumberland.

Dad never played cards, but I think he looked forward to those nights as much as we did. He had few other diversions. He was not an avid reader but never missed an episode of *Gunsmoke* and was captivated by *Saturday Night Wrestling*.

Once when Fred was in town, I commented, "Last week, I went upstairs to ask Dad something, and he was watching wrestling—carrying on like it was all real. I should tell him that all those shows are staged."

"Don't say that to him!" Fred exclaimed. "It might hurt his feelings. He likes believing it's real sports. Saying it's fake might ruin it for him."

At the time, my father's veneration of *Gunsmoke*'s Marshall Dillon was as puzzling to me as his worship of wrestling strongmen. Now I believe Dad revered he-men, guys like Alan Ladd who walked tall even if they were short—men like he perhaps envisioned himself.

On Taco Nights, as the smell of fresh-fried taco shells and spicy hamburger filling wafted through the small house, Ingrid would treat Dad like royalty. "Don't get up, Dad. How many tacos do you want?" She always served him or had one of her kids bring in his dinner and ice cream as he beamed.

After card games and ice cream one evening, Mom, Fred's wife, and I helped Ingrid clean up the dining room and dishes as the men joined Dad in the living room. The conversation turned to sports, then segued to showing off pushups. Fred attempted some, then the older boys. Suddenly, Dad dropped to the floor and managed a couple himself, his face red with the effort, but when he attempted a one-handed pushup, he crumpled to the carpet.

Embarrassed but unhurt, he seemed to see for the first time he was not able to power through a feat he had done so often when he was younger. I saw him deflate before my eyes, no longer the fearful, towering presence he had once been in my life. He was now an old, weak codger whom few sought out or wanted around. The first stirring of pity for him arose in me, but I never followed up on it, never tried to know who he really was. I always thought there would be time.

As I mulled over my own future, I calculated that higher education degrees were my ticket out of public-school teaching. When I was assigned two sections of reading, I had begun taking courses at Frostburg State in how to teach it. By the time we landed in State College, a master's degree in reading was doable in the two years it took for Don to complete his business degree. My plan worked. Don graduated and got a job with a prestigious Philadelphia accounting firm, and with a 4.0 grade point average on my record and a killer interview in a spring-green Ladybug suit, I managed to land an entry-level training-specialist position in a consulting firm in the Philadelphia suburb of Bala Cynwyd. I found my work absorbing, but Don soon knew he hated being a public accountant. One day he admitted, "My hand always shakes when I write numbers at work."

"Why do you think it happens?" He just shrugged.

When we weren't in State College with Sid, Don didn't try to be funny. There were days-long silent periods when he appeared depressed, but I could never draw him out to talk about his thoughts and fears. He could be affectionate, sometimes sketching cartoons of us as Little Bear and Big Bear, but our relationship was virtually sexless. Don never seemed to be in the mood for more than cuddling, and nothing I did seemed to arouse him. If I had known about homosexuals back then, I would have pegged him as a closeted gay man. A closer-to-home truth was that he and I simply had mismatched sex drives. Our marriage was failing.

My mind went back to all the stop signs I had run right through during our first summer living together in Bedford. I soon learned that the "job" taking care of his mother's house was her way of giving him a free place to live, and though he had no ambition to hunt for work, I was hired as a desk clerk at the New Bedford Motor Hotel after a one-day search. He was intelligent but had let a Penn State education slip through his hands and was only interested in returning because he knew I wanted him to. Worst of all, our sex that summer was more like a brief match-flame than fireworks and less frequent than a Bedford May snow. I had accepted the ring, but as all my alarm bells continued to ring, I had tried to give it back.

"You know it's never going to work, Don," I murmured gently. "Better to end this now."

"Oh, now you back out?" His voice rose. "My whole family is looking forward to this wedding." And the clincher. "It would kill Mom!"

Dorothy's disappointment wasn't the only reason I had set aside my misgivings. It was the devil's bargain I struck to escape my mother's control. I had also been embraced by his exuberant family, and I loved his mom like the mother I never had. I was twenty-three then, old enough to know better but not mature enough to grasp the full import of my commitment.

After four years of marriage, I began to see that though I was fond of Don and proud of his recent accomplishments, none of it was going to be enough. As I was trying to figure how to extricate myself from the mess I had made, the greatest trauma of my life captured my attention.

Chapter Twenty-Nine

Legacies

You've probably heard woo-woo stories like this before, but it happened to me the same way. An urgent voice calling, "Peggy, Peggy!" shook me out of sleep one morning. It seemed like a dream; the voice faded away as my eyes opened. I couldn't identify whose voice it was, but it felt like I should know. Fred's call came a couple hours later.

For years after my father's death when people asked how he died, I would say, "My mother killed him," and I believed it. I would describe how she treated him, especially at the end after his first heart attack as he frantically tried to keep some part of his business going. I described the contempt she showed him whenever he was forced to come into the kitchen for a meal. He would pull out a kitchen chair and sit down heavily, fold his arms in front of him on the table, and lay face down on them.

"Spates isn't really that tired," she once carped to me. "He's just playing it up for attention."

All my life my mother had never given much thought to cooking, and her fare never improved over the years. Dad once described to Fred a meal of beans and burnt hot dogs, which sounded even worse than what I remembered. His ex-wife probably contributed to his decline, but it was Dad's determination born of deprivation that killed him. Thanks to FDR's Social Security program and Dad's savings and rental-house income, he could have retired, but that was not Dad. He had to strive as hard as he always had, be the provider and strongman protector he had always been. He had been moving around eighty-pound putty cans in the shop when the sharp pains began. With Cindy's help, he just made it to the house to lie down before gasping his last breath. It had taken three heart attacks to fell my father. He was sixty-one.

His high blood pressure, undiagnosed for years, was a legacy of his own lineage that Fred and I would also inherit. How often had I seen him come in from an especially frustrating day in the shop, his face red and veins in his temples bulging? But I did not witness the incident that caused his first heart attack.

A couple years before he died, Dad and his worker, Ed, were preparing to unload sheets of glass, tipping the wooden crate forward slightly to remove the metal rollers underneath. They had leaned it too much, and the crate began to fall forward. Ed released his hold on the box, quickly stepping back out of the way. But Dad, foreseeing sheets of shattered glass and weeks of lost profit, braced against the 800-pound weight yelling, "Ed! Ed! Help me!" They managed to get the crate righted before all the glass fell, but the effort sent Dad to the hospital. A doctor called his attack a "wake-up call" and prescribed blood pressure medication and a vacation. After a brief visit to his sister's in Florida, Dad was back at work, being who he had always been.

His second attack less than two years later hit him harder. I went to see him in the ICU as he lay in bed, eyes wild and distraught, hands moving about nervously beside him, breaths quick and shallow.

Sitting beside his bed, I whispered, "Pop, I'm here."

He glanced toward me, his eyes not really focusing. “Peggy Dale, I can’t stop working.”

I patted his hand to calm him, an act I had never done in my twenty-three years. “Rest, Dad,” I comforted him quietly, “You can rest a while now.”

He closed his eyes, and his hands stopped moving. His breathing slowed. I sat with him for a while to make sure he was asleep before I left. That small, reassuring act was all it took to quiet him, to comfort his wounded spirit. Maybe it sent him back to when he was very young. Perhaps he knew then I loved him, that I would have been the daughter he needed if Mom had not set up the barrier between us.

After that second attack, I found out he hadn’t been taking his blood pressure medication. In my naiveté and ignorance, I called his doctor demanding that he do something. He gave me the impression this was an often-repeated conversation with his patients’ family members.

“I can’t make Spates take that medicine” he explained gently. “It often dampens sexual drive with older men like him.” The doctor couldn’t make my father do what he needed to do to stay alive; only my father could make that decision. After I left home, Bobby had mentioned to me that Dad had a girlfriend named Florence who lived in South Cumberland, so I wasn’t that surprised about the sexual comment, only that my father seemed to have decided that if he couldn’t be the vital man he had always been, he might as well die. Maybe he felt he had already lost too much. Dad’s fatal heart attack came six months after he left the ICU.

Don and I drove in from Pennsylvania, but Mom and I went alone to the George Funeral Home on Greene Street. A depressing old place with age-darkened stained-glass windows, its walls seemed to sag from the weight of decades of weeping mourners. White-haired, lugubrious Mr. George had seen a lot of the grief-stricken, and I'm sure he thought he knew how to offer the comfort each needed.

He ushered us into a viewing room near the main entrance, and Mom and I inched toward the casket, our arms around each other, bracing for the sight. When she saw Dad lying there amid white satin, her hand flew to her mouth, and she shuddered and leaned heavily on me.

She whimpered, "Oh, Spates, Spates, we were young together!"

I heard in her lament all my parents' promises and hope, loss and regret. They stood before me young, as if I saw their image in a new mirror. For that brief moment, I understood them, and I mourned with her all they had lost. Then I was back with Mom in the dim light of the funeral parlor.

I propped up my wilting mother and whispered, "Mom, he is not here. He's not here." I said it to remind myself as much as to calm her.

Mr. George approached and reached out to lay a comforting hand on my mother's shoulder, but I shot him a murderous look, and he backed away, leaving us alone. I wanted no one around to witness what might be one of her dramatic scenes. I kept saying quietly, fiercely, over and over, "He is not here. He is not here."

Finally, a calm came over her. "I know, Margaret, I know," she whispered.

We stood gazing at the ashen form, and I sensed something looked wrong. Then it hit me; it was his hands. Always lined and discolored from his work staining wood window frames and re-silvering mirrors, Dad's hands were pale and unblemished;

they were clean for the first time in my memory. I tried not to think how the funeral home got them that way.

For weeks after he died, Cindy had dreams with cathartic metaphors I envied. After the funeral as we sat in the kitchen of the Cresaptown house, reminiscing about our childhood, she confided, "I've been dreaming about Dad." I rubbed my arms, suddenly cold.

"He came dragging himself into the kitchen, walking slow and heavy. You know, the way he always did when he was exhausted?" I nodded, seeing the scene clearly. "Then he sat here at this table." She gestured toward the chair where he always sat. "He rested his arms on the table and slumped over them like he used to do." She looked over at the back door. "In the dream, I came through that door and walked past him into the living room without speaking. Then I realized that he couldn't be there, and I rushed back to speak to him, but he was gone."

I took her hand. "It's okay, Cindy."

"No, there's more." Her eyes were wide and moist. "Recently when I dream that I come in and see him there, I stop and put my arms around him and hug him, and I say, 'It will be okay, Pop.' And he nods and pats my arm and says, 'I know, Cindy, I know.' Then I walk into the living room, and again I remember and run back, and he's no longer there. But here's the thing. I don't feel so bad anymore."

I nodded. "You got to say goodbye."

I had no such comforting visions. My sleep was brief and troubled, and I woke from dreams of dark rooms and of watching funerals of strangers. Before Dad was buried, I wrote an epitaph for his gravestone:

Father, by the light that from your window fell,
We strive to keep your trust: to labor well.

"Tell me more about Florence," I later entreated Bobby, who was more than willing to share what Dad had confided in him, but I was shocked at what I learned.

"Dad began dating a year or so after his divorce from Mom. One lady was a waitress in Cumberland; he said she made the best fried chicken." Thinking back to Mom's cooking, I could imagine how much he valued a good meal.

"He was also friends with a retired Baptist minister and his wife, Florence. The guy was in a wheelchair, and one evening, he confessed to Dad that his wife had needs he could no longer meet. He appealed to Dad to 'be a comfort to her.' So, Dad dropped by every so often to 'comfort' Flo and have a homecooked meal."

Their liaisons continued after we moved back from Jacksonville, and Dad was still seeing her until he became too ill, a span of perhaps five years.

After Flo's husband died, Dad wanted to marry her, but she rebuffed his proposal. Maybe she was not prepared for the baggage that marrying Spates would entail, and who could blame her? One day soon after Dad's funeral, Fred and I visited her at her South Cumberland home. She seemed a nice enough gray-haired lady, around Dad's age. Her house reminded me of my friend Gail's, small but very orderly, cool, and clean. She was keen to show us around, and when she ushered us into her bedroom and noticed a small wrinkle in her white chenille bedspread, she smoothed it immediately and fluffed the spotless, ruffled pillow shams.

Flo implored me to keep in touch, but I was not inclined

to be charitable. After our visit, I concluded that she refused to marry Dad because she didn't want to disturb her comfortable, well-ordered life. I figured that if she loved him, she would have done it anyway. Knowing she refused to be Dad's second chance at happiness, I couldn't bear to be around her. I lived to regret that decision, not because I wanted to get to know her, but because it would have been an opportunity to learn more about Dad.

Dad's estate was to be divided equally among his four children. We knew Dad was tight; he was family-famous for it. Still, we were still surprised to learn how much was there for us to split. In today's currency, Dad was nearly a millionaire, and each of his children would inherit a quarter of that. We were also astounded that Dad's frugality had coexisted with startling generosity. When he died, he owned nine small houses, all except two earning rental income. Mom and Cindy lived in one of them, and Dad's longtime worker Ed lived in the other. I don't think Mom knew exactly what Dad owned or how much he was worth. He probably wanted her well clear of his finances. I'm not even sure she knew about Dad's arrangement with Ed, but he had told his sons.

Dad willed Ed the rental house he had been living in, and after the estate was probated, Fred and Bobby dropped by to give him the deed. Bobby was incredulous at Ed's reaction. "He didn't even invite us in or thank us, just took the deed and nodded before going back in the house." I don't think Dad would have cared. Ed wasn't the best worker, but Dad must have felt his loyalty was worth a lot to him.

At learning Dad had left her nothing, Mom was crestfallen and angry, but we knew what he wanted: that we should support her as he had done. After Jacksonville, Mom never earned a steady income, despite eventually achieving two college degrees. But to me, Dad left something more valuable, something that wasn't in the will. I wrote Suzanne, "Dad left letters, a diary, and I found out things I'll never fully understand. I've never experienced anything like finding out that I had something after I lost it. And yet, in a way, it's consoling. I did have a father, just like everyone else. I just never knew it."

In my letter, I sounded heartened by what I found, but as with many of my missives to Suzanne, my words masked anguished emotions. All those early years and even into adulthood, I was unable to form any parental bond with my dad. My childhood fear of showing him affection had persisted; I always felt about him the way Mom had worked so hard to make me feel. *Filthy old man.*

Unconsciously, I always knew he loved me despite all my slights, but somehow, it came through clear enough only after he died, when it was too late to tell him I loved him, too. I blamed myself for not figuring out what was going on, and guilt haunted me. So many questions came to me when sleep would not. Each of my siblings managed to form a positive relationship with Dad. Why hadn't I? I had no respect for Mom's opinions. Why had I embraced her hatred of Dad? Would self-absolution ever come?

By the time Dad died in 1971, the close correspondence between Suzanne and me was also dying. My letter informing her of Dad's death was among the last. We lost touch until I found her on Facebook many years later. After I left Tallahassee, we never met in person again.

Bobby came all the way back from his posting in Morocco for the funeral. Dad's four children stood together in our father's shop, the glass shop he and his father designed and built and slaved in so many years.

Bobby declared, "Any minute now, he'll come in and say, 'Okay, it's all over. I've got to get back to work now.'" We all admitted we'd been thinking the same thing.

Instead, we had to realize that we owned that shop, and not Dad. We owned it, and it all seemed so silly. That place should have ceased to exist when he died.

More jarring events followed in the years after Dad's death. The four of us inherited properties he spent his life accumulating, and after agreeing we had to sell them off, the only buyer who came forward for the Art Glass Company's building and stock was his old competitor, Jimmie Kamauf. Art Glass really did cease to exist then; it became the Reliable Glass Company.

"He's rolling over in his grave," Bobby mourned, but what else could we do? Dad's ghost must have haunted the place because in 1988, an inexplicable fire burned the building to the ground.

Bobby, Fred, Cindy, and I shared a sudden cash windfall from Dad's estate. I don't know how Bobby and Fred used theirs, probably for investments to benefit their families. But Cindy and I were each considering a different kind of investment, one that would bring about profound changes in both our lives.

Chapter Thirty

Highest Education

A year after the funeral, Cindy flabbergasted us all by eloping with a preppy-looking local boy named Ted. Her new husband had just begun an entry-level job with Martin Marietta Corporation in Orlando, courtesy of his uncle, a top executive there. Martin Marietta had recently completed work on Disney's monorail and was making a name in the corporate world with government space and missile contracts, so Ted had a bright future. But Mom was vexed.

"Did you know about this?" she demanded.

"You lived with her," I laughed. "Didn't you know what she was going to do? She sure didn't tell me." I don't think Cindy let anyone in the family in on her plans, but Mom didn't believe me. The wasp's nest was now officially empty.

Don's Philadelphia job faded away after a year. From colleagues, he learned that each year, big accounting firms hired young graduates from universities like PSU, worked them like blue-collar slaves for a year, then fired most of them, keeping only the most ambitious. Don may have been a victim of 1970s corporate policy, but he had made it clear to me how much he hated his job. I felt he wasn't trying very hard.

"I think I'll drive out to California," he announced. "I've

heard it's always sunny out there."

"Well, I'm staying here," I replied flatly. Don merely shrugged. He offered no protest when I declared I wanted to make our split official, and since he made no claim on Dad's inheritance, our divorce was amicable—at first.

For a year, we fell into an odd post-divorce friendship. I occasionally dated other guys, but he was my most frequent companion; I even visited him in California when he decided to move there permanently. His sister Audrey always laughed whenever I showed up with him at football games and family dinners. "You and Don were always the oddest married people," she grinned. "Now you're the strangest divorced couple." Perhaps our mismatch as marriage partners had been evident to everyone except me.

Don lacked the ambition I thought he should have, but I possessed enough for two. My title in my Bala Cynwyd job was Training Specialist, and I wanted to be the best one I could be (Mom's influence) so I could win a higher-paying job (Dad's impact). My company's contract was to train military pilots to use a computer-aided surveillance system, but its training approach was giving them user manuals I wrote. I felt there had to be a better way to prepare them, but I had no idea what it was.

One phrase that was all the rage in the corporate training literature was "instructional design." "A systematic strategy," they crowed. "Revolutionize your training" and "Boost corporate productivity," they promised. I decided that my inheritance from Dad would fund my next ambition, a PhD in instructional design from PSU. When Education Professor Keith Hall invited me to be his graduate assistant and prototype doctoral student for a new ID degree he was creating, everything seemed to be falling into place.

The first time I sauntered into Dr. Hall's Computer-assisted Instruction Lab, I felt I had entered a portal to the future—my own. Eight large screens the size of thirty-inch TVs—terminals they called them—were crammed into the small room, all connected by thick cables to an IBM 1500 mainframe computer that filled most of an adjoining room. At each terminal sat a grade-school student, eyes glued to the screen, holding a light pen in one hand and tapping on a keyboard with the other as drill-and-practice multiplication problems flashed on the screen. Cutting-edge technology, but what did it have to do with instructional design in corporate training?

Even more disappointing, Dr. Hall had no firm ID curriculum in mind except that half my courses should be in educational leadership and half in computer science. After I took PL1 and Fortran programming languages and saw the next course was Computer Operating System Design, I was done.

In an assignment that ironically proved useful in a different way than Dr. Hall intended, he had me peruse brochures from ID graduate programs around the country and complete a matrix of their courses, faculty, and degrees. I chose the one that stood out—at Florida State University's College of Education in Tallahassee, a five-hour drive from Orlando where Cindy and Ted lived—and applied to it. The uncommonly understanding Dr. Hall wrote me a glowing recommendation. FSU accepted me, and I lit out for Florida to spend the summer with Cindy and her husband and prepare for my next big venture.

Don wrote me from California, filling his letters with Big Bear-Little Bear cartoons. He invited himself to visit me in Orlando, and we were in the airport when he proposed for the second time.

As if I would make that mistake again!

"Don, you know we were miserable when we were married." I sighed. "Why not go on as we are?"

He stopped me on the landing of an empty stairwell, and taking my arms, pulled me close. "It would be different now," he pleaded. "I am different. I know what love is now." And he kissed me.

I was touched but unpersuaded. "Don, I'm sorry, but I'm never going to change my mind. It's just not going to happen."

He continued to write, visit, and propose, once even making sexual overtures. But Jay had taught me what sexual fireworks were, and Don wasn't capable of it. Who knows how long we might have played the Friends-with-Scant-Benefits game if I hadn't found my first semester at FSU so intensely demanding that I began worrying I had made the wrong move, that I wasn't smart enough to excel in this program? The neck-tightening tension I had felt as a teenager (*I'll never be good enough!*) visited once more and would not leave.

At the end of the semester—before I learned that I made straight A's—my high school chum Sally called from Virginia, and I blubbered out my worries to her. She dismissed them with her usual matter-of-fact confidence. "Hey, I'll come down; we'll stay with your sister in Orlando, hit some bars, find some cute guys. By Christmas, you'll be fine."

Cindy recommended a jumping joint in downtown Orlando: Rosie O'Grady's Good-time Emporium, a "meet-market" bar for locals and tourists. It boasted a barbershop quartet and a "Red Hot Mama" who wore theatrical make-up, sported a feather boa around her ample shoulders, and belted show tunes from her perch on a steep spiral staircase. At about 9:00 p.m., we joined a throng that descended on Rosie's. It was Nickel-Beer Night. I was sipping White Russians and scanning the crowd for possibilities. An olive-skinned cutie slouched against the bar across the crowded room talking with two other guys, and I pointed him out to Sally. "Good choice," she nodded. "Go for it." But I was suddenly shy.

Sally directed, "Okay, Peggy. Watch and learn." The guys were also sweeping the crowd for anything interesting, and when Sally, herself a head turner, caught the target's eye and raised her glass in a wordless toast, his eyes nearly popped out. The three of them quickly joined us.

The cutie, named Raoul, shouted introductions over the din. "This is Bob and Harry. We drove up from Miami for the Tangerine Bowl this weekend. We're crashing at his house." Harry raised the beer stein in his hand. It didn't take long for me to figure out that none of these guys was much of a conversationalist. I could have sat around the FSU Student Union for a few hours and had a better time. Bored, I ordered another White Russian and prepared to get thoroughly wasted.

Then I noticed a tall, grinning fellow with a full scraggly beard and neck-length blond hair pushing his way through the crowd balancing fistfuls of beer mugs. Under his denim jacket was a silk shirt unbuttoned halfway down to his belt to reveal an expanse of curly blond chest hair and several gold chains. *Well now, doesn't this look like a good time?*

"Bill! Where've you been, man?" Raoul grabbed one of the beers.

After beers were dispersed, Bill announced to the group, "Well, I'm going up there," and jerked a thumb behind us toward the staircase leading to the restrooms (clearly an ill-advised design choice for a bar). "Ask me why I'm going up there."

I eyed him, intrigued. "Okay, Bill, why are you going up

there?"

"Because it's there." Hands on hips, he assumed an intrepid-mountain-climber stance. It was probably the White Russians, but I thought it the cleverest quip I'd ever heard.

When he returned and we began talking, I was quickly swept into the current of his blue eyes. Despite his hippie appearance, Bill told me he was a high school industrial arts teacher in Miami. His thinning hair made him look older than me, but at twenty-five, he was nearly three years my junior.

We closed down Rosie's at 2:00 a.m., and none of us should have been behind a wheel, but Raoul and Bill persuaded Sally and me to give them a ride to Harry's place in an Orlando suburb. Despite Bill's magnetism and his pleas when we got there, I made it clear I had no intention of letting all those White Russians talk me into a sleepover with an out-of-town guy I had just met, even though the way he kissed when we got there was seductive in a way that was new to me. *What about this guy that makes me feel relaxed and excited at the same time?*

Bill begged, "At least give me your number so I can call you." *What a line!* I was floored when the phone rang for me at Cindy's house the next day.

"Come to Miami," he coaxed. "I'll send you an Air Southern ticket."

The few days Bill and I spent together just after Christmas offered magic that had little to do with the bright holiday decorations adorning every Miami street and neighborhood. We bicycled through the fragrance of hanging orchids at the Fairchild Gardens, window-shopped on the Miracle Mile in shirtsleeve weather, and snorkeled off a friend's yacht anchored at Dinner Key. I felt as if

I had been dropped into a painted Florida postcard. That night, an upscale dinner at the Coconut Grove Restaurant would have been enough without adding a once-in-a-lifetime performance by Milton Berle in *A Funny Thing Happened on the Way to the Forum* at the Coconut Grove Theatre. Milton even threw in a half-hour of standup after the show while we laughed until we were breathless.

That weekend swept away so many illusions. That I could be so seduced by someone the exact opposite of my dark-eyed Nick Prescott daydream. That I would ever find a man who made me laugh and whose intellect I felt matched my own. That I could resist the intense physical desire I felt for Bill.

Our lovemaking was an explosive chemical reaction, all-night passion that left me breathless and craving more. Even before that, we couldn't seem to stop touching each other, even holding hands while walking down the street—a first for me. And he was a new level of funny.

As we strolled hand-in-hand around Coral Gables on a Sunday afternoon, I glanced up at him. "Why don't men like to hold hands?"

He didn't miss a beat. "Because people would talk?"

That weekend we spoke of my doctoral degree and what I wanted to do with it, the master's program he had begun at Florida International University, our past regrets, and our dreams for the future. By Monday morning, Bill whispered, "I know you're the one."

Mentally, I began backing away, my ill-advised first marriage fresh in my mind. *Too fast!*

Even so, I accepted his suggestion that he drive to Cindy's house in Orlando for New Year's Eve, then follow me back to Tallahassee so we could have another weekend together. He was offering to make a round-trip drive the length of the state, about nine-hundred miles. No one had ever made such a full-court press to win me. Sally, triumphant, headed back north.

The Friday before spring semester classes began in January, the phone rang in my Tallahassee apartment. "Guess where I'm calling from?"

"School?"

"Nope, not even close."

"Not Orlando!"

"A lot closer to you," he laughed. "I'm at the Tallahassee Airport. Come and get me?"

That weekend, he cooked dinner for me and some fellow doctoral students, and after another night of fiery lovemaking, made breakfast with the dinner leftovers. With each moment we spent together, my resolve to avoid quick commitment began to soften; I was that easy.

My letters to him were on school notebook paper, and he promised that when he got back to his industrial arts shop, he would print some personal letterhead stationery for me. *Is there anything this man can't do?*

No social media in those days, but the news flashed through my family. Fred called from Annapolis to warn, "Be careful; go slow," and Cindy fretted, "He's a lot of fun, but isn't he a little immature?" I just smiled. Cindy had never met anyone with so much high-spirited exuberance that it spilled over in frequent puns and jokes, but I had already been married to immature. Bill was something altogether different. He was not only a rollicking good time, but he was also highly intelligent, ambitious, and in love with teaching—and me. After so many wrong turns and so much disappointment, I wandered into an Orlando bar and found my match. *Could he be the one?*

Don was dismayed. "But you just met him!" he protested. "I love you and if you'll just marry me again, I can prove it to you."

I sighed. "I've gotta go study."

My primary challenges that spring were statistical variance and covariance and applying for a summer internship in Minneapolis offered by the Control Data Corporation, but I managed to find time to exchange a stream of long, passionate letters with Bill, and we called so much that I wrote, "Our phone bills are going to look like the national debt." Ah, the days before cell phones.

One afternoon as Bill and I were on the phone talking about a future together, there was a knock at my apartment door, and when I answered, there stood Don. Bill was unamused.

"Tell him to leave!" he implored. "Right now."

"I can't do that, Lover. He's my friend."

"Well, he wants to be a lot more than that."

Bill was rarely wrong. Don was there to make another appeal for remarriage, but when he saw Bill's photo in my living room, his face fell.

"He looks like a hippie," he sneered.

"I know, and if that were really true, you wouldn't have a thing to worry about."

Bill and I were already moving fast, but after Don's sudden appearance, Bill upped the pace. On Valentine's Day, he flew in again. As we sat on the bed in my Tallahassee apartment, he smiled, and his hands shaking slightly, produced from his pocket not one small ring box, but two, both containing family heirlooms. One was a gleaming platinum band with two carats of diamonds, and the other a slenderer platinum band with three small stones in a tasteful setting. Before he could utter a word, I threw my arms around him, and he held me close for a moment and then pulled back to look into my brimming eyes.

"Does this mean yes?"

I chose the bigger one, of course.

On finding out I was marrying Bill, Mom sniffed, "You're still married to Don in the eyes of the Church, you know."

I glared at her. "Well, if that's how you're going to be, you needn't show up." I suppose she didn't want to be left out, so she said nothing more.

Our June wedding was at the University Baptist Church a couple blocks from Bill's childhood home in Coral Gables so that his mom's friends could see her only son wed. My own mother, looking dour as usual, drove from Orlando with Cindy, who served as matron of honor.

Six months after we met, Bill and I were newlyweds speeding my blue Corolla up to Minneapolis for my paid summer internship at the Control Data Corporation. A couple weeks after we'd settled into our Arden Hills apartment, I slammed the door on my way in from work. Bill was already home; he had been unsuccessful at finding employment.

Bill jumped up to greet me with his usual warm embrace. "Anything wrong, Lover?"

"Yes, there's something wrong." My tone was icy. "That stupid CDC lawyer I'm working with. The hell with him and his damned antitrust course! You're not working so you wouldn't understand."

He paused and blinked, taking in the blow of the unexpected insult. He had never met this version of his wife, though he would again. "You know I've tried, honey," he replied gently. "No one wants to hire someone who's leaving town in a couple months. Anyway, I'll be teaching this fall and . . ."

I cut him off. "Teaching shop. Right. I'm talking about real work."

I brushed past him to the kitchen for a glass of wine. I calmed down after a few minutes, though I never apologized, not for that slight nor others over the next months. That summer Bill encountered a Mom-molded Peggy for the first time.

Bill, a quick study, learned Basic Peggy. To patiently wait out these brief storms. To avoid sudden loud noises, which always made me jump and curse. Most of all, not to say anything I might view as criticism.

He had only one ask of me that summer, that I quit Don cold turkey. No calls, no letters, not even a Christmas card. Cindy took pity on Don and gave him my Minneapolis number, but when he called there, Bill hovered, demanding, pleading, "Tell him." And I did. Don's last letter was a cartoon of Big Bear crying.

On our return to Tallahassee that fall, we faced our next challenge: what to do about my mother.

Chapter Thirty-One

Alone

My relationship with Mom transformed slowly at first, then all at once. After Dad's death, sympathy and pity gradually merged with the anger and fear I always felt for her. I worried about the impact of Dad's death on her fragile psyche. With her old adversary gone, she had no one left to blame. When my siblings and I visited, there was consultation before we saw her and analysis afterwards, as if she were our patient rather than our parent. We knew what we had to do. We took over our father's caregiver role.

We established a trust from Dad's estate, enough to meet her basic needs and maintain the house, but our visits grew less frequent, not only because three of us lived so far from Cresaptown, but because she was hard to be around, always sad and distant, often angry and belligerent. Her perennially favorite topic was the ways in which her husband had wronged her.

More than once, I begged her to consult a therapist, but she always refused. Bobby felt that her time in Sykesville had taught her not to trust them, but Fred sneered, "She always thinks she's smarter than they are."

In my view, Mom's mental state lacked any characteristics that define illness like schizophrenia or bipolar condition. She could be irrational and dramatic, but she didn't hear voices, cut herself, or make multiple suicide attempts—though she talked often enough about death. She didn't do anything that would make her "crazy" by any expert's definition, only my family's. She was, however, always bitter and disappointed in her unrealized dreams—for herself and for me.

Then we got the call from Fred. "Mom's at Memorial Hospital; she's in a coma." Five years after Dad died and Mom was alone in the house that had been their battleground, she had collapsed from too many prescribed painkillers, kicked up with her daily intake of wine. The doctors said her liver stopped functioning and she would not last long. We all returned to Cumberland in funeral mode. She lay motionless in the hospital for days, her skin like yellow parchment. We were in the process of figuring out how to honor her wish to be buried in a Franciscan nun's habit when she suddenly emerged from the coma. The doctor was speechless, but I was sure Providence had given us a second chance to be a family. *This is a brand-new beginning. Things will be different now. We will all love each other as a family should.*

If that was Mom's maiden suicide attempt, she never tried it again, but we all agreed she could not be alone as she recovered. Fred arranged to sell the Cresaptown house, and Cindy and I decided we would take turns having Mom live with each of us. Bobby was still going from tour to tour with the Navy and not able to host her. Fred didn't offer. I proposed that Bill and I would have Mom first, and Bill blessed my plan. "Of course, Peggy; she's your mom, and it won't be forever." When Mom was ready to travel, we brought her to live in our Tallahassee home.

So many nights we would wake to the piteous sound of her

haunted dreams. Her cries were like something from a horror film, strangled and shuddering, as though she was battling with someone and trying to break free. The sound would wake us from a deep sleep. I'd drag myself from my bed, shuffle down the hall to gaze into the darkness of her room, and yawn, "Wake up, Mom. It's okay; it's just a dream." She always woke slowly, her dark eyes wide and frightened, looking like she had escaped from devils. She whimpered that she had visions of the "evil spirits on the second floor." Perhaps a metaphor for the evil spirit in her own father? No matter where she went or what haven she found, there would be no escape. The demons would always find her.

A live-in mother-in-law of any temperament can wear on a marriage, and Mom was still Mom, as critical and sniping as ever. She talked incessantly about her awful life with Dad.

"I should never have left Jacksonville," she moaned. "I had to live with that filthy old man who was so cruel to me and . . .

I snapped, "Find something else to talk about, Mom. We don't want to hear it."

But she always managed to return to the same tired topic. After six months, the sound of her voice set my teeth on edge, and I called on Cindy to take her turn.

Mom began agitating to get her own place. Fred, perhaps fearing she would end up homeless or living with him, filed the mountains of paperwork to get her qualified for social security disability due to medical conditions resulting from her coma. I noted that though the government labeled her permanently disabled, she retained enough mental prowess to write poetry and short stories and create paintings.

Her disability allowed her to obtain a government-subsidized apartment in Tallahassee where Bill and I and Cindy's family lived. She remained a gloomy presence at holiday gatherings and family celebrations, visiting most often with Ted and Cindy, who had a daughter and son.

We were all shocked when Florida's Child Services took a Child Abuse Hotline call accusing Cindy and Ted of neglecting and abusing their daughter. Child Services would not divulge the caller's identity, but when Cindy heard the details of the complaint, she informed them she knew exactly who had called and why, but they were still obliged to investigate. When they did, they found zero reason for concern. Later we learned that Mom had questioned Cindy and interrogated my four-year-old niece, though Mom didn't repeat the pillow technique she had used on me when I was about that age. Everyone, including my niece, denied any abuse or neglect, and neither Bill nor I ever saw any evidence of either. At the interviewer's questions, the precocious little girl responded, "Oh, you've been talking to my nanna."

Everyone in the family was as certain that Mom was the anonymous caller as they were that abuse or neglect was Mom's phantasm. Poor Ted was as innocent of the crime that Mom suspected as my father had been so many years before. Yet the old fear buried deep within my mother would not let her rest. She had repeatedly confided her fears to a senior-center counselor with scant training in such matters who finally advised, "You have no choice but to call the abuse hotline."

After that episode, we knew that Mom would always fashion a logic to fit her long-held fears. Her belief that fathers abused daughters and that no one would help was so ingrained in her that she saw it everywhere. Though no one was guilty of a crime, the hotline call automatically triggered a yearlong probationary period for my sister and her husband and an avalanche of ill will toward my mother.

Mom refused responsibility for anything, observing simply,

"I got bad advice."

I saw her less frequently, and after we moved out of Tallahassee, not at all. When she called, I kept our conversation short until finally, she stopped calling, though she continued to send long letters and all her new poems. Cindy never spoke to her again.

Mom quickly tired of wherever she was living, moving from one government-subsidized Tallahassee apartment to another, and finally relocating to Pensacola, where Bobby had retired from the Navy. Sometime in her wandering, Mom changed her name from Phrona to Francis, casting off at last a name she always hated. At first, I wondered why she hadn't also changed her erstwhile husband's name, but I figured that may have presented more problems than she was willing to confront. There was someone she hated more: the black-hearted Blackjack who had made her distrust all men and cast a shadow over her life she could never outrun. She would never return to his surname.

In the last brief paragraph of my mother's life, she was in a Pensacola nursing home near where Bobby lived, and I went to see her for what I knew would be the last time. By then, I was in my fifties and a successful professor; my first educational technology textbook had been a hit, becoming the bestselling one in a burgeoning field. It had been four years since I'd laid eyes on her and she had no power left to do much of anything to anyone, but even then, I feared what she could do to me with a word or look.

The nursing home was a jolt of contrasts. Outside its windows was a paradisaical setting of waving palm trees and tropical azalea bushes. But inside, Alzheimer's patients sat parked in wheelchairs in the hallways, calling out and weeping. An antiseptic odor mingled with that of sickness and adult diapers. I opened the door to her small, bare room and found her sitting on her bed, books and papers strewn around her. Even at eighty-three, she was still making grand plans for her next accomplishment.

"Mom? Mom, it's Margaret." She looked up wide-eyed and gave a shrill cry as she stretched out thin arms toward me. "Oh, Margaret, my sweet girl, I hoped I'd see you again!" She wept as we embraced. What a pale shadow of her former self she had become, just as my father had so many years before, the shadow she had made him.

Within weeks of my visit, she was gone, flown away home.

My mother found her final escape in 2001, mercifully leaving this earth just a week before someone had to try and explain to her what happened on September 11. She had already lived through Pearl Harbor; another attack on our home soil by an enemy no one had seen coming might have broken the fragile, fearful shell her mind had become.

She is with me still.

Twenty-five years after her death, her artworks hang in nearly every room of my house. In our foyer are her Grandma Moses-like images of deer gamboling in the snow. A placid painting of bowls filled with bright flowers glows on the dining room wall. In the family room hangs the acrylic portrait of Harvey, the pet rabbit I kept in the 1980s; she styled him with blue fur and pink eyes. Another bedroom displays Mom's colorful drawing of the cartoon Road Runner, capturing for me a nickname I earned in my childhood for donning my bathrobe and imitating his meep-meep run down the hall. Two large, blue-and-red tulip paintings that I once commissioned from her gaze out coolly, a little sadly, from a wall of our bedroom.

Some may think it bizarre that my admiration of her art could coexist with resentment and fear, but perhaps separating the parts of her complicated character is my way of celebrating her. I can point to her paintings and say, "These are my mother's." This artist was the real person, not the woman who shoved a pillow over my face and drained my security and self-confidence. My friends see her work and exclaim, "Wow, your mom was an artist!" That was Mom, not the woman whom my brothers always dismissed with "Oh, she was crazy" and whose funeral Cindy would not attend. And perhaps it's also a little of the white picket fence syndrome. I want my friends to think the best of me. Yes, my mom was an artist.

Hers was what one of the characters from her beloved *Spoon River Anthology* called "eagle souls that flew high in the sunlight." But the closer she got to the sun, the more it singed her wings, until all fell away, and she was alone. She had no wealth except her love of art and writing and reading, but she willed me those. I am compelled to admit that I became a successful author not despite her but because of her. Though I could not bring myself to write an epitaph for her as I had for Dad, I borrowed instead a stanza from "A Song of Eternity in Time," by Sidney Lanier, one of her favorite authors:

> A star that had remarked her pain
> Shone straightway down that leafy lane,
> And wrought his image, mirror-plain,
> Within a tear that on her lash hung gleaming.
> "Thus Time," I cried, "is but a tear
> Some one hath wept 'twixt hope and fear,
> Yet in his little lucent sphere
> Our star of stars, Eternity, is beaming."

Chapter Thirty-Two

The Suitcase

William Faulkner was dead on. The past is not past, he warned. I know now that the past lives inside us; the past is us. I learned it before death writes my final scene and someone else autopsies my life story. The day Bill packed his suitcase seven years into our marriage sparked a long-overdue self-examination. Casting about frantically for why I had treated my husband so hatefully, I landed on the one person whose influence I tried so hard to escape and ended up mirroring. "My mother made me do it." The insight that I was treating Bill exactly as my mother had treated my father was sufficient self-analysis, at least for a while. But even before Mom died nearly twenty years later, I came to see that blame wears badly on a self-image and that "I couldn't help it; I had a bad mother" is neither sufficient explanation nor particularly helpful in changing one's deplorable behavior.

Many of us from problematic families might agree with poet Philip Larkin. "They fuck you up, your Mum and Dad. They may not mean to, but they do." But I needed more than his simplicity. People often become absorbed with the study of genealogy, but I was never interested in simple lineage. I wanted to know what made my parents behave as they had, the motives and actions that had been confusing and inexplicable to me.

I had always perceived my parents as an imperfect glass, too damaged to be refinished. Then I saw clearly what I wished I'd seen before: that countless other lives shaped theirs, the ghosts I still see shadowing me when I gaze into our family mirror, long-dead kin, generations of relatives going back an infinity of years. As I peered into the jagged trajectory of my life, I saw it, the legacy not only of my mother and father, but of my grandparents and all our forebears, still casting their fractured shadows on me after so many years.

I came to see that I had been living two lives, Mom's and my own, as if I were an earthling in a science fiction story whose body had been taken over by an alien presence, the two of us battling constantly for dominance. I hated that Mom inhabited my life, yet I could not make her leave.

As my research progressed, I came to see that her actions had been motivated, at least in part, by an unspeakable past and a desperate need to make her children's lives different from hers, even though I ended up making some of the same mistakes she did and treated my husband as she had hers. I saw that her path, like Dad's, was shaped by that of her own parents, and that how far back that trail goes is an imponderable. What really matters is how far in the future it will continue.

After Dad's funeral, we four siblings and our spouses took our depleted spirits to Warner's German Restaurant. I expected the occasion would be a somber reflection on the torment in Dad's life, but I was in for a surprise.

After we ordered our steins of beer, slices of pizza, and tall, fluffy wedges of Warner's famous Bee Sting Cake, Bobby leaned forward, rested elbows on the red-checkered tablecloth, and began.

"You know, Dad always knew the best, cheapest diners when we were on the road together installing those church windows. I remember one place in Cape Charles that looked so dicey I was almost afraid to go in, but they had the best milkshakes I ever tasted." Soon we were all laughing and dabbing at our eyes, swapping remembrances of our Cresaptown childhood and our own favorite "Dad stories." I can't imagine what locals thought of the hilarity coming from our table as we sat there in our funereal black, but we needed the lightness of that moment after the gloom of that week. Anyway, the laughter of Dad's children was a better memorial to him than our tears around his tombstone.

Every time I saw Bobby after that day, he would steer our conversation toward stories of his travels with Dad and what he had learned of Dad's childhood and life with his own parents. "Did I ever tell you about Dad's days running moonshine with Granddad?" If I'd heard it, he'd tell it again anyway, because it was a good Dad story.

Over the years, Bobby added details about our father's background, and Fred supplied a little more, though I soon learned that neither of them knew much of Mom's history. My own investigations filled in a little of that. No matter how much I learn, the hold my mother has on me will never completely vanish no matter how many miles or years are between us. Not even death loosened it. I look in the mirror and she is there with me.

She lives in me. She is me.

Old men on their deathbeds and soldiers on the battlefield, they say, will cry out for their mothers. Some of us must wait until such moments to recognize the enduring connection we have with the woman whose heartbeat we hear next to our own before we are born. But I realized something about the strength of this imprint just before I turned twenty-one.

I was relieved of my wisdom teeth early one morning in State College when I was still a college student. After a breakfast of Novocain and blood, I arrived at my future mother-in-law's apartment to find her daughter Laura sitting at the kitchen table, perusing a newspaper.

"Ah, there you are." She looked up, grinning as she tossed her newspaper aside. "How do you feel?"

I allowed that I didn't feel anything; I had gotten a surfeit of Novocain.

"Let me see your sutures," she asked, rising to get a look down my gullet. A young nurse, Laura was interested in all things surgical. I tilted my head back and opened my mouth.

The next thing I saw was my mother's slender young face leaning over me. She had the light-brown hair and intense, worried-mother eyes I had seen so often in my childhood and completely forgotten until that moment. Laura caught me as I started to go limp, and using her nurse-training protocol, held my head and laid me down gently on the floor.

"Mom?" I murmured in a tiny-child voice, looking up through semi-conscious eyes. "Mama?" Then my vision cleared to see Laura's dark eyes looking down at me, not especially worried.

"You need to eat something," was her matter-of-fact advice.

In the decades since I stood beside my husband's suitcase, listening to his plaint, I have often been reminded of how much like both my parents I will always be. To my mother, I owe my defining temperament: intense and hyper-sensitive, trusting no one, quick to love, and quicker to anger. Always building my white picket fence, I care too much what others think. All the fear and doubt and self-loathing she acquired in her childhood, I learned in mine. Sudden noises still shatter my composure, making me brace for the lightning strike to come. *Is she angry again? Am I to blame?*

Like my father, I am hardworking but always anxious and worried I am not working hard enough. It is difficult for me to rest (though unlike him, I do take my blood pressure medication). Like each of them, the anger smolders deep in me and flares up suddenly, a combustible spirit easily brought to blaze by a feeling or word or look.

In my first university position, I remember waiting impatiently in my Dean's outer office, anxious to get back to the grant proposal I was writing but needing his decision on the budget. Each minute I sat there made me more frustrated at the time I was wasting. I fidgeted in my chair and fixated on the wall clock, watching unproductive minutes drain from my day. The Dean emerged from his office and motioned for me to continue waiting as he called in a student who had arrived after me.

As his office door closed, I jumped up cursing under my breath. "Let him write this damned thing himself," I muttered as I rushed out the door, startling his secretary. I was still steaming and cursing as I speed-walked down the hallway to my office. My colleague Elinor saw my red face and asked what was wrong.

"That fool knows I need his input, and I'm not waiting any longer," I raged. "I think I'll go back there and tell him what he can do with this damned proposal." I turned to go back, and Elinor stopped me with upraised hand.

"No, no, Peggy. Don't go like that," she offered gently. "Whom the gods would destroy, they first make mad."

Her wise counsel calmed me immediately and thank goodness

I had the grace to thank her. What I had been about to do might have forfeited everything I had built over so many years and all I aimed to achieve. After all, I was not even tenured at the time. *What if Elinor hadn't stopped me*? I cringed from my own destructive nature.

In the years since Bill's suitcase turned me toward the study of my parents and their family background, I have come to see that they had both achieved what they wanted from life, what they thought they wanted, anyway. The warning "Be careful what you wish for" comes to us from Aesop's fables, but an even darker version is purported to be an ancient Chinese curse, though who really knows what wise person first labeled it a malediction. "May all your wishes come true."

My mother wanted a little girl to whom she could give the security and love she was denied, shaping her daughter into a better version of herself. She yearned for freedom from the domination of men, to earn her own way, and decide how to spend both her money and her time. She burned to be educated and creative and to choose her own spiritual path. Her most fervent dream for her future, it seemed to me, was the freedom to fulfill herself. "Freedom is the word," her poem proclaimed. All her desires she was able to achieve to some extent. None of it was enough; none of her fulfilled wishes brought her contentment or immunized her against the nightmares.

My father's frantic need was for financial security, to be able to provide for himself and his family, yet even after achieving all of that, he never felt it was enough and continued to deny himself everything, even time to recuperate from illness. Long after his children each attained their own measures of success, he was mindful of his remaining dependent, his wayward ex-wife. Family came first, even her. The legacy of his life experiences left him always working, always driving at breakneck speed, always worrying that today would be the day it would all fall apart and leave him wandering by the river.

In pursuing their goals, they lost so much. Mom lost her marriage and the love of her daughters. Dad lost his life.

Both my parents lived long enough to see some of the first fruits of what they had sown along the way. Cindy became a talented nurse, Fred turned to the law, and I made my career in educational technology. On the day I received my PhD hood, my mother was unsmiling. Was she still thinking, "Just think what you could have done"? Had he been there, my father would have been so proud, standing in his brown suit and wide tie, beaming at me. Then he would have changed clothes and hustled back into the shop to work.

Bobby, though, who had quit school at fifteen, had the most remarkable path of any of us. He quickly obtained a GED in the Navy, and after rising to the rank of Chief Petty Officer and traveling the world, he retired from the military, moved to Pensacola, earned a business degree and an MBA, and became a successful businessman and college instructor. After a second retirement, he wrote *Navy Adventures in Morse Code*, a memoir of his early life in the military. His vivid, lively tales of Navy life for enlisted men gained him notoriety among the many retired veterans in Pensacola. He also became a Methodist Stephen Minister and hospice volunteer.

At Bobby's funeral, the church was crammed with friends and colleagues from his many careers, as well as his wife, five children, and numerous grandchildren. I spoke at his funeral of his adventurous life. As honor guard guns sounded a tribute over his flag-draped casket, I thought of my brother cruising South Cumberland in his Pontiac and contemplated what would have become of him—of all of us—if he hadn't pursued his uncharted course.

All four of us Cresaptown kids achieved so much, but there were high costs. Broken images, destroyed trust, companionship cast aside like used paper. All of us had failed marriages; even Bobby went off the rails and divorced his devoted Ingrid before realizing he had made a terrible mistake and begging her to remarry him. There were days we shed so many tears that we felt hollow, as if tears were all we were ever made of. There were regrets that tore at us and seared us and left us scarred inside.

"You've got to get tough in this world," my dad always cautioned me, and before he died, he knew I was heeding his advice. He saw how many challenges I had already overcome. Life would not defeat me; I would find a way forward, just as he did.

In the hard times, the times that seem designed to destroy us, some turn to Ernest Hemingway's lines from *A Farewell to Arms*: "The world breaks everyone and afterward many are strong at the broken places." Those who wield these words like a shield bear down and find comfort, anticipating that time to come when they will rise stronger having endured what beat them down. But I mark well that Hemingway wrote "many," not all, and some are, indeed, stronger but still show the breaks outlined in red with anger and pain. They are put back together but always fractured and fragile, like the broken and mended skull in my childhood nightmare.

Only part of the person I aspired to be survived the trauma that is my family legacy. Occasionally, irony still overwhelms me as I consider that my parents rendered impossible the powerful, fearless woman they wanted me to become. "Make the most money you can," my father cautioned. "Don't rely on a man," warned my mother. I chased their advice, and the professional and personal life I most wanted eluded me.

Bill had become the guy who lived in my house whom I yelled at a lot, but I was not angry with him; I was disappointed in myself for being afraid to take the path that would have meant less money and more reliance on him, and for listening to my parents, still in my head.

On that day the suitcase that changed my life appeared, I was frustrated with the direction my life was taking. I had all but stopped reading for pleasure, and there was neither poetry nor stories in my writing life, only lesson plans and instructional textbooks. My husband did not deserve the way I had been treating him any more than my father deserved the way my mother and I had treated him. When Bill confronted me with my own shortcomings, I, always so quick to anger and swift to reply, could say nothing in my defense.

He had been a good husband. The best. He didn't deserve to be married to my mother. I couldn't conceive of a life without him, couldn't imagine anyone better than him. I still can't. In that moment of bright crystal clarity, I saw it was time for me to stop living out my family's generations-long legacy and start making my own.

I grabbed the suitcase, rushed it back to the bedroom, and sprinted out again to wrap myself around him, my arms tight around his neck. Through tears, I begged him, "Give me another chance, please Bill. I'll do better, I promise."

My husband, the teacher, taught me a lesson about grace and compassion that day. As Don once said to me, I know what love is now. I grasped that I had to turn away from what had almost cost me everything and at the same time, turn back to examine the past I had fled. Everything flowed from that realization like a fast river out of a fiery forest. The story of the suitcase has become a symbol of my marriage's robust resilience and strong core.

My new path led to absolution for self-accused sins. I saw too late who and what built the wall between my father and me, and the guilt and anger burned the deepest part of me. But I finally absorbed that Dad had seen enough of angst and recrimination, Sturm und Drang; he wouldn't want more of that for me. He would want me to forgive myself and Mom as he had always forgiven everyone, as Bill forgave me. I came to see that by the time I knew them, my parents were the best version of themselves they could be, and if the transformation of death brings clarity, they know I was the best version of myself that I could be. I forgive them both for all they lacked, and the light mantle of their forgiveness has replaced my dark mourner's cloak of guilt.

Trauma in one's youth has a long, bitter afterlife. It can leave victims with post-traumatic stress disorder, a sad legacy memorialized in countless memoirs and novels; there is even a PTSD postage stamp. All the damage done to parents, they often pass on to their children. Many suffer, as I do, from the nonstop pursuit of unattainable perfection, the fear and shame, the desperate need for recognition. Still inhabiting my psyche, these traits can burst out suddenly, and once again I must learn the lessons I thought I had mastered. I escaped generational trauma but still have ghost pain, like feeling in a limb that was long ago severed.

Whenever I become tired or self-pitying, I profit from journeying back once again to commune with my ghosts before I turn forward, and the benefits of these visits have accrued. I recommend the trip. I am among those who imperiled my future by running from my past.

I'll always sense those shadowy figures standing behind me, and sometimes an ethereal presence overtakes me. I have learned so much about myself and about them, yet so much is still obscure. So many dark corners remain in the old mirror.

Three hand-drawn images of church-window designs from my father's collection, found in his shop after his death, are now on display in the home Bill and I share. Though faded, each design was once a brightly multicolored combination of geometric shapes within a long window with a gracefully rounded top. One window features a chalice, one a cross, and one a Bible.

In a window just up the stairs from those drawings hangs a large, colorful, stained-glass work—not Dad's but that of another man with an artist's heart and a craftsman's skill—placed in the pane of our house that can most often catch and transfer light. When the sun finds this window, the beams stream through it, hitting the beveled places in the stained glass and breaking up into colored shapes and lines in a confusion of tinted patterns on our shiny wood floors. I have conjectured that my love of all things multicolored springs from the richly hued glass I saw my father laboring over in his shop.

Now I wonder if my father ever sat down heavily on a pew in a church sanctuary and looked up at the windows he had worked so hard to fashion. Did he stop for just a moment to consider his creation, and did he observe the shards of colorful light streaming in and breaking up in jagged slivers before striking the polished pews, like his own shattered dreams, lying amid the fragments of broken glass on his workshop floor?

I like to imagine that he smiled and summoned strength from the sight of lasting beauty he had created in a house of worship, and I hope that he pondered the multitude of people over decades to come whose gaze would also rise and find comfort there. *Rest, Dad, you can rest now.*

Photo Gallery

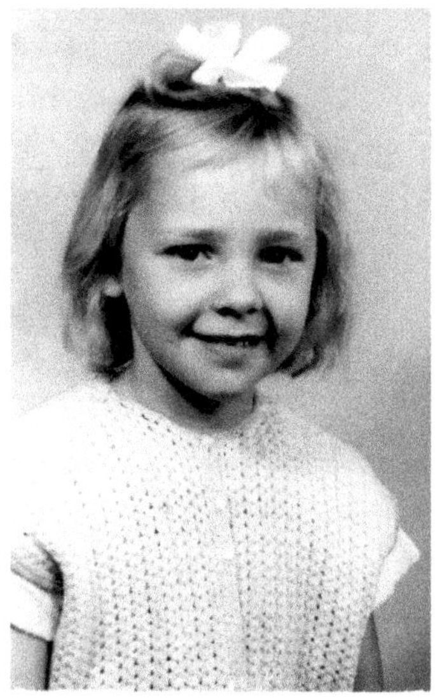

Peggy as Cresaptown first grader in Mom-crocheted vest, 1953

Grandmother Floda Mae Roy Pryor, with two unnamed children, perhaps siblings, date unknown

From left to right: Uncle Delos (Doss), Grandfather Robert, Grandmother Adeline, Aunt Beulah (Bee), Aunt Leona Agatha (Gay), Gay's first husband Joe Logsdon, Dad holding Bobby, circa 1939

Dad in his beloved Kissell, circa 1929

Dad and Gladys, his lost love, circa 1935

Grandfather Roblyer in Art Glass Company panel truck, 1953

Peggy and Cindy at Jacksonville Beach, 1956

Eleven-year-old Peggy in Holy Rosary School uniform, 1958

Peggy at Holy Rosary Church after First Communion, 1959

Tenth-grade Peggy at Allegany High School, 1962

Dad (Spates), formal picture, circa 1961

Mom (Phrona Catherine, in wig), formal portrait, circa 1972

Twenty-five-year-old Peggy with Nittany Lion on Penn State Campus, 1971

Peggy in Dutch Pantry waitress uniform

Peggy and Bill at Miami wedding, 1976

Peggy at Florida State University doctoral hooding, 1978

Thirty-one-year-old Bill in teacher's school portrait, 1980

Peggy and Bill at home, 1983

Peggy and Bill, Smokey Mountain trip, September 2025

Author's Note

My resolve to remain childless cracked when I was nearing forty, but I had waited too long to have a child in the usual way. With the help of an adoption attorney, we met Paige and became her parents when she was a day old. She was almost thirty when I began envisioning a kind of self-help manual, a how-I-did-it guide for her. I thought to pass on "knowledge nuggets" I had acquired along the way in my life, sage insights and helpful advice that helped me succeed and seemed worth sharing with her before I forgot it all. Such is the arrogance of the aging. I gauged that writing it might take a year. Such is the ignorance of the novice memoirist.

Some months into what turned into a six-year process, the book took a sharp turn and became considerably more than what I planned. I blame it all on my brother Bobby.

Bobby Roblyer (U. S. Navy CTRC, Retired) possessed an unparalleled knowledge of family background. He was the only one of us siblings who had spent so much time talking with Dad as they traveled throughout Maryland, West Virginia, Pennsylvania, and Virginia installing the stained-glass church windows they had made together. During these trips when he was a teenager, Bobby heard and absorbed the histories of our family. He became the closest to Dad and, perhaps, the only one of us who loved our father for who he was at the time we knew him.

In the years before Bobby died in 2019, I asked him to tell me more of the facts of our family history, and then I couldn't get him to stop. Dates, events, and stories streamed out of him, and he repeated many of them, using almost identical language in each telling. By the end, he was having short-term memory problems, but the past was vivid to him, and I think our talks became a practice exercise to keep him in touch with who he was. He didn't know everything, but he knew a lot, and Fred added a few details to some of Bobby's stories.

Bobby sat for a series of telephone and in-person interviews, telling the oft-repeated stories, occasionally adding others I had not heard before. There was a lot of laughter and wonder in those conversations and only an occasional regret. "I loved that man," he sometimes murmured mournfully, and then he wept, perhaps feeling that when he left home to join the Navy, he had deserted our father, leaving a space for misery to pour in like a burst dam. Bobby was always the heart of our family, there to console Dad at his darkest hour and to rescue Mom from Sykesville. Bobby adopted the attitude Dad had often modeled in stories from his life: family comes first.

Sometime during my conversations with Bobby, connections began to emerge, and a narrative of a memoir began to take shape in my head. It started with an image of faces behind me as I stood in a room lined with Dad's mirrors, faces of the long-dead who had so much to do with why I became who I am.

With Bobby's help, I began to understand a little more of what made my parents who they were, and I see them more clearly now, over fifty years after Dad's death and more than twenty years after my mother's, than in the entire time they stood before me.

Studying them in the context of our ancestors has helped me take a more accurate measure of myself and all my motivations and passions, disappointments and triumphs. Now I can understand my parents' path while recognizing why I left it.

I am writing these words because I was lucky, but many are not. My path is my own, and I can offer no unqualified counsel to anyone else clawing along their own rough course, but I can advocate for education because it paved a solid road for me. Mom always claimed it would free me, and she was right, though not in the way she thought. My college degrees gave me opportunities I would not otherwise have had and let me rise from the life my parents had known. Without the opportunities that came from education, I could not have afforded the luxury of researching my history, nor the free time to reflect on what I learned. I would never have met Bill. Most of all, I would not have acquired knowledge that grew into insight.

It would be lovely to be able to say that everyone in my family pitched in and contributed to shaping the account set down in these pages. But if that were true, it wouldn't be my family. Siblings become similar from shared growing-up experiences as well as shared genes. But because they come along at different times and follow diverging paths, they become as different as sparrows and seagulls. Despite our commonalities, we four siblings each flew in different flocks.

Some family members helped me with this story only a little, and Cindy, estranged from me after her divorce, not at all. Fred reacted to my desire to publish my growing-up story was as though I were about to expose family skeletons, rather than explore my own ghosts. "Why do you want to go airing our family's dirty laundry? Dad was always telling people things about our family. Why'd he need to go and do that? What business is it of anyone's what happened to us?" And the final stab, "It's not as though it will be great literature!"

The question that drove me and perhaps all those who write their family stories is, "Why should any of us take excursions from our birthplace and take few—if any—trips to an interior life, which is the most illuminating place we could go?" Pretending that the past never happened or that we should ignore its effects seems far more perilous than taking that inward journey. Unearthing our narratives can help us recognize the strong core that lives inside all our fragility. We might echo author Bruce Chatwin in *The Songlines* when he quoted anthropologist Spencer Wells. "One responsibility that we neglect at our peril is that of self-discovery. Once the document of our journey has been lost it will, like the footprints of our ancestors . . . be gone forever." We may not all be Thomas Merton or Tara Westover, but our stories are worth the telling as much as theirs and, we can dare to hope, worth the reading and sharing, even though they are not destined to join the literary canon.

My decidedly unsaintly mother, who always seasoned her Motherisms with a drop of acid, frequently intoned, "We live and learn, die and forget it all." Though it may be true that we won't—as far as we know—get a chance to do it all over again, I believe there is some redemption of joy and hope in passing along something of what we have learned before we leave. My story may speak to others who are seeking to escape, as I did, a predetermined path willed to them by intergenerational trauma.

And so, I suppose in the end, this became a self-help book after all.

M. D. Roblyer
Chattanooga, Tennessee

Acknowledgements

I have too many debts that can never be repaid, but some that brought this book to life can and should at least be officially recognized. My first thanks go to dear friends and early readers, Cara Cassell, Suzanne Hall, and Meghan O'Dea, who applauded all my drafts, even when no applause was merited. Special huzzahs to another reader, Debbie Stollenwerk, retired Pearson editor and gifted friend, for her wisdom on Catholic doctrine, dogma, and practice; to the talented Lisa Romeo, who helped me develop my story and weed out my story-telling inadequacies; and to Suzanne Woodham Juday, who kept every letter she ever received and was gracious enough to dust off all mine from her attic and send them back to me for use with my "little project."

Proofreading is a tiresome, tedious necessity. And its amazing to me that my friends Sherry Poff and Sally Richardson not only volunteered for some of the job, but did it admirably.

Thanks to all those who furnished facts and figures about the life and times of Allegany County and my deceased relatives: Kathy and Tom Cecil, Cresaptown Methodist Church; Kevin Kamauf, Manager, Allegany County Fairgrounds; Scott Llewellyn, Principal, Cresaptown School; Ashley Owlett, Postmistress, Tioga, Pennsylvania; Ruth Davis Rogers, City of

Cumberland Historic Preservation Planner; Ginger Winter, Cresaptown/Cuffy's Corner Reunion; Lisa Zakharova, Allegany County librarian; and especially my brothers, named by pseudonym in the chapters. I am also grateful to my gifted therapist, Dr. Gina Delgardo, and to Gene Roblyer, late cousin of the "western Roblyer clan," who lent constant encouragement.

I am indebted to Kevin Atticks and the Apprentice House Press team at Loyola University Maryland for choosing my Maryland story to add to their own. Special thanks to my development editors Abigail Szypula and Caroline Drennen for helping me strengthen my story's structure and prose, and to the amazing Eleanor "Del" Salvatore for her invaluable design work and promotional insights.

My website, which made me look better than I could expect, was designed and supported by neighbor, friend, and graphic artist Mark Cooley, owner of Cooley Design. To all friends at home and abroad who loved and buoyed me, I love you back despite your beginning every conversation in recent years with the same teeth-gritting question. "Is that memoir out yet?"

Finally, I acknowledge my love and gratitude for my husband, Bill (dubbed Captain America by my girlfriends), who makes possible every good thing in my life, and our powerhouse daughter, Paige, who inspired me to begin writing *Strong Glass*. I'll always be amazed I got so lucky twice.

References

Angelou, Maya. *I Know Why the Caged Bird* Sings. Random House, 1969.

Caro, Robert. *The Years of Lyndon Johnson: Path to Power*. Knopf, 1982.

Catechism of Christian Doctrine, Prepared and Enjoined by Order of the Third Council of Baltimore. The Catholic Publishing Company, 1959.

Chatwin, Bruce. *The Songlines.* Penguin Books, 1988.

Cronin, A. J. *The Keys of the Kingdom*. Little, Brown & Company, 1941.

Farrar, Jamaica Kincaid. *My Garden.* Straus and Giroux, 2001.

Ferber, Edna. *So Big* Double Day, Page & Company, 1924

Heinlein Robert. *Stranger in a Strange Land.* G. P. Putnam's Sons, 1961.

Hemingway, Ernest. *A Farewell to Arms*. Scribner, 1929.

Jones, Jessie Orton and Elizabeth Orton Jones. *Small Rain.* Viking Press, 1944.

Lanier, Sidney. "A Song of Eternity in Time."

Lanier, Sidney. "A Song of the Future."

Larkin, Philip. "This Be the Verse"

Lepore, Jill. "The Last Time Democracy Almost Died." *The New* Yorker, January 27, 2020.

Martignoni, Margaret E., Editor. *Children's Book of Illustrated Literature*. Grosset and Dunlap, 1955.

Merton, Thomas. *The Seven Storey Mountain.* Harcourt Brace and Company, 1948.

Mitchell, Margaret. *Gone with the Wind*. Macmillan Publishing Company, 1936.

Masters, Edgar Lee. *Spoon River Anthology*. Macmillan Publishing Company, 1915.

Pagels, Elaine. *Revelations: Visions, Prophecy, and Politics in the Book of Revelations.* Viking, 2012.

Roblyer, S. L. *Navy Adventures in Morse Code*. S. L. Roblyer Publisher, 2009.

Shakespeare, William. *Hamlet.* Act 3, Scene 1.

Shannon, William H. "A Note to the Reader." In *The Seven Storey Mountain.* Harcourt Brace and Company, 1998.

Spark, Muriel. *The Prime of Miss Jean Brodie*. Macmillan, 1961.

Tennyson, Alfred, Lord. "Crossing the Bar" in *Demeter and Other Poems*. Macmillan, 1889.

Wolfe, Thomas. *Look Homeward, Angel.* Charles Scribner's Sons, 1929.

Yeats, William Butler. "The Second Coming."

Apprentice House is the country's only campus-based, student-staffed book publishing company. Directed by professors and industry professionals, it is a nonprofit activity of the Communication Department at Loyola University Maryland.

Using state-of-the-art technology and an experiential learning model of education, Apprentice House publishes books in untraditional ways. This dual responsibility as publishers and educators creates an unprecedented collaborative environment among faculty and students, while teaching tomorrow's editors, designers, and marketers.

Eclectic and provocative, Apprentice House titles intend to entertain as well as spark dialogue on a variety of topics. Financial contributions to sustain the press's work are welcomed. Contributions are tax deductible to the fullest extent allowed by the IRS.

To learn more about Apprentice House books or to obtain submission guidelines, please visit www.apprenticehouse.com.

Apprentice House Press
Communication Department
Loyola University Maryland
4501 N. Charles Street
Baltimore, MD 21210
Ph: 410-617-5265
info@apprenticehouse.com • www.apprenticehouse.com

www.ingramcontent.com/pod-product-compliance
Lightning Source LLC
LaVergne TN
LVHW010602100826
845148LV00014B/2813

* 9 7 8 1 6 2 7 2 0 6 6 3 1 *